Fundamentals of Educational Research

)5

5

Falmer Press Teachers' Library

Series Editor: Professor Ivor F Goodson, Warner Graduate School, University of Rochester, USA and Applied Research in Education, University of East Anglia, Norwich, UK

Fundamentals of
Educational Research

Gary Anderson

with contributions by
Nancy Arsenault

2nd Edition

UK   Falmer Press, 1 Gunpowder Square, London, EC4A 3DE
USA   Falmer Press, Taylor & Francis Inc., 1900 Frost Road, Suite 101,
       Bristol, PA 19007

First published in 1998

A catalogue record for this book is available from the British Library

ISBN 0 7507 0858 1 cased
ISBN 0 7507 0857 3 paper

**Library of Congress Cataloging-in-Publication Data are available
on request**

Jacket design by Caroline Archer

Typeset in 10/12 pt Times by
Graphicraft Typesetters Ltd., Hong Kong.

*Printed in Great Britain by Biddles Ltd., Guildford and King's Lynn on
paper which has a specified pH value on final paper manufacture of not
less than 7.5 and is therefore 'acid free'.*

Contents

Contents

This book is dedicated to the educational researchers of South Africa in the hope that it will help them understand the challenges and opportunities in their new system of education.

Preface

In my view, the main reason to write a book is to say something new and to add value to what has already been said. This book is a sequel to a book I published in 1990, *Fundamentals of Educational Research*. The reactions to that book were mostly positive — I should say they were positive from those who really counted: the students learning about research. Some of my peers were less charitable as they seemed not to appreciate my attempts to make complex matters simple. The students, however, were the significant group to me, and I soon learned that there was a vigorous trade for the text by students and practicing researchers that endorsed a competitive, reader-friendly reference. They found *Fundamentals* more relevant to their needs and indicated that it was a useful and helpful book as they struggled to learn about research. They particularly appreciated the short length of the chapters that enable a beginner to cover a topic in one sitting. However, some students have progressed beyond the basic text and are ready for a slightly more advanced treatment of similar concepts. They are the audience for this book.

The second edition of *Fundamentals of Educational Research* has benefitted from the inquisitive world of graduate students at McGill University. Dealing with students is a good way to clarify one's thinking. I might know what methods to use, know what research questions to ask, know how to proceed towards the answers, but my students do not. Being uncontaminated by the social niceties of academe, they have little hesitation in admitting that they don't have a clue what I am talking about. So, as a teacher, I start over with new examples, alternate explanations and additional footnotes. If they see the light, then I am pleased and write a new page of notes to be used next year. If they do not, then I try again and search for new ways of clarifying a point. Additionally, the research world has evolved, qualitative methodologies have gained acceptance, and to remain current, over the past few years I developed handouts to give to my students to supplement *Fundamentals*. These resources ultimately grew into a large enough workbook that I had sufficient new material to justify a more advanced book.

Like my students, I am also a learner. I learn through reflection and dialogue with colleagues, by engaging in new and challenging research endeavors, and by trying new things in new circumstances. In so doing I develop new examples and illustrations of basic concepts. Over the past half dozen years, with my colleagues, I have conducted many research studies all over the world, and I have learned a great deal in doing so. The scope of the research includes case studies of girl child education in six countries in Africa, an analysis of human rights cases in the United

Nations and in selected countries, studies of education management development in various countries in support of the new government in South Africa, evaluations of PhD programs in management in Southeast Asia, evaluations of a variety of Canadian and international organizations, the development of new instruments and data collection and analysis techniques. I feel that I have now done and learned enough to make a new book worthwhile. This is not just a matter of minor refinement and updating of examples and references; it is a case of gaining new insights that are worth sharing. Books are expensive, and the reader needs to be assured that the sequel volume represents a worthwhile investment. I certainly believe this to be the case.

Finally, I have had a colleague work with me on this book. Nancy Arsenault is a former PhD student who became one of my best teachers. As any teacher knows, to learn a subject you really need to teach it. Nancy taught the research methodology course with me and in so doing, helped me to re-conceptualize many concepts that I would otherwise have continued to take for granted. We have worked collaboratively in reviewing each chapter and attempted to clarify the messages each chapter contains. Her additions and questioning have been invaluable. As one who is herself learning about research, Nancy can identify with the students' uncertainties and she has been an important bridge between me, the concepts and novices in the field. She has added many portions that cover areas that she and her fellow students want clarified. This book owes a great deal to her influence and the improvements found here are in no small measure a result of her contributions. She has co-authored two of the chapters and the glossary.

So, what does the second edition have that was not in the first? Essentially, this book attempts to round out and contemporize each topic without adding unnecessary detail or complexity. It takes a broader and deeper look at the various research paradigms, designs, tools and techniques to allow researchers to better respond to the research demands of today's world. I maintain my belief that this text should be short, yet provide all the essentials with enough breadth and depth to develop a well rounded researcher. Current references are provided in case the reader wishes to pursue specific topics in greater depth and lengthy exhibits have been moved to the appendix to keep the chapters themselves short. Finally, previous topics have been revisited and expanded and new chapters included adding valuable new perspectives, approaches, and a wider range of examples.

Both Nancy and I have learned a great deal in writing this book and we hope that you will find it to be a useful learning tool.

Gary Anderson
McGill University
and *Universalia Management Group*

Part I

Introduction to Educational Research

Chapter 1

The Nature of Educational Research

How you see the world is largely a function of where you view it from, what you look at, what lens you use to help you see, what tools you use to clarify your image, what you reflect on and how you report your world to others. Thus, an empirical researcher will see only those things which are conveniently measured in empirical ways. A sociologist will only be concerned with patterns affecting groups and will have little chance of learning about individual motivations except as they relate to group behavior. The behaviorist will focus on reporting and controlling behaviors, whereas the anthropologist's concern will be on the underlying meaning. Thus, research reflects the values, beliefs and perspectives of the researcher. This is not the same, however, as saying that research is subjective. For valid research, similar approaches should lead to similar conclusions, but different approaches can hardly be expected to lead to exactly the same conclusions. These different approaches cannot even be expected to ask the same questions, let alone realize similar answers. Thus, few researchers are truly unbiased or value-neutral, obviously carrying a baggage of beliefs, assumptions, inclinations and approaches to reality.

Beginning researchers should understand this interaction between the answers, questions and who is asking them. When reviewing previous research one should attempt to understand the researcher's perspective on the world as well as the results and conclusions. In coming to grips with your own research you must clarify your own preferred way of viewing the world: What questions are important to you? What are your approaches to knowledge? What personal strengths do you have that can help you adopt a particular methodological approach? With what types of studies would you prefer to be associated?

Traditional Approaches to Knowledge

There are five main ways in which the human race approaches knowledge. The first is the method of tenacity where people hold to the truth merely because they believe it to be true. They have always known it to be true and so even contrary evidence is dismissed out of hand. This method is nothing more than blind stubbornness, but it is responsible for many prevalent beliefs, some true, others erroneous. It is not an approach to knowledge which need concern us as researchers.

Another fundamental way of knowing is based on authority. People rely on experts to gain understanding and guide their behavior. In any family or work setting the views of those endorsed as knowledgeable have credibility and are believed.

On the broader scene, certain acknowledged experts are also believed. Thus, if Linus Pauling believes in vitamin C, that is good enough evidence for me. If the Bible says it is true; it must be so. The only utility of this approach to the researcher is that it sometimes poses questions which bear researching: Does vitamin C really cure colds?

The rationalist approach to knowledge adds thinking and deduction which, in some instances, can lead to useful generalizations or predictions. It is based on the notion of logic which links truths and enables us to predict situations which may not have been directly observed. If A causes B and B causes C, then A probably also causes C. This approach is under utilized in the educational research literature, but it is a vital one. The rationalist approach helps extend theory and sets up questions that can be addressed by the researcher. It is the fundamental approach of educational philosophers and is also used in evaluation studies and contract research.

A related method might be termed insightful observation. Insightful observation is used by intelligent people who are capable of gathering information from their experience then drawing useful generalizations and conclusions from these observations. Unlike the former method, this incorporates some observational basis, albeit unsystematic. Furthermore, it assumes values and contradictions that surround all aspects of our lifeworld. This approach is used by some researchers to formulate logical questions and suppositions for more systematic research and analysis. As a way of developing questions, it, too, can be useful to science as demonstrated by the recent research on folk remedies and natural medicines.

Finally, the scientific method incorporates observations and data which are systematically collected and analyzed in order to obtain understanding of phenomena based on controlled observation and analysis. It is this final form which represents research and the research method in its most widely understood meaning. Unlike the other methods, the scientific method builds in self-correction. New evidence is constantly brought to bear and existing generalizations are constantly modified and corrected to accommodate this additional evidence. However, it is also fair to say that most research and especially contract research and evaluation also incorporates some of the useful features of insightful observation and the rationalist approach. Philosophical inquiry does not typically involve systematic observation and relies entirely on a rationalistic approach. For this reason, some people would question whether philosophical inquiry should be called research.

Dominant Paradigms and Approaches to Research

This book focuses on two dominant research paradigms: the *positivist paradigm* and the *post-positive paradigm*. The dominant paradigm influencing educational research is what is popularly referred to as the scientific method. It stems from the branch of philosophy known as logical positivism. It asserts that things are only meaningful if they are observable and verifiable. The so-called scientific method formulates a hypothesis from theory and then collects data about the observable consequences of the hypothesis to test its validity in the real world. This method originated in the physical sciences and then was adopted by educational psychologists who dominated the field of educational research for most of this century. The approach is inherently quantitative, emphasizing measurement of behavior and prediction of future measurements. The underlying assumption is that mathematical models exist and need to be uncovered, and any limitations are a result of faulty measurement, imperfect models, or an inability to control the extraneous variables. However, there have been criticisms of the positivist paradigm. One is that observation is not value-free, as the positivists assert. Indeed, what one observes, not to mention how we observe it, implies a set of values in the observer. Furthermore, some of the most important things in human behavior are things that cannot be directly observed, such as intentions and feelings.

These criticisms led to a paradigm commonly referred to as *post-positivism.* This paradigm accepts values and perspective as important considerations in the search for knowledge. What you see is dependent on your perspective and what you are looking for. The post-positivists are inclined to working in naturalistic settings rather than under experimental conditions. The approach is holistic rather than controlling and it relies on the researcher rather than precise measurement instruments as the major means of gathering data. It emphasizes qualitative rather than quantitative measurement where the approach emerges according to opportunity, and those being studied are assumed to have something to say about the interpretation of data. It has many elements of insightful observation though in its best manifestations is grounded in theory. Both of the first two paradigms are what might be referred to as academic research, because they share the academic agenda of the advancement of knowledge that can be generalized to the world.

As well as these two dominant paradigms, educational research is affected by two differing approaches: the *academic research approach* and the *contract research approach*. Unlike academic research, contract research places value not on a detached or disinterested quest for truth, but on the need of the sponsor to know. The contract research approach is a utilitarian approach which assumes that useful knowledge is that which influences practice, and the contract researcher is able to serve a client who needs this knowledge to make informed decisions about educational practice, policy on programs. It includes such considerations as the cost of different courses of action and it is designed to examine past practice in an attempt to improve how things are done in the future.

Many beginning researchers confuse the two approaches, and consequently get into difficulty because they mix their perspectives. They embark on academic research that searches for ungrounded knowledge, but do so because they expect that it will influence someone such as their employer or someone they do not even know: 'Once I diagnose the problems of education in Indonesia, the government will surely change its policies!' If you wish to engage in academic research, do it for the personal pleasure it brings. If you wish to do contract research bear in mind that it can only be successful if the agenda is not yours. Exhibit 1.1 compares the academic and contract research traditions.

This chapter explores the nature of educational research, the four levels of research and introduces terms which refer to common methodological approaches. It then defines some basic concepts useful for further study of educational research.

Exhibit 1.1: A comparison between academic research and contract research

Academic Research	Contract Research
1 Is sponsored by an agency committed to the general advancement of knowledge.	1 Is sponsored by an agency with a vested interest in the results.
2 Results are the property of society and the research community.	2 Results become the property of the sponsor.
3 Studies rely on the established reputations of the researchers and are totally under their control.	3 Studies follow explicit terms of reference developed by the sponsor to serve the sponsor's needs.
4 Budget allocations are generally based on global proposals and accounting is left to the researchers.	4 Budget accountability is directly related to the sponsor and relates to agreed terms of reference, time frames and methodologies.
5 The conduct of research is based on 'good faith' between funder and researcher.	5 The work is contractual between sponsor and researcher.
6 The research produces findings and conclusions, but rarely recommendations except those related to further research needs.	6 The research includes applied recommendations for action.
7 Academic research tends to extend an identifiable scholarly discipline.	7 By its nature, contract research tends to be interdisciplinary.
8 Academic research is typically focussed on a single set of testable hypotheses.	8 Contract research frequently analyzes the consequences of alternative policy options.
9 Decision-rules relate to theoretically-based tests of statistical significance.	9 Decision-rules relate to pre-determined conventions and agreements between the sponsor and the researcher.
10 Research reports are targeted to other specialized researchers in the same field.	10 Research reports are intended to be read and understood by lay persons.

What is Educational Research?

Research in education is a disciplined attempt to address questions or solve problems through the collection and analysis of primary data for the purpose of description, explanation, generalization and prediction.

Research is fundamentally a problem-solving activity which addresses a problem, tests an hypothesis or explains phenomena. I prefer the problem-solving formulation which relies on a series of specific questions addressed by data collected for the purpose. In this traditional research approach, hypotheses are derived, tested under various conditions, then accepted or rejected, generally in accordance with pre-established conventions. This approach is best suited for certain problems and methods rooted in experimental studies, but is of limited use for the more general problem-solving addressed here. The formulation of research problems and questions is a more general and generalizable approach to research and is the one followed in this text. Succeeding chapters are devoted to the task of formulating researchable problems, suitable research questions and deriving methodologies with which to explore them.

There is another domain of investigation which some scholars consider research. It includes philosophical analysis, especially conceptual analysis, the situation of educational issues within a philosophical tradition, the examination of epistemological and axiological assumptions, criticism and so forth. I view such activities as scholarly, but not as research in the sense in which it is used in this text. The principal difference is the lack of primary data in those approaches which rely entirely on critical thinking and analysis of existing literature and theory.

Exhibit 1.2 lists ten characteristics of educational research which extend the definition noted above. Unlike other forms of knowing, research relies on systematic and objective observation, recording and analysis. It seeks to answer the questions

Exhibit 1.2: Ten characteristics of educational research

1 Educational research attempts to solve a problem.

2 Research involves gathering new data from primary or first-hand sources or using existing data for a new purpose.

3 Research is based upon observable experience or empirical evidence.

4 Research demands accurate observation and description.

5 Research generally employs carefully designed procedures and rigorous analysis.

6 Research emphasizes the development of generalizations, principles or theories that will help in understanding, prediction and/or control.

7 Research requires expertise — familiarity with the field; competence in methodology; technical skill in collecting and analyzing the data.

8 Research attempts to find an objective, unbiased solution to the problem and takes great pains to validate the procedures employed.

9 Research is a deliberate and unhurried activity which is directional but often refines the problem or questions as the research progresses.

10 Research is carefully recorded and reported to other persons interested in the problem.

and address the problems posed by inquiring minds and strives to find general principles and theories which can lead to the prediction of behaviors and events in the future. The goals of research have to do with understanding, prediction and ultimately control. These notions rely on controlled and accurate observation and the recording of information. Only in this way can prediction be accurately measured and assessed. It is important to understand that the researcher should be unbiased and not have too strong a vested interest in the outcome. It is natural for people to do research in areas towards which they feel a certain value commitment, but it must not interfere with one's ability to preserve objectivity. People with a mission should engage in volunteer work or religion; they should not pursue research to justify their causes.

Research is a scientific process which assumes that events in the world are lawful and orderly and, furthermore, that the lawfulness is discoverable. This is the meaning of determinism and the researcher acts in the belief that the laws of nature can be understood and ultimately controlled to at least some degree. In a nutshell, educational research is the systematic process of discovering how and why people in educational settings behave as they do.

Our assumptions and perspectives underlying nature and research are fundamental to our understanding and progress. Very often shifts in assumptions have lead to important discoveries. The assumption that learning must be controlled by a teacher who feeds information to students has helped preserve the nature of schooling as we have known it. A shift in such an assumption leads to fundamental questions about the nature of schooling. Early research on teacher effectiveness focused on the teacher, but a shift to learning and study of the learner paid greater dividends in helping us understand the teaching–learning process.

Research takes many forms and it incorporates many tools, methods and techniques with which we attempt to understand the world around us. All research relates to questions or problems which present themselves and to which the researcher seeks answers and understanding. Why are school classrooms organized in seats and rows? Why is formal schooling arranged in different levels which take place in different buildings and incorporate slightly different methods? Why do some children learn easily and effectively while others have learning difficulties? Why do some school administrators attend inservice education while others do not? How do young children best acquire a second language? How can we help developing nations build educational institutions which respond to indigenous needs and reflect indigenous capabilities?

Levels of Research

There are essentially four levels at which educational research takes place: descriptive, explanatory, generalization and basic or theoretical (see Exhibit 1.3). Descriptive research has two major branches — historical and contemporary. Historical research attempts to describe what was, whereas contemporary research describes what is happening now. While descriptive research is the first and most elementary level of

Exhibit 1.3:   The four levels of educational research

Level	I	II	III	IV
Research Type	Descriptive	Explanatory (Internal Validity)	Generalization (External Validity)	Basic (Theoretical)
Major Questions	What is happening? What happened in the past?	What is causing it to happen? Why did it happen?	Will the same thing happen under different circumstances?	Is there some underlying principle at work?
Methods/ Approaches	Case study Content analysis Ethnography Historiography Needs assessment Observation Policy research Polling Program evaluation Sociometry Survey research Tracer studies	Case study Comparative Correlational Ethnography Ex-post facto Historiography Observation Sociometry Time–series analysis Tracer studies	Casual-comparative Experimental Meta analysis Multiple case Study Predictive Quasi-experimental	ABAB designs Experimental Meta analysis Policy research Time–series analysis

research activity, it is of major importance for understanding and the accumulation of knowledge. A great many contemporary and past educational phenomena are not well understood because they have not been sufficiently described. A great many questions in education are descriptive. How were schools organized in colonial North America? On what activities do principals spend their time? What do teachers actually do in a classroom? What types of programs are offered by leading universities in adult education? What are the backgrounds of teachers of mathematics? What are the concerns of teachers, parents and students? What are the learning needs of beginning educational administrators? These and thousands of other questions are not necessarily well understood in the literature and for this reason descriptive research needs to take place if we are to gain understanding of the state of education in our world.

Fundamental to good description are good measurement and observation. Unless we can accurately describe our findings and observations objectively they will have little meaning for others and will be of no general use. Statistics can be used to quantify and simplify description by grouping observations and describing in a few words, symbols or numbers that would otherwise take a great deal of prose. In some cases, photographs, videos or films can be used to describe educational situations. Descriptions can also be enhanced and brought to life through the use of quotations, including stories and, as is the case in qualitative research, subjective interpretations by the researcher. Regardless of the approach — qualitative, quantitative or both — without good descriptions it is impossible to move to higher levels of research.

Explanatory research asks the question, what is causing this to happen? Why does one school get better results than another? How does a given principal motivate the staff while another is unsuccessful at doing so? Does a French immersion program lead to greater French second language competence than the traditional program? Is a given type of schooling an effective way to expend taxpayers money? Explanation, sometimes called internal validity, focuses on understanding what is happening in a given observable setting. Thus, our interest is understanding what goes on in a given classroom or school but not necessarily its implications for the world at large. That becomes the third level of research.

Generalization attempts to discover whether similar things will happen in new situations. Building on the explanatory level, an attempt is made to generalize to a new situation. This, of course, begins to lead to prediction and ultimately to control of effects. Our interest is to push the explanation to see how far the results can be generalized. For example, will an approach that taught Johnny to read also help him with mathematics? Will the technique for motivating a school staff apply in another setting? While our interest is in generalization, it does not necessarily try to explain why the generalization occurs. So, for example, if we wanted to predict the level of the tides we could do so easily with a computer model that would enable accurate predication into the future, without any understanding whatsoever of the law of universal gravitation. Discovery of the law leads to the fourth level of research.

Basic or theoretical research attempts to discover underlying principles which are at work. Basic researchers hold that the proper role of science is the study of basic scientific questions regardless of whether their solution has practical application. What are the underlying dimensions of school climate which lead to school effectiveness? What is the relationship of intrinsic and extrinsic rewards to performance? What are the characteristics of educational leadership? Often such basic and theoretical research is conducted in experimental settings, using contrived situations and perhaps even animal experiments in order to isolate the underlying principle. Such basic research has been motivated by a desire to understand theory but as is the case in the natural sciences, such understanding has often had important applied consequences. The study of x-rays and microwaves in physics has led to medical and kitchen applications which were not the primary motivation for exploring the phenomena. Similarly, Skinner's reinforcement theory developed with animals has had profound educational applications. While philosophy does not typically incorporate primary source data, empirical evidence, or observation, it is included as an associated discipline since it relies on similar approaches to other forms of theoretical research.

Research Disciplines and Fields

Education is a broad field and in the past it often borrowed its methods and approaches from the traditional academic disciplines such as the physical sciences, history, psychology and anthropology. Now that the study of education has matured, researchers often adhere to fields of study that have developed their own agendas and approaches. For example, the American Educational Research Association has divisions that deal with such themes as: administration, curriculum studies, learning and instruction, research and measurement methodology, history and historiography, the social context of education, and school evaluation and program development. The specific concerns of these fields often focus on particular levels of research. The methods and approaches also cover a wide spectrum so the beginning researcher is advised to consider the traditions that have emerged in the field where your work is to be located.

Relationship Among the Levels of Research

The various levels of research are by no means discreet. Furthermore, they often build on one another in an interactive way. It is fair to say, however, that one cannot explain without being able to describe, nor can one easily generalize without being able to explain. Theoretical principles have a scant chance of being discovered and understood unless one has a thorough knowledge of relevant generalizations and their limitations.

Generally speaking, educational researchers should attempt to go beyond the strictly descriptive level in their work. Description is the proper domain of pollsters and those who conduct surveys, but in most worthwhile research, an attempt is made to explain and interpret the data. Such explanation relies on a knowledge of theory and prior research and its application is the mark of the experienced researcher. Such a person can relate the present study to previous research in the field, link sets of findings and extend the basis of general knowledge.

The type of research one does is greatly dependent upon the research culture prevalent in the institution where the study is being carried out. Contributions to existing research teams, who explore similar themes, will generally enable one to make a greater contribution than doing an independent and isolated study. Furthermore, the higher levels of research require a great depth of experience either in the form of an extensive published literature, successive studies done by an individual researcher or numerous studies done by a research team. In general, the beginning researcher should obtain a thorough grounding in the lower levels before the higher levels of research are attempted. One of the most difficult challenges of all for the beginning researcher is to select an appropriate problem and pursue it at an appropriate level. At this stage, it is fair to say one cannot do the higher levels of research until he or she has mastered the rudiments of the descriptive and explanatory levels.

Basic Concepts

Pilot Study

A pilot study is a small scale study conducted prior to the actual research. The entire pilot study is conducted in order to test the procedures and techniques to see that they work satisfactorily. Additionally, pilot studies are used to test questionnaires and other instruments and to see whether there is any possibility that worthwhile results will be found. If promising results do not appear in a pilot study, researchers sometimes reconsider the rationale, design, or viability of their study. Thus, pilot studies provide an excellent way of avoiding trivial or non-significant research.

Primary and Secondary Data Sources

A primary source of data is one where the person providing the data was actually present, whereas a secondary data source is one where the data comes from one who was not present. For example, a child's test results are primary sources, whereas a teacher's recollection of how well a child performed is a secondary source. Research studies are primary sources if one consults the original account such as found in a research journal. Descriptions of research studies reported in a book are secondary sources since they are described by the author of the book rather than the person who conducted the research.

Variable

A variable is a characteristic that can assume any one of a range of values. Nominal variables are those which do not have a numeric or quantitative implication such as eye color, race or gender. Ordinal variables can be rank ordered, but do not imply an equal interval between the levels being ranked. For example, common performance grades on exams such as A, B and C are ordered, but the difference between a B and an A may be different than the difference between a C and a B. Sometimes these are grouped into intervals such as ages 21–30, 31–40, etc. These are called interval variables. Ratio variables are those that are created during the research by dividing existing ordinal variables. Cost per pupil is an example. In general, nominal variables are used in the construction of frameworks or the division of samples into comparison groups. Ordinal and ratio variables are used for statistical analysis.

Reliability

Reliability refers to consistency in measurement. In common terms the reliability of a test is the extent to which subsequent administrations would give similar results. A test which is not reliable will give different results every time it is taken. Accepted practice uses such measures as test-retest reliability coefficients to indicate reliability. This is equivalent to the correlation (see Chapter 12) of test results obtained on two separate occasions. In qualitative research, reliability suggests that different qualitative researchers would come to the same conclusions given exposure to the same situations.

The extent to which data relate to objective criteria will improve reliability. When the data are based on personal impressions they tend not to be reliable. However, when they relate to counts or physical measurements or the number of correct math problems, they are generally reliable. For example, it is much more difficult to get agreement on the artistic merits of a work of art than it is on the technical competence of a draftsman. The data used in educational research must be reliable if the analysis is to have any meaning. If we do not have reliable measurement tools, we can't have much confidence in our results.

Validity

Validity is the complement to reliability and refers to the extent to which what we measure reflects what we expected to measure. Thus, an IQ score is assumed to be a measure of intelligence and is assumed to be a valid representation of intelligence in quantitative terms. Similarly, the enrollment of a school is assumed to be a valid measure of its size. Validity to the qualitative researcher generally refers to the extent to which the stated interpretations are in fact true. Two forms of validity — internal and external — concern the researcher. *Internal validity* refers to the validity of data measures as described above. Internal validity also relates to issues of truthfulness of responses, accuracy of records, or the authenticity of historical artifacts. There is a related validity problem known as external validity. *External validity* refers to the generalizability of the obtained results. Are the results obtained with a sample of 100 principals similar to the results expected from all 1243 principals in the province or state? Can the results of studies of school effectiveness in Montreal be generalized to schools in Toronto or Boston? We require internal validity to be confident that the results obtained are true for those participating in a study; we need external validity to be in a position to generalize them.

Unit of Analysis

Researchers must be clear on their unit of analysis. That is, they must decide from the sources of data and sample selection procedures what unit is being selected as opposed to the one which is desired. It is the actual unit which must be used in the analysis. For example, if five classrooms are chosen, the unit of analysis is the classroom, and the study should be of classrooms. It is not a study of individual children, even though many individual children are involved. For that purpose, the unit of analysis would be children and individual children would have to be selected for the study. Even though you have many children involved, if you have selected classrooms you can only legitimately deal with the number of classrooms chosen. This tends to be a great limitation on the generalizability of most research and many researchers violate the principle of unit of analysis by collecting data in one way and then attempting to analyze it and generalize from it in another.

Units of analysis can range from nations or provinces or schools to individual teachers and pupils. Each of these levels has an appropriate place in research, but when the nature of the questions and methods of analysis comprise a collective, such as a nation, then the data used in the study must be overall data for the nation, such as gross national product or size of the population. If one wants to use the results of academic achievement tests in referring to a nation, one would have to use the average score for the nation.

Statistical Significance

Quantitative research follows the probability laws of applied statistics. These indicate whether relationships and values observed would be likely to occur by chance alone. A trivial example is useful to help understand the concept. If you were researching the question, 'Does stereoscopic vision (seeing with both eyes) help score points in basketball?', you might take an expert like Wilt Chamberlain, blindfold one eye and let him shoot from the foul line. If he shot 100 times, he would undoubtedly get some balls in the basket. Now remove the blindfold and let him try again. If he scored 50 with one eye covered and 95 seeing with both eyes, we would be inclined to say that sight helps. What if he scored 60 blindfolded and only 65 with both eyes? Then we would be less sure. Obviously, there would be variations in performance every time he did the task. These chance variations can be monitored under the two different conditions and the probability of each score can be calculated. Even with no real difference in performance there will be a difference in the actual scores obtained every time the task is performed. The greater the difference in scores, the more likely that stereoscopic sight helps.

A statistically significant result is one which is unlikely to have occurred by chance alone. Thus, the observed relationship or difference is assumed to be a real one. One can never be absolutely sure in dealing with the laws of statistical probability, so researchers generally adopt some level of confidence in their result. Universal levels of confidence are 0.05 and 0.01. These imply that any observed relationship or difference would be expected to occur by chance less than 5 per cent or 1 per cent of the time. In other words, there is a 95 per cent chance that the results observed are real, rather than statistical aberrations. In polls, researchers generally describe the confidence in their results by saying that the actual result is within x percentage points 19 times out of 20.

It should be emphasized that statistical significance has little to do with educational significance. Results which might be highly statistically significant may have few implications for researchers or practitioners. Differences can be very small and still be statistically significant, too small to have much practical application. There are other procedures which can be used to estimate how powerful the results are but they are beyond the scope of this text.

Conclusion

There are many routes to knowledge. People learn through observation, reading, discussion and debate. Much of what is to be learned is already known by others and it is a case of accessing this knowledge and learning it. Some things, however, are unknown. They must be discovered independently. That is the function of research and is part of its excitement. As a researcher, you are on a quest which, despite no small share of frustration and hard work, leads to the discovery of new knowledge which can be passed on to others. The anticipation, the discovery and the potential contribution is what makes it all worthwhile.

The competent researcher, unlike the untrained person, is a skilled observer, familiar with the patterns and theories that govern human behavior and sensitive to recognizing which manifestations are important and which are routine. He or she knows how to observe, record, analyze and share this world view, so that other researchers can criticize, replicate and extend this new knowledge. Indeed, the human species differs from other forms of animal life in that humans are able to learn from the experience of others. Information is collected, analyzed and communicated, and over time the body of accumulated knowledge increases and provides the basis for societal progress.

While research is a means to discovery of new knowledge, there are differing research paradigms and many approaches to research. The research approach used tells something of how the researcher views the world. In examining research it is useful to bear this in mind. What assumptions is the researcher using? Out of what traditions have the questions and approaches emerged? What would happen if the assumptions and approaches were changed or traded in for alternatives? These types of questions often generate new avenues of significant research and should be borne in mind when defining a research problem.

For many readers of this text disciplined research is a new activity requiring the learning of many new concepts and skills. Often this is done while one is trying to formulate and develop a research problem and proposal, and the challenge is to learn what you need while progressing with your own research. As you develop your interests, consider how each approach to research relates and how it might change the perspective and formulation of your research topic.

Reference

Skinner, B.F. (1938). *The behavior of organisms*, NY: Appleton-Century-Crofts.

Chapter 2

Research Ethics

All human behavior is subject to ethical principles, rules and conventions which distinguish socially acceptable behavior from that which is generally considered unacceptable. The practice of research is no exception, but like most fields of human endeavour, acceptable standards for research on human subjects have evolved and become more formalized over time (Frankel, 1987).

Until relatively recently, many researchers considered their work beyond scrutiny, presumably guided by a disinterested virtue which in their view justified any means by which to reach the end. Thus, in 1932, 399 semi-literate black men with syphilis in Tuskegee, Alabama, had treatment withheld, but were monitored for 40 years merely to study the progression of the untreated disease. Although it had become apparent by the mid-1940s that mortality rates for the untreated people were twice as high than for the control group, the experiment went on until its exposure in the *New York Times* in 1972. Closer to home, during the period 1957–60, Ewan Cameron at McGill's Allan Memorial Institute in Montreal administered psychedelic drugs to 52 unsuspecting patients in order to carry out brainwashing experiments for the Central Intelligence Agency of the USA. These experiments were also disclosed publicly for the first time in the *New York Times* in 1977, but it was not until 1988 that the survivors received settlement. Alas, such travesties are not confined to the fields of medicine and psychology. In education, countless children have been routinely forced to learn nonsense syllables; native children have been taken from their parents and punished severely for speaking their mother tongue; generations of left-handers have been forced to write with their right hands; most children are at some time asked to participate in questionable experiments in teaching methods and all of us are called upon incessantly to fill out meaningless questionnaires. Who bears the responsibility for ethical research? What principles are required to protect the innocent from such abuse?

The Need for Codes of Ethics and Controls

Throughout this century the pendulum for ethically responsible research has shifted from the moral arena to the legal arena. Historically, ethical responsibility for a study rested solely with the researcher; this is no longer the case. The onus has shifted from the individual to regulatory bodies who sanction submissions for research projects according to approved guidelines and regulations.

The need for regulation and codes of behavior emerged from revelations of the atrocities committed by the Nazis and immoral behavior in the name of research. The Nuremberg Code of 1947 for biomedical research is one of the important codes and was the first to focus on the importance of informed consent as discussed later. The Helsinki Declaration of 1964 provided guidance in such areas as the use of animals for research purposes. Perhaps the earliest code in the social sciences was the 1953 code relating to research, teaching and professional practices developed from over 1000 case studies submitted by members of the American Psychological Association (APA) through a research study launched in 1948. The American Sociological Association (ASA) adopted a formal code of ethics in 1969 followed four years later by the APA whose ethical code for research with human subjects has become the major standard in use by social scientists. In addition, researchers following the contract research approach have adopted standards of professional conduct to help ensure that minimal levels of competence are met. The development and adoption of codes and procedures has been an important step mainly because it has alerted people to the problems and issues to consider. The actual judgments involved are still often difficult. Furthermore, the control continues to rest ultimately with the individual researcher and to a lesser extent with a better informed public.

One question remains. Does the regulation and control of ethics make research more ethical? Not necessarily. One of the greatest challenges researchers face today is complying with one set of guidelines for all people. Should a graduate student researching the range and usefulness of extracurricular school activities in a school district be forced to comply with the same ethical requirements as a doctor who is testing a new drug on an AIDS patient? Obviously not, for the purpose and impact of the research and the consequence of error vary considerably from project to project, discipline to discipline, institution to institution. In the long-term, excessive regulations and approval procedures may in fact hinder the very process it is designed to help. Participants may become apprehensive and reluctant to give willingly of themselves when forced to engage in complicated bureaucratic approval processes. Researchers, frustrated by lengthy, slow and sometimes irrelevant ethical approval processes may decide to change their vocation, or worse cheat the system!

Who Bears the Ethical Responsibility for Research?

The responsibility for ethical research ultimately lies with the individual researcher. Historically, it was presumed that qualified people with the authority to conduct research would conduct themselves morally and professionally. As this has not always been the case, the responsibility for ethical practice in research has moved a self-regulated moral arena into a multi-faceted legal arena. There are two sets of governing norms: ethical standards and professional standards. Today, regulatory bodies set standards of conduct, require certificates of ethics and have the power to veto research projects. Today's researcher is bound by these regulations, as well as their personal codes of ethics.

The network of regulatory bodies is extensive. Research institutions, research councils, community and professional boards, and sponsors of the research all impact the process to some degree. Most universities have developed review procedures which follow the spirit of the requirements set by the major research councils such as the Social Sciences and Humanities Research Council of Canada, the Medical Research Council of Canada or the Natural Sciences and Engineering Research Council of Canada.

In practice, each major research organization must have a research ethics committee charged with the responsibility to scrutinize every piece of proposed research and grant written permission before a study may proceed. Furthermore, most funding agencies will not fund research unless it has a certificate of ethical responsibility, complete with signatures of all members of the ethics committee. Thus, accountability rests with a group of peers willing to place their names as guarantors of the ethical standards of the research. Such practices now extend to virtually all institutionally-sanctioned research involving human subjects, including that conducted by graduate students.

Governments are also involved in controls. In the United States, the Department of Health and Human Services and the National Institutes of Health have developed regulations for grant recipients. In general, they require that institutions receiving grants provide for an institutional review board to assume the protection and welfare of research participants.

Ethical Standards

All people involved with research, the research community, funding agencies, governments and the public share certain common concerns. These concerns raise several general considerations which must always be addressed. The specific considerations and acceptable standards for ethical research are as follows:

- that risks to participants are minimized by research procedures that do not unnecessarily expose them to risks;
- that the risks to participants are outweighed by the anticipated benefits of the research;
- that the rights and welfare of participants are adequately protected;
- that the research will be periodically reviewed; and
- that informed consent has been obtained and appropriately documented.

Informed Consent

The most fundamental principle for ethical acceptability is that of informed consent: the involved participants must be informed of the nature and purpose of the research, its risks and benefits, and must consent to participate without coercion. There are six basic elements which must be respected when seeking permission from persons who consent for themselves and from people who give consent for those who cannot provide consent themselves, such as minors:

- an explanation of the purpose of the research and the procedures that will be used;
- a description of any reasonably foreseeable risks and discomforts to the subjects;
- a description of any benefits that may reasonably be expected, including incentives to participate;
- a disclosure of any alternative procedures that might be advantageous to the subject;
- an offer to answer any questions concerning the procedures; and
- a statement that participation is voluntary and that the subject is free to withdraw from the study at any time.

In practice, many situations require that an informed consent form be duly signed before a participant is permitted to participate. Such a form should describe the purpose of the research, its benefits, the nature of the tasks to be performed, the rights of the participant to withdraw and the names of the person and institution conducting the research. This makes everything clear and provides a degree of proof that the person was informed and consented to become involved. Naturally, the information needs to be suited to the language, culture and age of the participants. Participants who are coerced to get involved, such as prison inmates, or those in search of monetary rewards, are not assumed to have consented voluntarily, so in recent times such groups are rarely used in social science research. The Food and Drug Administration in the United States no longer permits data obtained from captives to be admissible in human trials of new drugs.

Unfortunately, the best intentions behind the principle of informed consent have not necessarily led to more ethically defensible outcomes (Adair, Dushenko and Lindsay, 1985). In practice, it is relatively easy to get participants to sign an informed consent form, particularly because of their inherent trust of a scientific leader whose individual attention to the participant becomes a subtle form of coercion.

Use of Volunteers

Most social science studies ask people to volunteer as participants. This raises four major ethical problems. First, the people most inclined to volunteer tend to be the more powerless in society. They look up to the researcher and in some cases, such as when students are involved, the researcher has a position of power over the 'volunteers' who are really subjected to coercion. A second and related problem is that of feeling obliged to participate. A researcher, with permission from a sponsor, may arrive at a location and make a verbal request for people to participate in a pre-approved study. Peer pressure or an expectation that one should participate may cause some people to join the study who would otherwise not take part. A third ethical problem is that people may volunteer with the expectation that they may be helped. A researcher may describe a new experimental allergy treatment to a patient and inadvertently offer hope to those who have not been successful with previous options. Finally, the fourth issue relates to labeling participants. By identifying people as having certain attributes, deficits or potentials, you may unwillingly affect their lives.

Honesty, Trust and Betrayal

Investigators should be honest and open. Some experiments call for the use of deception or telling the subject that the purpose or method of the experiment is one thing when in fact it is quite another. Deception is seldom warranted and in the rare instances when it is, the potential benefits from the research should exceed any known risks. Furthermore, the investigator should take special steps to explain the deception after the experiment and restore a relationship of honesty.

Right to Discontinue

Ethical research practice requires the researcher to respect the participant's right to discontinue at any time. This is an important safeguard, particularly when individuals feel that ethical principles have been or may be violated. It is frequently used by people filling out questionnaires (who merely leave offensive questions blank or do not return the questionnaire), but is not as easily exercised by persons who are captive in a group such as a school class. There are also subtle forces between researcher and participant which generally make it difficult for the participant to stop unless there is good reason.

Debriefing

Once the data are collected, ethical practice suggests that the investigator informs participants about the experiment and clarifies any questions which may arise. The debriefing also permits the researcher to provide additional information which if given in advance may have biased the results. In studies which employ questionnaires or tests it is advisable, when possible, to offer participants a summary of results.

Confidentiality

Confidentiality involves a clear understanding between the researcher and participant concerning how the data provided will be used. Confidential information implies that the identity of the individual will remain anonymous. It assumes as well that the reader of the research will not be able to deduce the identity of the individual.

Information may be quoted and reported, but the identity of the individual should be protected. While it is the duty of the researcher to protect the identity of individuals, there is a distinction between one's public role and private life. It is generally agreed that reports on the behavior of people in public office performing their role can be disclosed, but their personal life should be protected.

Right to Privacy and Access to Personal Records

The right to privacy is an important ethical consideration and implies that the individual concerned should decide what aspects of their personal attitudes, opinions, habits, eccentricities, doubts and fears are to be communicated or withheld from others. There are major international codes of human rights such as the United Nations' Universal Declaration of Human Rights that hold privacy as a basic right and this has been incorporated into all codes of research ethics. One-way mirrors, concealed microphones, video cameras and many other technical devices are all formidable threats to privacy. It is understandable that in the interest of furthering our understanding, for example consumer product testing, or in the interest of scientific rigor, these devices can be useful. However, when these methods are used, special care must be taken for informed consent.

Access to personal records, both as a primary or secondary source of data, must be approached both ethically and legally. When evaluating the need to access a data base, for example student records, the researcher must ensure that confidentiality is not breached, harm will not come to any individual, the privacy of the individual is protected, and if possible consent should be obtained. Also, in today's world of high technology, researchers must ensure the integrity of their data base and ensure computer files are protected and limit access exclusively to those who need to know. In general, it is advisable to apply and use codes as early as possible in the research process.

Respecting the Participant's Time

Although seldom mentioned in standard works on research ethics, it is unethical to waste the participant's time by asking him or her to complete irrelevant questions or participate in studies which by their nature cannot lead to significant results.

Risks/Benefits

In any social science research the potential benefits must outweigh the risks to individual participants. There are occasions, such as in medical research, when the risks are high but are tolerated because of the potential to aid great numbers of people. While difficult to assess, the importance of the benefit is an essential consideration in certain types of research.

Exploitation, Exclusion and Vulnerable Populations

Certain groups of people at times may be more vulnerable to damage as research subjects due to their age, limited mental capacity, psychological disposition, gender, culture or medical disposition. Location of the subjects is also a concern. Isolated populations, such as prisoners and institutionalized people, can be considered vulnerable due to their inability to remove themselves from the research setting. In some instances, specific populations such as minorities, women or children have been excluded from the research arena, thus creating an imbalance in the opportunities for all to benefit from the research advances. All researchers must exercise caution to avoid exploitation and take special care in selecting and dealing with various research populations.

Risk to Cultural and Proprietary Values

Special care must be taken in dealing with sensitive populations whose cultures are fragile. Removing archaeological artifacts, the inappropriate storage or display of sacred objects, or taking photographs in certain cultures are examples. Common courtesy dictates a need to understand what one is doing and to go as far as possible to protect cultural values. Similarly a researcher should not impose foreign values or introduce disruptive ideas when performing a research role. There is a place for educating people of all cultures, but it is not a legitimate part of the researcher's role.

Different Countries and Cultures

Research involving people in different countries and of different cultures requires special care. When researching people of different cultures both at home and abroad, informed consent can be difficult for two reasons: a) linguistic barriers, and b) people in other cultures often have difficulty understanding the nature of research and its uses. Researchers who operate in other countries and with other cultures generally have an advantage of wealth, power and information. It is therefore, willingly or unwillingly, possible to coerce subjects to participate. An important safeguard is to involve researchers from the other culture to inform you about the norms of the country, to assist with the task of briefing and debriefing participants, and to aid with interpreting the results. Some African countries, such as Kenya, require 'research permits' which raise additional questions for people who may suspect the researcher is a government spy.

Professional Standards

In addition to the ethical standards that affect all research, professional bodies have established standards of professional conduct that affects research. These typically apply to the utilitarian forms of research such as contract research. For example, the Joint Committee on Standards for Educational Evaluation serves 15 professional associations of educators and psychologists. In 1994, that body published its *Program Evaluation Standards* (2nd ed.), which identifies four types of standards for professional evaluators: utility, feasibility, proprietary and accuracy. The utility standards are intended to ensure that an evaluation will serve the information needs of intended users, and include seven elements such as standards for report timeliness and clarity. The three feasibility standards are intended to ensure that an evaluation will keep disruption to a minimum, be diplomatic and frugal. The eight proprietary standards are intended to ensure that an evaluation will be conducted legally, ethically, and with due regard for the welfare of those involved in the evaluation, as well as those affected by its results. The accuracy standards include 12 components and are intended to ensure that an evaluation will reveal and convey technically adequate information about the features that determine worth or merit of the program being evaluated.

Professional and Ethical Problems

Ethics are complicated. No single law exists to regulate research ethics, nor is this particularly desired. Today's ethics are rooted in both moral and legal grounds, and despite the best intentions of individual researchers and the collective body of research councils, institutions, boards and committees, problems exist. It would be impossible to identify every situation where an ethical dilemma may surface; therefore this book restricts itself to presenting six more common problems that confront researchers. For additional information interested readers are encouraged to consult Burgess (1989) or Punch (1994).

The Research Topic

The Kinsey studies on human sexuality used research to explore personal behaviors some of which themselves were contrary to law, religion or social custom. At the time, no one had valid data on the prevalence of such behaviors, and publication of the report caused considerable concern in certain quarters. Was the topic ethically viable given the societal norms which prevailed at the time of the study? It is the responsibility of the researcher to answer this question, and in concert with the affiliated ethics committee, decide on the line between what is reasonable to research and the concerns of those who might not want to know.

The Research Procedure

The most prevalent ethical issues relate to the procedures used in conducting human experiments. The most difficult cases often use deception, and the most celebrated example is the series of experiments by Stanley Milgram conducted between 1960–64. Milgram involved volunteers who believed they were administering an electric shock to a learner involved in a learning task. Whenever the learner, who was in an adjacent room, made a mistake, he was 'punished' with an electric shock. Volunteers were asked to gradually and continually increase the shock level up to the highest level labelled 'dangerous'. The learner was actually an experimental confederate who cried out in pain but was never really shocked. The true purpose of this experiment was to research obedience and explore why some people refused to follow the 'orders' while others carried through. Critics charged that great harm may have been done to those who discovered that they did this terrible thing to another human. Milgram established elaborate debriefing, counseling and follow-up investigations in an attempt to safeguard the participants.

Similar charges may be made against Robert Rosenthal's studies of 'self-fulfilling prophecy' in which teachers were told of the latent talents of selected students who, according to Rosenthal's early reports, did improve subsequent performance, presumably because of the experiment's influence on the teachers. There are issues in this regard even when deception is not used. Terman's long-term study of genius (1954) identified selected individuals who were followed for years. One cannot help wonder how that identification affected their lives.

The Sponsor

Sometimes it is not just the topic, but also the sponsor which creates issues. In the early 1960s, the US Department of Defense launched Project Camelot, a research project to uncover the determinants of revolution in various Latin American countries. Once the intent became known, Project Camelot was quickly condemned by social scientists who viewed it as an attempt to intervene in the affairs of other countries through the results of research. In this case the motives of the sponsor were suspect, though by itself the topic may have had scientific merit. Shortly after the outcry Project Camelot was terminated.

Free and Informed Consent

Free and informed consent implies that research participants have knowledge about the study and agree to participate without coercion. In many instances, particularly in North American institutions, this consent is formalized in writing. In other cultures, oral consent is more important. It is the responsibility of the researcher to obtain consent from all those who participate.

What happens however, when during the research process, you gain information relevant to the study through informal or unplanned conversations? The value of these communications may not be known until later when you are engaged in the analysis and you are constructing a framework for understanding. Is it unethical to use this information? Yes and no. If the information gathered is used personally, to help you as a researcher understand the phenomena you are exploring, then it is not unethical. If on the other hand, you wish to quote something a specific individual said, or you change your research plan because of this information, it is your duty as a researcher to try and return to the source to obtain written consent.

Obtaining more than you asked for

One particularly difficult and sensitive ethical issue concerns what to do when you get more than you bargained for! This concern is particularly relevant to evaluation researchers and certain qualitative human science researchers. It is not uncommon for a researcher to enter the field with an ethically sound study sanctioned by all the regulatory bodies, personal scruples intact and then, while collecting data, the researcher is made privy to other information. This may be a result of building relationships and developing confidences, it may be that certain people feel the need to provide you with contextual information to enhance your understanding, or on other occasions, participants may have a personal agenda and will use an evaluation to air dirty laundry and address problems which they feel contribute to the subject at hand. To complicate matters, qualitative researchers in search of understanding, may feel compelled to follow some of these leads to see if they are in fact related, in some macro-way, to the study.

Ethical choices must be made about what to do with this additional information. Evaluation research has uncovered practices which range from wastage of public funds to the implementation of harmful educational procedures such as labeling children. The decision of a researcher not to publish an evaluation study might be faulted for not identifying and alerting people to these harmful effects. In other situations, the researcher may innocently discover unsavory evidence of fraud, nepotism or personal misconduct, to name a few. Delicate decisions must be made about what, if any action should be taken, with whom, and how the information should be shared.

Conflict of Interest

Conflict of interest exists when a researcher's personal interests influence the objectives of a study, the ability to make fair judgements or relationships are put at risk. Naturally, many people enjoy doing research in their field where they have both a personal interest and subject expertise. Caution must be exercised, however, with all aspects of the study design to avoid any conflict of interest. Educators, for example, may find it easier and more desirable to research students in their classrooms; however, this should be discouraged as the roles and responsibilities of researcher and educator may become incompatible or worse, have a negative impact on the children.

Conclusion

The responsibility for ethical research has moved from the sole domain of the individual researcher to the collective domain of regulatory boards, councils and committees who control both ethical and professional standards. When developing a research proposal, consider the implications of the topic, the methodology you intend to employ and its relationship to the various principles articulated here. The ultimate responsibility for ethical research lies with you, the researcher. You should be able to answer any question raised by the issues listed in this chapter. You should also find out the rules and procedures governing ethical approval at your own university or institution and take early steps to fulfil their requirements. These procedures often take considerable time, so it is wise to think ahead and not jeopardize your research on the failure to comply with a technical requirement.

Ethical principals are intended to guide the behavior of researchers and offer security and protection to participants. However, no listing of principles of ethics can cover all eventualities. The principles discussed in this chapter provide a framework within which proposed research may be examined. Ethical responsibility begins with the individual researcher and the researcher is the main determinant of ethical standards.

References

Adair, J.G., Dushenko, T.W., & Lindsay, R.C.L. (1985). Ethical regulations and their impact on research practices. *American Psychologist, 40*, pp. 59–72.

Frankel, M.S. (Ed.). (1987). *Values and ethics in organization and human systems development: an annotated bibliography*. American Association for the Advancement of Science.

Terman, L.M. (1954). The discovery and encouragement of exceptional talent. *American Psychologist, 9*, pp. 221–230.

For Further Study

Burgess, R.G. (1989). *The ethics of educational research*. London: Falmer Press.

Punch, M. (1994). Politics and ethics in qualitative research. In Denzin, N.K. & Lincoln, Y.S. (1994). *Handbook of Qualitative Research* (pp. 83–97). Thousand Oaks, CA: Sage.

The Joint Committee on Standards for Educational Evaluation. (1994). *The program evaluation standards: How to assess evaluations of educational programs,* 2nd Ed., Thousand Oaks, CA: Sage.

The Medical Research Council of Canada, The Natural Sciences and Engineering Research Council of Canada and The Social Sciences and Humanities Research Council of Canada (1996). *Code of conduct for research involving humans.* Minister of Supply and Services Canada 1996: CAT. NO. MR21-13/1996 I.

Chapter 3

The Research Process

Gary Anderson and Nancy Arsenault

Research is a dynamic activity that travels a long and winding trail from start to finish. It is not a single event, rather, the act of doing research is a process. And like instructional design, evaluation, decision-making and planning, the research cycle has a set of basic elements that interrelate and interact with each other. The purpose of this chapter is to look at the research process first from a conceptual perspective, then from a planning perspective. While it provides an introduction to some of the topics that are discussed in other chapters, it is both an overview and an integration of the whole research process.

The Research Process

All research involves certain common elements such as defining the questions, reviewing the literature, planning the methodology, collecting and analyzing data, and disseminating findings. At first glance, this may seem like a rather logical, straightforward process, but it is not. Research is dynamic, it evolves as activities unfold and the elements of the research process interact and impact on one another. Time is required to allow research questions to develop, literature to be searched, data to be collected, interpreted and analyzed, and findings disseminated.

Exhibit 3.1 illustrates the major components of the research process. The inner four circles represent the core required research activities. They are joined by a circle of arrows to portray the fact that these core activities are not linear, they are interactive. Consider this scenario: you have just submitted a research proposal to a funding agency with specific research questions, a defined methodology and a proposed budget. Your study is approved but the funding allocation has been cut in half. This one lone external factor will force you to reconsider your project. You may abort the study, you may decrease the sample size, or you may choose to weigh the pros and cons of an alternate research design. Anything is possible. The most immediate external factors that affect the research process are: opportunity, peers and mentors, institutional requirements, experience of the researcher, literature and emerging research questions. You may want to think of these as the micro-forces that affect the research process. The macro-forces — ethics, human resources, values, and the environment — also influence the research process and shape the

Exhibit 3.1: The research process

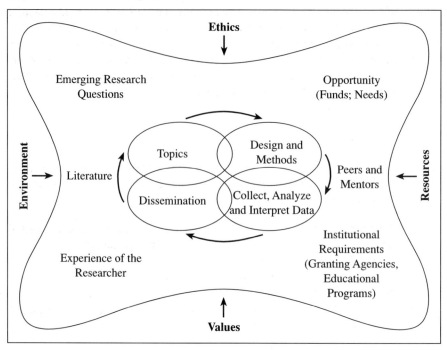

context. If a research project is to succeed you must be aware of how these micro- and macro-forces can both positively and negatively impact the research process. Let us consider them in more detail one by one.

The Core of the Research Process

Topics

The decision to embark on a research project may be motivated by personal or professional reasons and is influenced by all the macro- and micro-forces in the conceptualization. Whatever the reason, the topic will have to be identified and massaged and from there, research questions and sub-questions developed. Student research topics often relate to current or anticipated work environments, whereas topics for career researchers are driven by market demands, whether economically or socially conditioned.

Design and Methods

The choice of research design and methods should be largely influenced by the desired end product, (e.g. a thesis, or consulting report) and the best way to answer the research questions. However, in reality many researchers start with their pre-ferred methods and then go searching for questions that fit. This is all right providing they do not try to answer questions for which their preferred methods are ill-suited. Ideally, all researchers would have the capacity to work within different research tra-ditions, research designs, and use a variety of tools and techniques. Having diversity in your research capacity will permit you to complete a range of studies on your own, or contribute your specialty to a research team.

Collect, Analyze and Interpret Data

All research requires data to be collected, analyzed and interpreted. Essentially, these are technical skills one can learn which should improve with experience. When you collect data you must consider the following questions:

- What type of data are required (i.e. statistical, qualitative, census records)?
- Who will provide the information — the study population?
- Who will collect the information?
- When, where and how will the data be collected?
- What instruments are required?
- What limitations, constraints, approvals and ethical standards are required?
- What resources are at your disposal?

Disseminate Findings

There are a multitude of ways to disseminate research findings including detailed research reports, executive research summaries, theses, dissertations, monographs, conference presentations, oral briefings to stakeholders, and journal articles, to name a few. The focus of Chapter 7 is to elaborate on these forms of scholarly communication. As a researcher you have an obligation to share your work, for that is part of the mission inherent in scholarly research.

Forces Affecting the Core Research Processes

Opportunity

The research world, like the business world, is competitive. Whether you are a student competing for funds from an international, national or local funding body or whether you are a consultant bidding for a contract, you must seek out, be able to recognize and act on possible research opportunities. What types of opportunities exist? Opportunities manifest themselves in different ways and your ability to take advantage of them will depend partly on your needs. You may be invited to join a research team, an outstanding professor in your area of interest may be returning from sabbatical leave and be available to discuss your research interests or, better yet, agree to be your supervisor. You may also stumble upon a particularly exciting line of research which you did not know existed, or you may be the lucky recipient of a scholarship. Keep your eyes and ears open — for when opportunity knocks, you want to be there to open the door!

Peers and Mentors

Peers and mentors are vital to surviving in the research world and enjoying the experience. Peers, in this context, are defined as anyone close to you who cares about your research activities. This may be a friend, fellow student, colleague, spouse or family member. Depending on their knowledge of your research area, peers can help in a variety of ways, for example, helping you search for information in the library or proofreading your work. The most important role of a peer, however, is support — physical, emotional and/or mental. Every research project presents new challenges, new learning opportunities, and new sources of frustration, even for the experienced researcher. Having peers to share your highs and pull you through your lows is extremely important.

Mentors are another indispensable resource to both the novice and experienced researcher. The role of a mentor is to provide challenge, vision, leadership and support. As a student, your mentor will most likely (but not always) be your research advisor. As a professional, your mentor will most likely be a senior colleague and is often the person with whom you work most closely. Mentors help guide you through the research process, share their experiences and point out opportunities and obstacles. Mentoring relationships can have a lasting impact on both parties. This chapter, for example, is a product of a mentoring relationship between two people, a career research consultant/university professor and a doctoral candidate. The months that preceded writing this chapter were spent examining the research process from two perspectives, the novice and the expert. Together, the research learning needs of the graduate student were analyzed, a concept map for the research process was developed (Exhibit 3.1), and the focus for a new chapter emerged.

All graduate students who engage in research may not develop a mentoring relationship with a particular individual, but every student does require a research supervisor. Choosing a supervisor is a critical factor in succeeding as a graduate student, yet many students select their supervisor in haphazard ways. Some university departments will assign you to work with a specific professor, however if you can avoid it, it is better to not have a supervisor assigned to you. Knowledge of your subject area is of course important, but it might be less important than the supervisor's individual qualities, especially at the masters level.

Finally, do not be afraid to shop around for a supervisor, or PhD committee members — in leading universities it is expected. It can also be extremely difficult for some students to approach a professor to discuss research possibilities when their ideas are green, their experience is limited and they have difficulty articulating their needs. Think of each meeting with a professor as a learning opportunity, a chance to share your ideas and refine your thinking. This way when you receive a polite 'thanks but no thanks' and a referral elsewhere, you can avoid being personally disappointed. Accept the situation for what it is, an inappropriate or untimely match. Appendix 3.1 offers a checklist of strategies that will help you prepare for your meetings when you set out to choose a research supervisor.

Institutional Requirements

The research process is also affected by your institutional context. All institutions have formal requirements that you must respect as a researcher. At a university these may take the form of ethical approvals, faculty guidelines or thesis requirements. Agencies that fund research also have certain rules and regulations to be followed and the prudent individual will seek out, in advance, the institutional guidelines that could impact his or her research efforts. As well as these formal rules, the informal norms can have a profound effect. Some universities disfavour certain approaches — many a social researcher has been denied tenure in a university with a behaviorist orientation. Some departments have built their reputations from particular perspectives, and they will not look favourably on a newcomer who comes with a challenging paradigm. These influences are very real and are an important force on you and your research.

Experience of the Researcher

All professions have a range of people, from novice to expert, who possess varying degrees of skill and ability. The research community is no exception. An experienced researcher may bring to the research environment expertise with a particular type of research method (i.e. case study, experimental or evaluation) and be gifted with certain tools of the trade (i.e. an ability to write, interview or develop effective questionnaires). The available skill set will be a major determinant of the research any person does and will also spill over to those around. Sometimes the team synergy kicks in to enable a broader attack; often the limitations on experience of the researcher limit the research process.

The ideal scenario is for experience to change through a learning process. The novice is particularly advantaged as he or she is usually keen on learning and committed to success. More importantly, however, new researchers bring a fresh set of eyes, new perspectives on old problems, they see the world through a clearer lens, one which has not been tinted by the realities and pressures of the research community. The lack of research experience may require that novices take longer to complete a research project, but their research, guided by an effective supervisor, can contribute to the most fundamental reason to do research, building knowledge.

Literature

The never-ending research literature should be a major force on the research process. For the experienced researcher, reading goes with the territory and new contributions published in the literature raise new possibilities for research. For the novice, it is a question of catch-up. Every student requires a thorough search of previous theory and research related to the problem. In the early phases of the research process, searching the literature helps you refine your topic, develop research questions and ground your study in one or more academic fields. As you progress through the research process, the literature informs you in new and exciting ways adding insights and refinements that help your research take on new shape and additional life.

Emerging Research Questions

Where does one get a research question? More often than not they come from unexpected places: concerts are a good source; so are long walks through the forest or paddling a canoe on a tranquil lake. We also get some in discourse with colleagues, or from our work and writing. Our different activities each bring new areas of the brain into the picture which is why some of the best research ideas come from other arenas. Students are another excellent source of emerging questions precisely because they come from another place without the rigid paradigms of the field. Their questions often stimulate interesting avenues of inquiry.

Resources

The type, availability and amount of human and fiscal resources have a tremendous impact on the research process. Royal commissions will spend millions of taxpayers' dollars to investigate a particular phenomena over several years, only to have the government disregard the recommendations. Alternately, many graduate students are faced with financing a small study, as part of their educational costs, to complete their graduate degree. Remember, if you want to study education in China, you probably have to go there. Do not plan a study of education in the South Pacific unless you can afford to board the plane!

Values

Values represent the intrinsic beliefs we hold as people, organizations, societies and cultures. Values are held close to our hearts and impact the decisions we make, the way we approach situations, the way we look at the world, and the way we process and reconstruct knowledge. The positivist approach to research has claimed to be value free. The whole premise behind experimental research is to isolate, examine, and manipulate variables outside their real world context. But even this is not value free, for the researcher brings to the research setting a set of personal values which impacts on the types of decisions made and the directions the research takes. The qualitative research community, and anyone involved in human science research, recognize that it is impossible to do value-free research. Values, like politics, are ever present and will impact on the research process. Rather than deny their existence, prudent researchers will attempt to understand and make explicit, their personal values while at the same time, seek to understand the values held by people, organizations or cultures being researched or supporting the research.

Environment

The environment, as presented in Exhibit 3.1, represents the social, economic, political and technical forces which impact on the research process. Depending on the nature of your study, these forces may have a varying degree of influence on your inquiry and like values, environmental forces both shape and define the research context. The impact of stakeholders — people with a vested interest — are a prime example of an environmental force that can influence a study. Another is time. Research themes come into vogue and provide tremendous opportunities for people willing to jump on board.

Planning a Research Project

All large projects can be enhanced by planning; research is no exception. Many studies are jeopardized by failing to address the various steps required, neglecting to allocate sufficient time and resources for the project, and by not recognizing that 'life is what happens between a plan'. Research can be exceedingly time consuming, particularly for the inexperienced researcher. However, if you plan your activities in advance and remain alert to the 'change factor', you will succeed.

Some people claim not to plan. While this may be correct at one level, they probably do plan, though they may not verbalize it or write it down. The approach recommended here is to take a pro-active approach to planning research and physically create yourself a workplan for each study you undertake. The single greatest benefit associated with planning is that it establishes where you are now and where you want to be at the end of the project. For example, as you read this book you may have just entered graduate school and this is your first course (candidate A) or, you may have finished most of your course work (candidate B) and are thinking about the research project required for your thesis, monograph or dissertation. If the goal is to complete a masters degree, candidate A and B will travel different paths to reach their goal, their time-lines will be different, and no doubt, the required human and financial resources will vary. In essence, just as no two individuals will plan their graduate degrees exactly the same, no two researchers plan a study exactly the same way.

The other major benefit of planning your research is that it forces you to think through the entire process while factoring in vital information about resources and time-lines. Creating a personal workplan is a challenge. Gaining consensus for a workplan that requires the approval of multiple stakeholders or a large research team can be a nightmare! But, the fact that you commit your ideas to paper means

Exhibit 3.2:   Generic steps in the planning and research processes

The Planning Process	The Research Process
Clarify or define the problem/need	Think about the research Specify the project time frame Identify the topic Define the research questions
Gather information	Conduct a literature search Write a literature review
Identify strategies, tools, and methods and then consider alternatives and SWOT (strengths, weaknesses, opportunities, threats)	Select a research design Define a study population Develop data collection instruments Discuss the limitations Forecast the ethical issues Project how the data will be analyzed Create the budget
Implement	Collect data Analyze and interpret data
Evaluate	Write and disseminate research findings Identify lessons learned

you now have a document for discussion. The mere act of discussing a research plan can be extremely informative to the astute researcher who will note how people interact, who holds the political clout, where the potential stumbling blocks can be found, or what constraints have been overlooked, to name a few.

So how does one go about developing a workplan? First, it is important to realize that there are numerous planning models and some approaches will be more appropriate than others, given the context of a particular project. You may be familiar with terms like Management by Objectives (MBO), Total Quality Management (TQM), Performance Evaluation and Review Technique (PERT), Critical Path Method (CPM), Decision Tree Analysis (DTA), Program Planning Budgeting System (PPBS) and Zero-Based Budgeting (ZBB). These are all names for various planning models that exist and, while they vary in detail and approach, there are certain generic elements common to all. Understanding the link between the five fundamental steps in the planning process will help you with the task of creating your own research workplan. Exhibit 3.2 shows the parallel between the fundamental elements of the planning process and critical steps in the research process.

While this type of comparison may be too explicit for some people, it highlights the essential elements which must be considered when planning research. Again, it must be emphasized that although this information is presented in a compare-and-contrast fashion, it does not necessitate a linear work sequence. Indeed, to avoid tedium, the nature of the research process is such that a mix of activities is recommended. Appendix 3.2 offers a generic planning guide to a 12 month research project.

The table was built based on a typical thesis or dissertation, assumed to last one year. The checklist can be used to plan the research study in advance and allocate time accordingly. The novice researcher may be shocked at the number of things to do and more so at the total time it will require to do them all. Bear in mind that a master's thesis may represent a year's work and a doctoral dissertation even longer, so considerable time is expected.

For Further Study

Burns, M.L. (1994). *Values based planning for quality education.* Lancaster, PA: Technomic.

Cole, A.L., & Hunt, D.E. (Eds.). (1994). *The doctoral thesis journey.* Toronto, ON: Ontario Institute for Studies in Education Press.

Madeson, D. (1983). *Successful dissertations and theses.* San Francisco, CA: Jossey-Bass.

Ogden, E.H. (1993). *Completing your doctoral dissertation or masters thesis in two semesters or less (2nd Ed.).* Lancaster, PA: Technomic.

Lock, L.F., Wyrick, W.S., & Silverman, S.J. (1993). *Proposals that work: A guide for planning dissertations and grant proposals.* Newbury Park, CA: Sage.

Chapter 4

Defining a Research Problem

The old cliché that a problem well stated is half solved, applies perfectly to educational research. It may be easy to decide on a general area of research interest and to have some idea of the general thrust of a research study, but it is not nearly so simple to state the problem in terms which limit the problem without robbing it of its significance. Many graduate students spend months refining a problem, only then to abandon it as once it has been adequately articulated it loses its appeal. The task of defining a research problem requires a combination of experience and intuition, and efforts spent in developing the required skills are useful even though a specific problem may be abandoned. Developing research problems and conducting the study is analogous to attempting to build your own house. While we all have at least a general idea of the kind of house we would like to live in, we are differentially equipped to build it. Some people will have a very clear idea of the specific requirements for the house — of how it will be sited, of its proportions, space allocation and style. Others will have only vague ideas and will require considerable assistance from professionals in order to come up with an appropriate design. Needless to say, basic building skills, experience in the use of tools and the ability to develop and follow a plan are essential if the task of construction is to be accomplished. The first effort, of course, should be more modest than later efforts because it is a learning experience and training ground in the necessary skills. The most successful beginning house builder will follow the established models and will break new ground in only minor ways.

To put the task of writing a thesis in perspective, there are more than 20,000 articles published in educational journals each year and there have been over half a million masters and doctoral theses written in North America alone. The next thesis will add one more small contribution to a vast and expanding universe of knowledge. Despite the vast quantity of work, there are rarely major individual breakthroughs. Thousands of studies add up to very little in the way of concrete knowledge. Rather, there tend to be modest advances which together, over time, add up to a better understanding. In this context, a graduate student thesis should not be viewed as a *vade-mecum*. It will not be the definitive work that will revolutionize the field of education, and if viewed as such, the author can only be disappointed. Treat your thesis for what it is: a good if modest contribution to the advancement of knowledge, but one of the most significant steps in your own education. The purpose of this chapter is to help graduate students define a research problem that will do this for them.

Approaches to Thesis Research

There are essentially three general approaches to an education thesis. One involves a prescriptive method that follows established models adding some small nuance of difference to previous work. This often assumes a building block notion of knowledge: that numbers of studies on a similar topic will together add up to a complete fortress of knowledge about the subject. More importantly, it is a good way of teaching and learning basic research skills while making a more useful contribution to the advancement of knowledge than would be made by creating totally new questions, methods and research tools. This, in its most disciplined and highly developed fashion, is closest to the approach of physical science and is most often used in educational psychology. In many universities, research shops attack a given theme over a period of years. Generations of graduate students follow similar procedures and each adds a new bit to the accumulated wisdom. As previously noted, this prescriptive approach is a good way to learn about research. For the new researcher, the path is clear, having been walked before by your predecessors. One knows the limits of the field, the preparation which must precede formulating the problem and what type of problem will be accepted. As for the research itself, models are there to follow. Furthermore, the fact that other researchers are interested in the problem and there are generally funds for the research, the novice can have support while proceeding with their problem through to a logical conclusion. For those who do not join a research team such an approach is still partially possible by referring to exemplary published studies and existing models from the literature.

A second approach is a more individualized approach, often followed by students to address a topic of individual interest. Most students are inclined to develop research interests out of their experience rather than through exposure to the research literature, so many adopt problems without regard to their standing in the field. They select the problem and work back to the literature trying to find studies which support their interest. Problems so defined may integrate various methods, fields of study and sources of data and are generally less likely to be at the higher levels of research (generalization and basic) than those following the prescriptive approach. In its best form this approach borrows the procedures and methods of the prescriptive model, but does so over time and across space. The individual approach lends itself well to explanatory research and a wide range of descriptive studies. Its difficulty is in its lack of boundaries and lack of focus. It is very easy under this approach to take on too large a problem and never get closure on it.

The third approach, which is not really an approach at all, might be termed muddling-through. I have included it because it tends to be one of the most common ways in which graduate students write their theses. In short, the muddling-through approach takes a general topic area, begins doing research and collecting data, and probably does not define the problem sharply until after the study is almost complete. Then it must be rewritten and recast in terms that relate to the problem which has now been defined. It is recommended only for those who have unlimited time and resources and who thrive on inductive solutions to life's problems.

One should not assume by the foregoing that research is merely a static and deductive process. On the contrary, good research is characterized by an evolving dynamic such that the research problems and questions may only be articulated fully when the study is far advanced. The ongoing process of collecting and analyzing data, endless discussions with others who bring new perspectives to bear and limitless personal thought and deduction may transform a routine problem into something new and different. In an extreme example, I was conducting research on the letters of nineteenth century Canadian Governors General when I uncovered in the National Archives a previously unrecorded diary which led me in a totally new direction on a new problem (Anderson, 1984).

Asking the Right Question

What is an appropriate research question? This is the fundamental issue for most researchers. There are two considerations, the topic and the scope. With respect to topic, you need a question which will sustain your interest and one in which your colleagues or supervisors can assist you. You should also consider its relevance and potency in the field of research at this point in time. This is where a sound review of the research literature is important (see Chapter 8). It should tell you whether your topic is timely or whether interest in it has waned. You might also want to review recent theses in your university to see whether others might have begun related explorations which suggest the utility of continuation.

Once you have defined a general topic area, the problem is to formulate the specific research problem or questions with just the right scope. It is easy and tempting to 'research the world'. That is, it is simple to ask a question so broad that it will always contain more meat. For example, 'what is an effective school?' Such questions are good topics for a speech or a book, but they are too big to be useful research questions. By the same token, a question which is overly specific can easily be addressed, but it may have no relevance beyond the immediate situation and little interest except to those directly involved. The challenge is to ask a question at the right level of breadth or abstraction.

It is relatively easy to generate research questions but less easy to generate questions at the right level of abstraction for your resources and abilities. To choose a problem which is overly specific is to rob quantitative research from any generalizability. To select a problem that is overly broad, particularly in qualitative research, will hinder your ability to resolve it. The challenge, therefore, is to choose a problem at the right level of abstraction.

It is useful in thinking of research questions to think in terms of a ladder of abstraction as summarized in Exhibit 4.1. The illustration shows that a given area of interest can be expressed on a continuum from the highly specific to the very general. You will find it useful in defining research questions to learn how to change the level of abstraction. Take any researchable question and make it one level more specific or one level more general. You may continue this exercise until you have a whole hierarchy of questions ranging in specificity. In general when you design a

Exhibit 4.1: Research questions at different levels of abstraction

1 What major factors enhance the transfer of training from school to daily living?

2 What major factors enhance the transfer of second language learning to daily living?

3 What major factors enhance the transfer of French learned as a second language to daily living?

4 What major factors enhance the transfer of correct usage of the subjunctive tense in French to daily living?

5 What major factors enhance the transfer of correct usage of the subjunctive tense of the French verb *être* (to be) to daily living?

research problem, you will have subquestions. Experience and counsel from those who know about research will enable you to choose the level of abstraction suitable to your capabilities and resources. It will also show you that even though you may have a fairly narrow and specific interest it relates to a more general sphere of research interest.

Characteristics of a Good Thesis Research Problem

The ten important characteristics of a good research problem for a thesis are summarized in Exhibit 4.2. The list enables one to examine any research problem and see the extent to which it measures up. Obviously, few problems will achieve all ten characteristics but good problems should fulfill most of these requirements. A few words are in order about each of them.

Exhibit 4.2: Characteristics of a good thesis research problem

1 The problem can be stated clearly and concisely.

2 The problem generates research questions.

3 It is grounded in theory.

4 It relates to one or more academic fields of study.

5 It has a base in the research literature.

6 It has potential significance/importance.

7 It is do-able within the time frame, budget.

8 Sufficient data are available or can be obtained.

9 The researcher's methodological strengths can be applied to the problem.

10 The problem is new; it is not already answered sufficiently.

1   The Problem Can Be Stated Clearly and Concisely

Unless the problem can be stated clearly and concisely it is probably a poor problem or a non-problem. The best way to test the problem statement is to write it into a concise sentence or paragraph and to share it with others. If the problem cannot be stated in a clear paragraph it has difficulties and will not endure as a suitable problem. Of course, it is not easy to express complex issues in simplistic terms and it may take many weeks and countless drafts before the statement is satisfactory. Good critics are essential. If your spouse or mother cannot understand it, it is probably flaky.

2   The Problem Generates Research Questions

The problem should generate a number of more specific research questions. These turn the problem into a question format and represent various aspects or components of the problem. The research questions make the more general statement easier to address and provide a framework for the research. Formulating these questions can be a challenge, particularly specifying them at the right level of abstraction.

3   It Is Grounded in Theory

Good problems have theoretical and/or conceptual frameworks for their analysis (see Chapter 6). They relate the specifics of what is being investigated to a more general background of theory which helps interpret the results and link it to the field.

4   It Relates to One or More Academic Fields of Study

Good problems relate to academic fields which have adherents and boundaries. They typically have journals to which adherents relate. Research problems which do not have clear links to one or two such fields of study are generally in trouble. Without such a field it becomes impossible to determine where, in the universe of knowledge, the problem lies.

5   It Has a Base in the Research Literature

Related to the former points, a well-stated problem will relate to a research literature. Tight problems often relate to a well-defined body of literature, written by a select group of researchers and published in a small number of journals. With some problems it might at first be difficult to establish the connections and literature base, but there should be a base somewhere. See Chapter 8 for a further discussion of this issue.

6   It Has Potential Significance/importance

This is the important 'so what' question: Who cares once you solve the problem? Assume that you have solved the problem and answered the questions and then ask yourself if you are any further ahead. At the very least, the problem must have importance to the researcher, but ideally it should also be of consequence to others.

7   It Is Do-able Within the Time Frame, Budget

There are logistic factors in terms of your ability actually to carry out the research. There is no point pursuing a problem which is not feasible to research. Do not do a study of education in India unless you have the means to go there and collect data — which may require years to collect. This factor helps explain why few theses relate to longitudinal data. The only exceptions come from research shops where there is a long history of collecting and studying data on a defined population. Terman's study of genius (1954) in which a defined sample was traced over 30 years, is a good example.

8   Sufficient Data Are Available or Can Be Obtained

In some cases, there are insufficient data to address the problem. Historical persons may have died, archival materials may be lost, or there may be restrictions on access to certain environments. As noted, it is difficult to conduct research on a distant country unless you can go there and collect local data. One under-used approach is to use an existing data base. Some data banks have been developed over many years and contain many opportunities for exploration of new questions and issues.

9   The Researcher's Methodological Strengths Can Be Applied to the Problem

As well as being grounded in a discipline, a good problem generally relates to some sort of standard methodology. This might be historical, or comparative or empirical, but it should build on the strengths of the investigator. There is no point conducting research on a problem that is best addressed with statistics if statistics are not your strength. Consider your problem carefully and ask whether your background is appropriate to tackle it.

10   *The Problem Is New; It Is Not Already Answered Sufficiently*

While this is often a concern to new researchers, it is generally not an insurmountable problem. Once one knows the field, it becomes clear what has been done and what needs to be done. The danger applies mostly to problems that are stated prematurely without adequate knowledge of the field. If you know and can analyze the relevant literature you can often easily identify the most logical steps that need to be researched.

Some Finished Examples

The suggested approach to defining a research problem is to develop it to the stage where it can be written in what I call a problem statement. It consists of a concise paragraph or two followed by specific research questions that can further define the study as specified in Exhibit 4.3. I have found that four to eight questions are about the right number, but these are generally broken down into many more subquestions.

Exhibit 4.3:   Components of a problem statement

---

1 Note that each problem has a title. You need a title on yours and the title should convey, clearly and succinctly, what you are researching.

2 The next section of the research problem statement is what amounts to a rationale for the problem. This might take various forms. It might relate to experience and common knowledge about the importance of the topic, or, it might include some reference to prior research or general literature. If you do quote prior literature, note that this is not a review of literature. What you are searching for at this stage is a few authoritative references which establish the legitimacy of this field of inquiry and of your particular problem definition.

3 Normally, a second paragraph specifies the purpose of the study. Various forms of statement might be used, but by completing the sentence 'The purpose of this study is . . .' you will have communicated what you are trying to do. You should be able to complete that sentence clearly so that any reader will understand what your study is about.

4 The third section of the problem statement includes the research questions. In most cases, there are four, five, or six major questions and generally there are subquestions related to each of these. You have two challenges in developing research questions. First, you must break down the problem into the large elements. You are attempting to have questions of the same level of abstraction and size proportions. The subquestions are definitely subsumed under the major headings. The second challenge is to sequence your questions into a logical order. Typically, the first question is background and required knowledge for later questions. You may need advice on appropriate sequencing in order to make this work. Generally, the major question that relates to the purpose of your study is the last question stated.

While the problem often appears straightforward, once it has reached its final form, the process of defining the problem can take many months. Often the problem gets changed and refined as the study occurs, so the final form does not emerge until the study is finished.

Over the last several years, I have worked with my students to express their research problems in the suggested format. All types of problems incorporating all sorts of research approaches lend themselves to this type of expression. I have found that it forces you to define your problem precisely and eliminates the frequent pattern of lengthy rambling around the problem without ever coming to grips with its essence.

Exhibits 4.4 and 4.5 present problem statements from graduates who have worked under the author's supervision. The desired format is for the researcher to introduce the problem by providing a paragraph of rationale for its study which might include reference to prior research and theory, followed by a concise paragraph on the purpose of the study, followed by research questions and subquestions. Students find it difficult to define the purpose and are encouraged to do so by completing the sentence 'The purpose of this study is to . . .' It is not easy to express the purpose in a single sentence in this way, but if you can do so you generally know what you are doing.

The particular examples shown here have been abstracted from more lengthy proposals or completed theses and in some cases I have omitted the rationale and reference to previous research. These examples represent one masters and one doctoral study. Interested readers can locate Arsenault's subsequent Ph.D dissertation in *Dissertation Abstracts International* (see p. 52) to see how the research problem evolved from the M.A. level to the Ph.D. The first edition of *Fundamentals of Educational Research* provides additional examples of problem statements for those who want more.

Conclusion

Probably one of the most important skills you can develop as a researcher is the ability to frame good research questions. Test the question you explore with the ten characteristics of a good thesis research problem (Exhibit 4.2). If your problem does not work, it might be its level of abstraction. Consider raising or lowering the level of abstraction of the problem you state (see Exhibit 4.1 on levels of abstraction). Please bear in mind that even the most experienced researchers revise their problem continually, even in many cases after they have analyzed their data. Until you know exactly what is going on, you might not be able to frame it in the best way. Exhibit 4.1 identifies the parts of a problem statement.

There is probably nothing in one's university education that can compare to the preparation of an original research thesis. It involves a lengthy commitment and difficult challenges. One not only learns a great deal about a narrow area of content, but more importantly, one learns how to write a coherent and purposeful report.

Exhibit 4.4: Understanding older adults in education: Decision-making and Elderhostel

---

The interest, research, and speculation on the motives of adults who participate in education has spanned five decades (Romaniuk & Romaniuk, 1982). An impressive list of researchers have examined various populations to describe, theorize, and provide models which explain why adults participate, or do not participate, in educational activities (Boshier, 1971; Boshier & Collins, 1985; Cross, 1981, 1992; Darkenwald & Merriam, 1984; Havighurst, 1969, 1976; Houle, 1961; Merriam & Caffarella, 1991; Morstain & Smart, 1974; Scanlan & Darkenwald, 1982). So why do another study? The social context for learning has changed, as have the opportunities in human science research. The way we view the world today is different than our forefathers and the role learning plays in our lives has changed. Today, 'life long learning is not a privilege or a right; it is simply a necessity for anyone, young or old, who must live with the escalating pace of change — in the family, on the job, in the community and in the worldwide society' (Cross, 1992: xxi).

This research contributes to the limited body of research aimed exclusively at the education of older adults and focuses on a new area of understanding, decision-making. This study seeks to discover more about retired learners and build on the existing base of literature in the fields of adult education and educational gerontology. It is anticipated that the discoveries from this study will assist agencies, organizations and community groups who offer educational programs, for the retired, better understand what factors are important when selecting an educational program. This qualitative investigation hopes to open the door to understanding the decision-making process and lay the foundation for my doctoral study which will quantitatively examine, in greater detail, the decision-making process.

The Research Questions
The purpose of this study is to gain understanding about how older adults, who are retired or contemplating retirement, make decisions regarding their educational experiences. Together, with Elderhostel participants, this study seeks to establish a typology of the older adult learner based on five research questions:

1 What factors influenced the participants decision to select Elderhostel as an educational venue?
2 What factors influenced the participants choice of a specific Elderhostel program?
3 How are the decision-making factors sequenced and prioritized in the minds of the participants?
4 Does the order of the decision-making factors change with each program registration, or do they remain the same?
5 Do certain types of Elderhostelers make similar program choices?

Arsenault (1996, pp. 7, 10, 32)

Most people learn new things about themselves, their strengths and limitations and develop their self-confidence. At its best it is a rewarding and exhilarating experience. At its worst it is an unbearable chore. In large measure the particular research problem is what makes the difference. You must live with the problem a long time, so make sure you choose it well.

Exhibit 4.5: Equal educational opportunity for students with disabilities in Canada. Volume 1: Research report

The purpose of this study was to conduct a systematic comparison of the legislative action of each province and territory in Canada, as of December 31, 1992, relating to the provision of equal educational opportunity [EEO] to students with disabilities. In order to fulfil this purpose, a framework for the analysis of legal rights for students with disabilities was constructed and used to undertake a content analysis of the legislation in each jurisdiction and provide a comparison of the results.

Given the purpose of this study — to identify, analyze and compare the EEO rights provided for in each jurisdiction in Canada, it was decided to formulate each major research question in terms of three subquestions, corresponding to these three elements of the purpose statement. These subquestions are organized sequentially, that is, the second depends on the first and the third depends on the second. Thus, the first subquestion defines rights; the second analyzes the legislation in each jurisdiction to measure the extent to which these rights are found; the third compares the results of this analysis across jurisdictions.

Specific Research Questions
How does the legislative action in each jurisdiction provide:*

1 Non-discrimination?
2 Access to action in each jurisdiction provide for access to schooling?
3 For identification and placement?
4 Legislative action in each jurisdiction for service delivery?
5 Parental participation?

* For each of these major questions, the subquestions were as follows:

a What are the specific rights which define *parental participation*?
b To what extent does each jurisdiction provide for such rights?
c How do all jurisdictions compare in terms of the provision of such rights?

(W.J. Smith, 1993, pp. v, 68–69).

References

Anderson, G. (1984). The Diary of James McGill Strachan: A Trip to the Mingan, 1849. *Atlantic Salmon Journal, 33*(2), pp. 12–14.

Arsenault, N. (1996). *Understanding older adults in education: Decision-making and Elderhostel.* Unpublished M.A. thesis. McGill University, Montreal, QC.

Smith, W.J. (1993). *Equal educational opportunity for students with disabilities in Canada. Volume I: Research Report.* Unpublished doctoral dissertation, McGill University, Montreal, QC.

Terman, L.M. (1954). The discovery and encouragement of exceptional talent. *American Psychologist, 9*, pp. 221–230.

Chapter 5

Research Information

Research should never take place in a vacuum; it is a field whereby knowledge is developed and added to by researcher after researcher. Educational research is a cooperative activity and contributing researchers are obliged to know the previous research in their field before embarking on a new line of inquiry. Just as it would be ridiculous for a biologist to go into a strange environment and begin applying his or her own names to flora and fauna, it is folly for an educational researcher to embark on a study without first becoming familiar with prior research.

In education, it is surprising that so many graduate students begin developing problems and go forward with research plans without an adequate understanding of what has gone on before. The purpose of this chapter is to serve as a quick reference tool for beginning researchers interested in finding information in their field of potential research. It begins by discussing the types of research knowledge then outlines where to look for research information.

All research projects should begin with a preliminary investigation of the field to find out whether the territory has been covered before and whether there is previous knowledge and experience to guide new investigations. Good research begins with determining what has been researched before, what types of studies have taken place, when they were conducted, how and by whom. The challenge for the novice researcher is cutting through the great quantity of previous knowledge to find out what has been done to date and to familiarize oneself with the major conclusions. In this sense, searching out previous research is an important aspect of data collection and is therefore a legitimate research activity. It involves collecting data, weighing its importance and relevance, and classifying it for future use.

Searching sources of research information is often a significant learning activity that helps define, refine and shape our view of our own research problem. Very often, as a result of the search, the problem is recast and sharpened. Thus, long before a formal review of research takes place, exploration of prior research and its interaction with the research problem is a crucial step in the overall research process. But just how does one find out what has been researched before?

The Six Types of Knowledge

Chapter 1 identified five main ways of knowing. There are also different types of knowledge, and it is important, when searching research information sources, to understand the type of knowledge that is being pursued.

Historical knowledge of research is the history of investigation in a particular field. In various eras researchers see the world through the particular lens considered appropriate for the time, and their research reflects this perspective. In psychology, for example, the study of intelligence evolved from a philosophical analysis on the nature of man to a systematic approach to measurement of peoples' abilities. Any researcher working on intelligence should be familiar with this historical evolution in the field. So it is with any research topic. Many topics have their popularity at a given time after which interest wanes and the topic remains relatively dormant until another era when it is picked up and examined using different frameworks and approaches.

When you look at published research, keep its historical context in mind and be aware that approaches to learning, research paradigms, and research methodologies evolve over time. This will enhance your understanding of the materials you read, give you possible insights into your own problem, and it will protect you from embarking on a path which has been pursued and abandoned in some previous era.

The second important type of knowledge is *axiological knowledge.* That is, what might be called the theory of experience. In Chapter 1, it was termed insightful observation. Axiological knowledge is found in the literature written by practitioners whose many years of experience lead to important conclusions and generalizations. Many educational research journals are written by practitioners for practitioners. They talk about the problems of school discipline, how to implement curriculum, ways of organizing schools and so forth. These articles tend not to be based on previous research but rather on the experience of the author. Beginning researchers should recognize that this literature is not, technically speaking, research literature. It is a literature from the world of practice; it bares some relationship to research but should not be the sole source of prior information leading up to your research problem. Thus, you should recognize axiological knowledge for what it is and not use it as if it were theory or prior research.

Theoretical and conceptual knowledge provides the structure within a particular field of inquiry. It generally results from a critical analysis of prior research and theory and provides the constructs leading to pursuit of interesting research questions. In this way it grounds your research in antecedent research that has generated contemporary constructs guiding subsequent investigation. Research not based on theory is generally strictly utilitarian and is often suspect in academic circles. Thus, in your study of prior knowledge you should attempt to identify appropriate theoretical and conceptual frameworks which bare relation to your problem.

Prior research studies are an essential starting point for any research investigation. These studies are plentiful in most fields, and the challenge is to identify specific studies which are valid and have particular relevance to the specific type of problem you wish to investigate. Prior research studies help illuminate related theory and often show the sequence of studies and their historical evolution. It is often difficult to identify previous studies which have an exact match to your interest. Rather, there are many studies which relate to part of your problem and are within the general boundaries. Deciphering which elements of previous research are relevant to your study often helps you crystalize your thinking and shape your conceptual framework. You may need to move to a higher level of abstraction (see Chapter 4) but you should be able to locate research studies which are in the same area as your interest. Note, however, that studies in different fields can be highly informative if they encompass a common element. For example, studies of gender equity can be informed by those dealing with racial equity. Studies in quite different fields may contribute insights on relevant research methodologies.

Reviews are another indispensable type of knowledge. As the name implies, a researcher gathers significant studies in a particular field, critiques them and writes a review. It is important to become familiar with the reviews in your area of study, for they have the advantage of pulling together a lot of specific pieces of research and casting them into frameworks and levels of generalization which might be more helpful than any specific study alone. Reviews exist in most fields of investigation, but again, you may have to change the level of abstraction to find one which is relevant to your needs.

The final type of knowledge identified here is *academic debate*. Very often new lines of research inquiry give rise to debates in the literature. Some journals publish these debates which typically take the form of critiques of prior articles. In some cases, over the course of a year or two, some journals will publish critiques accompanied by rebuttals from the original researcher. The academic debate, therefore, goes back and forth and moves the thinking forward in the field under discussion. In areas where these debates exist, it is wise to familiarize yourself with them. This may help you avoid embarking in a direction which has already been well discussed, researched and rejected.

In your search for knowledge about your topic, you should pay attention to these six types of knowledge. You should attempt to identify relevant literature pertaining to each of the six types. If you do so, you will have a complete perspective on your problem and be in a good position to know where you can move forward with your particular research contribution. The remainder of this chapter outlines the sources of information related to these six types of knowledge.

Sources of Research Information

Ask an Expert

Even in this technological age, the best overall source of information continues to be people. The smart researcher will consult an expert in the field and find out from him or her where to go from there. By asking someone who knows the field, you can find out the titles of significant books, journals and specific articles, the names of important researchers, identify key conferences and get direction about where to find unique research information. This will save a great deal of time and will help you in the difficult process of evaluating the quality of the research you review. Some experts maintain bibliographies in their field which can be most helpful. However, to provide good guidance, the expert will require a clear idea of the particular problem you would like to pursue. As a start, I suggest you ask an expert to recommend a small number of key writings. By seeing what an expert considers the best work in the field you will develop a notion of whether or not it is for you.

Libraries

The majority of research information can be found in libraries. A library which specializes in education holdings is generally easier to use than a general library containing all subject matters. Once you identify a suitable library for your work, it pays to become thoroughly familiar with it. You should spend time in the library, find out how it is organized, where the various materials are. Browse the various sections of the library and sample the different types of materials, so that in future, you will know exactly where to find the type of information you are seeking. A library tour or orientation session is an excellent way to become familiar with library holdings. Questions should be directed to the reference librarian, who has in-depth knowledge of the holdings. Remember, however, that you need to state your requirements in ways that the librarian understands. Thus, the more familiar you become with the general tools and terminology, the easier it will be to get professional help.

The Library Stacks

Knowing where to look for information is only part of the problem; you must also know how to search out research literature. Perhaps the best way to get a feeling for the field and the type of research done is to conduct a manual search. One of the easiest ways to get a feel for the literature is to visit your library, locate the section which pertains to your interests and literally browse the stacks for interesting titles. Extract the books that catch your fancy and set them aside for review. Once you have browsed the books, then move to the journals and again, look for interesting titles. Larger libraries often place all their current periodicals (within 12–18 months) on display in a separate location. Find this location, walk the aisles, and within an hour you will know what journals are available. Peruse the most current editions to learn the scope and focus of the journal, examine titles of articles, then if a particular publication seems interesting, you can locate the entire selection elsewhere in the library. Many journals publish annual indexes to previous issues. Once you locate one of these, you can merely consult the corresponding issue for each year and this saves you from the necessity of examining each individual copy.

Books

University libraries contain vast numbers of books on every conceivable topic and they are often the starting point of people looking for previous research. Unfortunately books are not generally a good source of information on prior research. In the first place, books, with rare exceptions, are dated and much of the information they contain was written at least five years before the publication date. Generally speaking, research information tends to be current and directed to a more specific audience than are books. Thus, books tend to give summaries and general backgrounds of research information, but they do not provide the primary research material which is so crucial to someone exploring research in a specific field. However, they are excellent sources of information about broad areas of study. Books are a good source of theory which is essential in determining the nature of a conceptual framework and thus the structure of a research review. For these reasons, one should consult books for general background, but should not spend too much time searching books for research findings.

There are, of course, exceptions to the general rule. Encyclopedias and handbooks, for example, contain summarized information which generally has been written by leading authorities in the discipline. The *Encyclopedia of Educational Research* is an example. One advantage of such publications is that they distill countless research contributions into generally more interpretable and digestible summaries and often project emerging directions and areas for further research. A number of other books and periodicals provide excellent sources of information about the more important journal literature and they will be discussed later.

Periodicals

Periodicals, more popularly known as journals, are the major information source of prior research literature in a field. There are currently upwards of 1000 journals in the field of education. These are published a number of times a year and are sent to subscribers, including libraries. Due to the diversity of their target audience, journals vary greatly in nature. Certain journals are targeted to researchers and the academic community, others are more pragmatic and supply 'how to' and 'what's happening' information to the practitioner. The novice must be aware of these differences and learn how to decipher research journals from those that are devoted to publishing articles of fact and opinions about a topic — axiological research.

The most significant journals to the researcher are those which report on research studies and their findings. Articles in research journals usually include a brief review of prior research, as well as methods and procedures used in the study being reported, its findings and conclusions. Like everything, however, journals vary in quality. Assessing the quality of various journals can be a challenge. The best journals are refereed, meaning that an editorial board or group of professional peers reviews each article and decides on its quality and suitability for publication. It is common practice to have blind reviews; that is, the reviewers do not know who submitted the paper.

One indicator of quality is the acceptance rate of articles. The best education journals accept as few as one to two per cent of the manuscripts submitted (e.g., leading journals of the American Educational Research Association, the American Psychological Association, etc.). However, with over 1000 education journals, many of the less discriminating accept half of what they receive. Clearly those which can afford to be selective tend to have higher quality than those that publish practically anything. Another index of quality is how often various journals are cited in later publications. Obviously, the most frequently cited journals will be general rather than in a specific or narrow field, but all journals have a certain status which experienced researchers know. Researchers are most keen to publish their work in the most prestigious journals and what appears in the lesser publications may already have been rejected from the better ones. Appendix 5.1 lists some leading educational journals and describes what they publish. Note that most of these journals are supported by universities or professional associations which help ensure their overall quality and continuity.

So how do you learn about the scope of various journals? First it is important to know that at the front of all journals, you will find information describing the scope and aim of the journal, subscription and publication information and often the names of the editorial board. Many journals also publish information for authors and manuscript preparation guidelines annually (some in every edition). This is a rich source of information for the researcher trying to understand the publication. The fastest way, however, is to ask someone who is an experienced researcher in your general area of interest. This will save a great deal of time. There are occasions, however, when you have no one to ask and must judge for yourself how a journal is contributing to knowledge in the field. When reviewing a journal ask yourself, is this advancing knowledge by reporting on research and theoretical developments, or is it advancing knowledge by sharing experiential information? Both are valid and useful types of information; however, the former is more useful to researchers.

One major advantage of journals is that they are published periodically and more frequently than books, and thus the information they contain is far more recent. Most research journals have a publication cycle of about a year, so articles appearing there represent papers written about a year earlier. However, be forewarned, papers accepted by journals often reflect research conducted a year or so before that, so in fact, journal information may be two years old as compared to book information which is likely to be five years old. Finally, students often learn of articles in obscure journals which are difficult to obtain. Chances are that if the journal is for a localized audience it will not be as consequential as will a national or international journal. In general, my advice would be not to bother with lesser journals unless one's topic is exactly matched by an article there. There are, of course, small circulation journals catering to highly specialized audiences which are also noteworthy. This is certainly the case for some foreign journals which may be difficult to find. When in doubt about the quality and relevance of a journal, ask an expert in the field.

Dissertations as Sources of Information

Previous student theses and dissertations are a natural source of research information. Doctoral students generally explore new areas and if you share a similar research interest, their work may provide great insight into research questions, methods and findings. The limitation of dissertations, of course, is that they represent student work, albeit work conducted under supervision. At the very least, the reference section of a dissertation is a marvelous source of information that may direct you towards interesting studies that support your area of research.

The major listing of doctoral studies is *Dissertation Abstracts International*, a monthly periodical which includes titles, key words and author indices for doctoral dissertations in over 350 institutions in North America and abroad. Abstracts of the dissertations are provided in the publication and complete copies of dissertations may be ordered on microfilm or hard copy from University Microfilms of Ann Arbor, Michigan.

The best starting point is to review the theses and dissertations done in your own university. They will indicate the types of research emphasized in the institution, acceptable approaches, topics which have been supported by your department, and help you identify the professors who supervise research in your area of interest. It is also useful to examine a few of the best theses or dissertations from your department, even if their topic differs from your own for it can alert you to such matters as: level of discourse, organization of ideas and audience. One asset of recent dissertations is that they are often more timely than either journals or books and they are also more complete. In addition, dissertations should contain copies of the research instruments, which otherwise are often difficult to find.

Government Documents

Depending on the nature of your research, you may find government documents a useful source of research information. Governments everywhere are constantly publishing information, some of it is research based while other publications are not. Some of the most useful types of information are census statistics, policy documents and evaluation research information. It is important to know that large libraries often have a special section that houses government documents. The reference librarian in charge is particularly well versed in these special publications and, in my experience, speaking with her or him about your research requirements is far more effective than searching a data base. Unfortunately, much of the useful literature is among the grey literature (see later section) which is much more difficult to access. One final point, once you locate a specific government document, write down the publishing information, for often you can obtain an original copy of the document by simply writing the responsible department and making a request!

Ancestry Method

Another approach with which you should be familiar is known as the ancestry method. Once you find an article of relevance, check its references and, in detective-like fashion, trace down the various journals and articles cited there. The journals identified may provide other sources of articles related to your topic. Search out reviews, dissertations and other sources of bibliographies using a similar technique.

You may find that tracing an author or two through various reference lists helps you identify other authors who research in similar areas and you may discover that certain theories are advocated or supported by all. This type of search can be extremely helpful when first developing your theoretical and conceptual frameworks. In the final stages of an advanced review, electronic citation indexes provide a convenient way of searching out all the publications of a particular author.

Previous Reviews of Research

In general terms, the fields are so vast and there is so much information that it helps to use the work of those who have already accessed and evaluated it. Often leading scholars review previous research. Such research reviews assemble the information, put it into context and often order it in ways which are helpful for someone attempting to conduct a study. These reviews may be published in handbooks and encyclopedias or they may be found in journals or other publications devoted to the purpose. The most significant of these is the *Review of Educational Research*. Of course, every research article, dissertation or research report normally contains a review of prior research, so this aspect of previous studies should be especially noted. If a relevant high quality review is found, one needs to devote most energies to updating it, working from the date of publication, or a year or two before, until the present.

Conference Proceedings

A number of associations of educators and researchers such as the American Educational Research Association (AERA) hold annual conferences. Their published programs indicate the name of researchers and papers to be presented. When the proceedings are made available they have the great advantage of representing work done within the year and, thus, are a good indication of what research is in vogue.

So how does a new researcher identify relevant associations and learn about upcoming conferences? Again, ask an expert. They are a rich source of information for this type of information. A second technique is to browse the bulletin boards in and around graduate departments at the university. Often the information about upcoming conferences is posted. Once you learn of an upcoming conference, you need not attend the conference. It is acceptable to write, or request via electronic mail, a copy of the conference proceedings or a copy of a specific paper. This often yields access to a research paper a year or more before it reaches the pages of a journal. It also connects you to researchers in the field who you can then contact for further information or advice.

Finally, search the Internet. Many associations are now on-line with their own home page. Once you know the name of an association, it is quick, easy and inexpensive to access information of past and future conferences. Depending on the sophistication of the association's web site, some information can be downloaded directly, other information can be requested via electronic mail.

On-Line Data Bases

Thanks to the technological advances in the computer industry a tremendous amount of research information can be accessed through on-line data bases. A research data base is simply a bibliographic listing of information that informs you where to locate information such as academic and professional journals, technical reports, special publications, books/chapters in books, conference papers, literature reviews, government documents, theses and dissertations, bibliographies and more! Appendix 5.2 lists 19 different on-line data bases that are useful to educational researchers; however, it is important to keep in mind that this is only a sample of what exists. There are, of course, many more on-line sources out there and as you begin to define your research project more closely, the relevant data bases can be identified by your local reference librarian.

Perhaps the most useful data base in education is the Educational Resources Information Clearinghouse (ERIC) which indexes over 700 periodicals and hundreds of thousands of research papers, projects and reports in education. The International Development Research Centre (IDRC) in Ottawa, Canada, has a similar data base related to international research. A unique index is the Social Sciences Citation Index (SSCI) because it categorizes documents based on the works cited in them as well as their topical focus. Using SSCI you can look up an author and find out which articles have cited that author. This is, in effect, the reverse of a manual ancestry search as it works from an article forward to others which refer to it and presumably build on its research. The identification of a definitive study can therefore lead to all kinds of spin-offs. The important thing to remember when selecting a data base is that the periodicals contained within are similar in nature and many periodicals are listed in a variety of data bases.

The major difficulty with on-line information searches is that they do not evaluate the information they contain, so you often receive lists of many in-house documents and reports which are of limited validity and limited use for your purposes. It is also difficult, with some on-line data bases, to control the quality of information.

Generally speaking, there are three on-line data bases readily available to most students. The fastest way to access a data base is via the Internet, all you need is the name (e.g., ERIC) to get started. The second way is to use computerized data bases created by libraries which identify, describe and provide call numbers to help you locate materials that are available in hard copy within that particular library system. This method replaces the old card files that listed and categorized library materials. The final method, and one of the most useful, is using a system especially created for a particular library system. McGill University, one of Canada's leading research universities, has such a system called PERUSE. What PERUSE does is to apply a special software package (OVID) which provides an interface between a multitude of select data bases and merges them into one search program that uses similar search codes.

Fundamentally, all these systems are the same. They permit the inquirer to search for information via key words, title, author or subject. Boolean logical operators, (such

Exhibit 5.1: Searching a computerized data base

- Define your area of interest and prepare a list of key words

- Ask your reference librarian how to explain the search codes for an on-line data search

- Select your data base (e.g., ERIC, LSI, PsycINFO, EDI, AST)

- Search each of your key words individually, then use your boolean operators to create possible combinations

- Try limiting the dates in the field (e.g., 1950–1975; or 1990 to present)

- Once you have a data file with 100–200 entries begin to examine the descriptions and abstracts

- Highlight any study that is of possible use

- Print a copy of your search

- Repeat your search in another data base

as, *and*, *or*, *not*), are used to combine terms precisely. You may also truncate symbols and limit searches. What differs between library to library, data base to data base, is often the computer codes which accompany the use of the boolean operators. Alas, this may mean you have a need to learn how to use several systems. The good news is that fundamentally, the 'think process' is the same and therefore, once you understand one on-line search system, learning the others is not quite as grueling as it may first seem. Exhibit 5.1 highlights a basic sequence that can be followed when performing an on-line data base search.

It is important to keep an interdisciplinary perspective in mind when searching on-line data bases, for the study of education cannot be done in isolation of other disciplines. Think back to the Elderhostel study cited in Chapter 4 (Arsenault, 1996). The purpose of this study was to gain an understanding of how older adults make their choices regarding their educational experiences. This particular research problem searched four data bases: ERIC, Medline, PsycINFO, and Current Contents. Similarly, the literature review in Smith's (1993) dissertation accessed ERIC, LPI and SSI. The reason it is so important to search related data bases is because systems are not inclusive unto themselves. Just as no library houses every holding, no data base can list every on-line reference.

Grey Literature

Finally, there is a vast quantity of what is known as 'grey literature', which takes the form of reports and manuscripts produced for a specific purpose but not generally found in libraries. This can be a rich field of information, particularly on certain topics (e.g., education in developing areas), but the difficulty is accessing it. A few sources such as ERIC index such material, but more typically they are not listed. Some specialized library collections, such as those found in specialized research centres, gather such materials, but more frequently you will have to talk to people 'in-the-know' and use grape-vine sources to obtain this type of information. The Government of Canada has a large number of research studies and consultant reports which are theoretically available through the Freedom of Information Act. However, you must know what exists in order to request it. Some of the grey literature represents proprietary information of various types and this is always difficult to access. Institutions such as the World Bank publish various versions of research reports and country studies, but the versions available to the public are available later than the confidential versions, and they typically omit information whose circulation is limited to the involved government.

What to Do with the References You Locate

Once you have located a useful study, it should be photocopied and classified in a system for future reference and retrieval. Photocopying a single copy for individual research purposes is permissible under the copyright laws and saves considerable time over making notes by hand. Be sure that the full reference source is on the title page, and if it is not, be sure to write down the particulars in order to refer to it later. Your time in the library should be spent in scanning and retrieving information, save the in-depth reading for a later time.

Conclusion

Finding research information is not an event; it is a process that takes place throughout the duration of your study. Indeed, for experienced researchers it continues throughout one's whole career. In practice, the student of research conducts a thorough search of relevant literature up front as the proposal is being formulated. This is then updated periodically as the research is underway. Students should go back to their literature searching once the thesis or dissertation is written. This will make sure that the most recent work is included, and it will enable you to incorporate related literature that only becomes relevant once your findings are known.

In conclusion, a thorough knowledge of the field being investigated is essential if your research is to make a significant contribution. You cannot do justice to a topic in the absence of knowledge of what has gone on before. By using the significant efforts of others you can design a better study and ground it in the field you are investigating.

Reference

Review of educational research. Washington, DC: American Educational Research Association.

Chapter 6

Research Frameworks

Much of good research follows a framework developed from prior theory and research or by thought and rational deduction and this framework serves to clarify the problem and help determine the best approach to its solution. Thus, the work of an excellent researcher is organized inquiry. The questions, the way they are framed, the combinations of concerns are not random. They represent approaches which help the researcher do significant research and which enable the reader to understand the point. Educational research is not the only activity organized in this way. Education itself follows organized models. There are concepts and objectives and activities, assignments, tests and exams all of which fit together in a coherent fashion. While the approach can be inductive or discovery-oriented, the result should relate to some established framework.

Frameworks range from simple one-dimensional lists to elaborate multi-dimensional models with layers of intersecting parts. Even a simple scheme is better than none at all. In selecting a principal for a school, it is better to rate the applicants on a list of characteristics than it is merely to accord each a global rating. Such a list leads to improved agreement among various raters (reliability) and also more precise estimations of background and performance on each characteristic (validity). More elaborate and improved frameworks would take into consideration which of the characteristics are most important for the particular position available. So, for example, bilingualism might be very important in one setting and less so in another. The purpose of this chapter is both to emphasize the importance of conceptual frameworks and to provide examples and knowledge of the types of framework which have proved successful in the past. For any researcher, the development of a suitable framework is part of the process of planning and clarifying the research problem and conducting the analysis. As in any problem-solving endeavour, problems which seem overwhelming can often be tackled once they have been broken into their constituent parts and the interrelationships among the parts have been graphically and conceptually arranged.

Some theoreticians use paradigms to explain their theories. These are often elaborate diagrams with flow paths and arrows. They often clarify relationships among loosely coupled systems and can suggest research questions and lines of inquiry. They sometimes have the advantage of situating research into a theoretical context, but in my experience, they are generally unhelpful in tightening the questions and level of understanding. This is why I use the term *framework*. A framework is a model which allows the researcher to explore the relationships among variables in a logical and prescribed fashion. It clarifies questions by relating questions and their constituent subquestions and it summarizes the overall concept being investigated. This chapter restricts its treatment to simple one and two-dimensional frameworks which are generally adequate for most research purposes.

Whatever framework one uses for a research study, the development of research questions and subquestions will facilitate the task of conducting and writing it. My experience suggests that conceptually sharp research questions can serve as the foundation for most types of research. If the study relates to a conceptual framework, the questions will fit into such a structure; if there is no other research framework, then research questions become the framework. Examples of such questions have been provided with the sample problem statements outlined in Chapter 4. Let me emphasize that such questions are difficult to resolve and phrase. Often they evolve and get refined as one grapples with the analysis of data and the writing of results. Thus, they may not emerge in final form until the study is virtually complete. Sharp questions indicate the potential of a good study; weak questions suggest a study that may not have been worth conducting. Let us move on now to various other types of frameworks.

The Importance of Definition

Some researchers do not do justice to their studies because they fail to define their terms. This is not necessarily a simple matter because concepts in education are often expressed in non-technical terms making them difficult for the researcher to deal with. It often takes considerable research just to break a concept into components which can be clearly described and more work if the researcher desires to express such components in measurable terms. Furthermore, complex concepts and the imprecision of language sometimes result in confusion about research results. The findings might appear clear when expressed in words, but the words used by the researcher might apply to different concepts than those in the minds of the readers.

In research, even seemingly simple concepts may, after a little thought, be found to be complex. For example, school effectiveness seems simple at first glance but the concept of effectiveness as it applies to schools has many meanings. There have been thousands of studies on school effectiveness, but much of this research is hard to compare since definitions of effectiveness are not stated or not subject to reliable and valid measurement. By definition, the effectiveness of something is the extent to which its objectives are achieved. The many types of objectives for schooling leads to many meanings for school effectiveness. Is it the proportion of students who achieve high school graduation? Does it imply a qualitative dimension and the acquisition of certain competencies? Does it include the school leaver's success in further education, employment and life in society? To study a concept like school effectiveness, one must clarify what is meant. A school may be highly effective in some respects and deficient in others.

This notion of defining a concept by subdividing it into components is a common practice in educational research. The components can be defined and measured more validly than the overall concept. For example, it is relatively easy to establish the dropout rate in a secondary school, as the answer can be expressed in a per cent, number or ratio. It is slightly more difficult, but feasible, to determine whether graduates of the school can read and at what level, since there are reasonably reliable and valid tests to measure such a component of effectiveness. It is more difficult still to assess the development of morals, values or character, but even that can be defined and measured to some degree. The impossibility is to attempt to apply a single score to the global effectiveness of the school. To do that requires you to apply a set of educational values to the issue. I might prefer a school where everyone graduates; you might favour one where only some graduate, but with high academic standing; someone else will prefer the school which instills certain religious beliefs in those who attend; others might value athletic development.

The solution to this problem is to define your terms carefully and work with a multi-faceted definition of effectiveness. Thus, effectiveness becomes a multivariate concept with a variety of components which can be joined together or not depending on your purpose. It then becomes possible to analyze various components of effectiveness and to obtain understanding of relationships derived from research. As this example illustrates, many concepts can be clarified if they are broken down into components which convey a shared meaning. The components are derived through the analysis of the literature and what people have said about the concept, as well as by rational logic which breaks up the concept into its constituent parts. As the process develops, the researcher then attempts to define the concept in words which incorporate these components. The purpose of research is to convey understanding to others and the only way of doing so is to provide clear definitions which enable other researchers to understand what is meant by the concept being researched. Even if others use different definitions, they will at least be able to compare and see where the results might converge or where they might differ. Thus, in all research, it becomes important to define the crucial terms related to the research being carried out.

One-Dimensional Frameworks

Clarification of definitions by breaking concepts into their constituent parts represents the most basic type of framework. This is a one-dimensional framework and it can be made to apply to many types of description. For example, the size of a school can be described in many ways — the number of pupils, the number of classrooms, the size of the physical plant, the number of staff and so on. Each convey part of the notion of size, but collectively they communicate a clearer understanding of the size of an educational institution than any one of them in isolation. Major advances in research often rely on something as simple as defining concepts in such a unidimensional fashion.

Thus, the starting point for the research is often the formulation of a one-dimensional framework. Definitions are one way of sub-dividing concepts; time is another. Chronology in historical research is a good example. If events are arranged

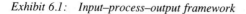

Exhibit 6.1: Input–process–output framework

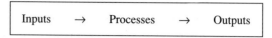

by dates, one can analyze and interrelate events, causes and effects. Undoubtedly the most common one-dimensional time-based framework is the pre-test–post-test experiment in which something is measured before an educational intervention and again afterwards. One might assess arithmetic performance, provide a special teaching program and then measure the performance again in an attempt to attribute any change in scores to the teaching program.

Exhibit 6.1 illustrates another type of one-dimensional time-based framework, the input–process–output model which is applicable to all types of education. This model simply takes the educational process and breaks it into what goes in, the process of education and the outputs achieved. Some researchers have done major work merely by examining the input and output sides of the framework. Called a black box model, it avoids the complex job of trying to define and quantify terms like curriculum and instruction. My own masters study (Anderson, 1966) used just this model to relate such inputs as teacher qualifications and salaries and the socio-economic characteristics of communities to school outputs defined in terms of high school leaving marks and pass rates. This was done using the school as the unit of analysis. Naturally, the inputs, including finances, qualified teachers and so forth have a direct relationship to the processes that go on in schools but in the black box model one need not describe or quantify these processes.

The one-dimensional model can either take a concept and break it into its constituent parts or it can examine a process such as that described in Exhibit 6.1. In either case, understanding can be attained by conducting research within the structure provided by the framework.

Two-Dimensional Frameworks

While often helpful, one-dimensional frameworks are limited in that they do not permit analysis of the interrelationships between sets of related variables. Two-dimensional frameworks are among the most common in educational research.

One of the most common and useful frameworks is formed by dividing the data sample into groups with like characteristics. Exhibit 6.2 outlines a typical framework of this type. In this example, one dimension is formed by grouping the sample into a useful number of groups, in this case formed by splitting the sample into three groups representing high, middle and low socioeconomic status. The other dimension in the example is a two-level nominal variable, gender. The data in the six cells formed by the intersection of these characteristics are the averages for people in that cell. For example, if we were interested in the performance on a test that relates to a new educational program, we could record scores and calculate the group means for each of the groups represented by cells in the table. The research

Exhibit 6.2: Typical two-dimensional framework for cross-tabulations or analysis of variance

Nominal characteristic (e.g., gender)	*Ordinal Characteristic (e.g., Socioeconomic Status)*		
	Low	**Middle**	**High**
Male	Data for low male	Data for mid male	Data for high male
Female	Data for low female	Data for mid female	Data for high female

question would be: 'How does test performance relate to gender and socioeconomic status?' If one were to use analysis of variance, it would be necessary to have the standard deviation of the groups assigned to each cell as well.

You can make your own two-dimensional frameworks to serve the particular needs of your research. For example, a one-dimensional framework that uses definition to break something into discrete components can be combined with another dimension such as size, or time (e.g., pre–post). Thus, the intersection of the two one-dimensional frameworks creates a series of boxes or cells in which two conditions exist.

As these illustrations show, two-dimensional frameworks enable us to have a more precise understanding of the dynamics of the situation than obtainable with overall global descriptions alone. There is no limit to the possible configurations which can easily be tailored to the particular purpose at hand.

The Logical Framework Analysis (LFA)

Some frameworks are highly conceptual and these can be the most useful. One of the most powerful frameworks for investigating educational processes is the logical framework analysis designed by the United States Agency for International Development. The LFA is not just a research framework, but it provides a structure for project planning and evaluation research. It is a difficult framework conceptually, but because of its importance, it is described together with an example.

The logical framework is essentially a planning and evaluation model which contains 16 cells arranged in two dimensions as described in Exhibit 6.3. On the vertical dimension, the bottom level lists the inputs which are the activities and resources that go into a project or program. The outputs are the first level of results that we expect from our investment. In a school, the inputs are such things as school buildings, curricula and teachers, and the outputs are the number of students graduated. In this sense, this is an extended version of the framework shown in Exhibit 6.1. It differs, however, in that the vertical dimension extends beyond the closed system of the school. The graduates graduate for a purpose such as to enter professions and trades. That phase in turn leads to a longer term goal such as community prosperity which could be stated as the goal of our school.

Exhibit 6.3:   The logical framework

Narrative Summary	Objectively Verifiable Indicators	Means of Verification	Important Assumptions
Program goal:	*Measures of goal achievement:*		*Concerning long term value of program/ project:*
The reason for the project, the desired end toward which the efforts are directed (program or sector goal), and for which the project is a logical precondition.	Conditions which will indicate that the goal has been achieved.	The way that the indicators can be objectively verified.	
Project purpose:	*Conditions that will indicate purpose has been achieved:*		*Affecting purpose to goal link:*
That which is expected to be achieved if the project is completed successfully and on time. The 'real' or essential motivation for producing outputs.	End of project status. The objectively verifiable condition which is expected to exist if the project achieves its purpose. The signs which will indicate that the project is a success.	The way that the indicators can be objectively verified.	An event or action, over which the project team has little control; a condition which must be assumed to exist if goal is to be achieved.
Outputs:	*Magnitude of outputs necessary and sufficient to achieve purpose:*		*Affecting output–to–purpose link:*
The specific kind of results that can be expected from good management of the project inputs.	The magnitude of the results and the projected completion dates.	The way that the indicators can be objectively verified.	An event or action, over which the project team has little control; a condition which must be assumed to exist if purpose is to be achieved.
Inputs:	*Resources and expenditures for each activity:*		*Affecting input–to–output link:*
Activities and resources necessary to produce the outputs.	The types and cost of resources for each activity with target dates.	The way that the indicators can be objectively verified.	An event or action, over which the project team has little control; a condition which must be assumed to exist if outputs are to be achieved.

Exhibit 6.4:   The vertical logic of the logical framework

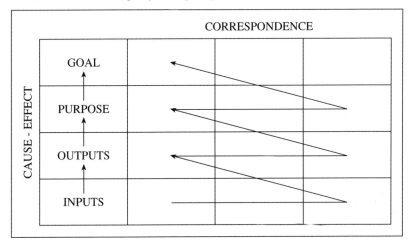

Unlike most other frameworks, the LFA helps systematize and apply a rational approach to knowledge with a research base. The rational part of the model is its logic. The various cells are interrelated in the vertical dimension and also inter-related horizontally. Turning first to the vertical logic (see Exhibit 6.4), it is assumed that if we contribute certain inputs we expect certain outputs. Thus, there is a neces-sary and sufficient relationship between inputs and their corresponding outputs. At the next level of vertical logic we again assume a causal inference. If we achieve those outputs, then it is assumed that we have achieved the purpose. Continuing the final step, it is assumed that if we achieve the purpose, we are expected to achieve the goal. As we move from the lower level (inputs) to the highest level (goal) the relationship tends to become more loose, less causal. This is similar to the ladder of abstraction noted in Chapter 4.

The horizontal logic works a bit differently. For the relationship to hold we rely on certain assumptions which are outlined on the far right for each level. These assumptions are the factors not controlled by the project but which influence its implementation and chances for success. For example, in the school example, we assume that there will be jobs available for the graduates in professions and trades. This would be an assumption at the goal level. The horizontal dimension is an explanation of how we measure the various inputs and outputs. The second column includes what are called objectively verifiable indicators. These are predetermined reliable and valid measures which indicate the status of input or output delivery, the achievement of the purpose or the attainment of the goal. The third column explains how they will be measured. Thus, filling in all 16 cells provides a whole logical plan of the project or program and indicates how it can be monitored at the different levels.

Exhibit 6.5 illustrates the LFA in a practical example. The Eastern Townships region in Quebec is becoming increasingly French-speaking and the English com-munity, once in the majority, has been experiencing difficulty in assimilating and

Exhibit 6.5: Logical framework analysis for Eastern Townships French second language program

Narrative Summary	Objectively Verifiable Indicators	Means of Verification	Important Assumptions
Program goal: To maintain English school system in Eastern Townships.	*Measure of goal achievement:* • Schools stay open with sufficient numbers. • Parents positive to FSL.	• Enrollments. • Attitude tests.	*For achieving goal targets:* • Lack of in-school French learning is a constraint to graduates staying in the Townships.
Project Purpose: To significantly increase French language competence of LDSB graduates.	*Conditions that will indicate that purpose has been achieved:* • Grade 6 grads. functionally bilingual.	• Standardized tests. • School records. • Success in secondary school French.	*For achieving purpose:* • English rural schools will continue to exist in Quebec. • Program will be effective in teaching French.
Outputs: To produce elementary school graduate competent in French.	*Magnitude of Output:* • 120 children graduate per year from 9 schools beginning in 1986.	• Enrollment statistics.	*For achieving outputs:* • Program will be accepted by government.
Inputs: • FSL Coordinator. • Program development resources. • Teacher training and selection. • Full day bilingual kindergarten.	*Implementation Target:* • Bilingual kindergarten by 1980. • New program developed on following schedule: 1 1981 2 1982 3 1983 4 1984 5 1985 6 1986	• Reports of coord. • Teacher and principal report. • External evaluation reports.	*For providing inputs:* • Extra teachers can be funded. • Government will allow program to be offered.

preserving its access to jobs and opportunities. To help address the problem of a lack of French competence among English school graduates, the Lennoxville District School System introduced a program of bilingual education which it was hoped would encourage school graduates to stay in the Eastern Townships and become gainfully employed (Anderson, 1985). The adopted program provided a bilingual full-day kindergarten followed, in the later grades, by one hour each day of intensive French. The expectation was that this treatment would lead to school graduates competent in French who would remain in the region and would be able to find employment. Exhibit 6.5 illustrates the logic of the LFA approach for this experiment. Note how the LFA is logically organized so that the inputs are assumed to lead to the outputs, purpose and goal. Note also how the effectiveness of schooling is to be measured. The measurement constitutes an agreed-upon definition of what the parents considered successful bilingual education. The purpose, of course, goes beyond the final examination and becomes an interesting research question which is observable and measurable. One should pay particular attention to the fundamental assumptions listed on the right hand side. The logic of the Lennoxville experiment relied on these assumptions and they were fundamental to the research program which evaluated it.

Conclusion

In conclusion, a successful research strategy is facilitated if structured into some type of framework which relates previous research and present understanding to new questions which can then be adequately explored. The development of a new framework or the application of an existing framework to a new group or setting often constitutes the basis of significant research which extends understanding and knowledge. If the ultimate purpose of research is generalization and prediction, conceptual frameworks greatly facilitate its achievement. They presume more complex patterns of interaction than a simple A causing B. Rather they infer that various dimensions of A have various types of relationships to the multi-dimensions of B and, furthermore, that the relationship may vary with other conditions which can be viewed as multi-dimensions of C.

References

Anderson, G.J. (1966). *A statistical analysis of input–output differences among Quebec Protestant secondary schools.* Unpublished M.A. Thesis, McGill University, Montréal.

Anderson, G.J. (Ed.). (1985). *Lessons in policy evaluation: A report on the Lennoxville district French second language program 1979–1984.* (Monograph). McGill University, Faculty of Education, Montréal, Montreal, QC.

Chapter 7

Scholarly Communication

Educational research has been portrayed as an activity whereby society accumulates knowledge. Knowledge is accumulated through the written word and researchers have an obligation to record and communicate their findings. There are various ways by which researchers spread their results. Their own teaching is an obvious method. There are also scholarly conferences where academics in each discipline gather annually to hear the latest results and findings from leading researchers. Researchers also publish research papers, reports and books which convey research literature. While some communication about research is in oral form, by far the most prevalent communication medium is the written word, whether in print form or through electronic or optical retrieval systems. For this reason, the researcher must know how to communicate. There are two aspects to the task, scholarly conventions and literary excellence. There are established scholarly conventions for making references, constructing tables and organizing results that prescribe how one conveys research information. The conventions followed by researchers have been developed over the years, and the new researcher is obliged to learn and follow them. Mastering these conventions is part of the socialization of researchers and denotes attainment of professional status as a researcher. There are also the literary conventions of the language which also need to be mastered if one is to convey information concisely, yet completely and clearly.

The purpose of this chapter is to give new researchers a quick introduction to the task of research writing. It is in no way considered a replacement for some of the contemporary definitive works on these matters (see Gowers, 1954; Strunk & White, 1979; Williams, 1981; Zinsser, 1980), but it does attempt to provide a few quick principles which will help people get started and pointed in the right direction. There is a great deal to learn and many beginners become discouraged because every time they put the pen to paper, they seem to be violating some rule of scholarly style or writing protocol. The chapter first deals with the process of scholarly publication. It then goes on to describe the mechanical aspects of scholarly editorial style, giving a brief synopsis of some of the main conventions. It then discusses writing style and offers some tips on how to write and improve your writing. Finally, it goes into the conceptual area of organizing research writing so that it suits the medium and the needs of its audience.

The graduate student who prepares fellowship and research grant applications begins to know some of the substance of the life of an academic. Most scholarly publication processes involve similar steps. The three most common places to publish — conferences, journals and books — are discussed briefly.

Conferences

Annually, professional associations host conferences to unite their membership and share recent developments in the field. Once the association sets a theme for an upcoming conference, a *call for papers* is sent out inviting interested parties to submit a proposal for a paper they would like to present. In some cases the submission is merely a title but more frequently it is a page or two describing the research and its contribution. These submissions are made about six months before the meeting is held. A review panel then goes over the submissions and selects those that it considers most worthy of presentation. Very often such proposals relate to research which is in progress but not yet complete. Acceptance of this submission implies a commitment to complete the research prior to the conference. The presenter is then scheduled a slot in the conference program and generally arrives with copies of the paper in hand. A short presentation, generally about 20 minutes, is made and sometimes there is an appointed discussant or questions from the audience are received. Copies of the paper are normally available for distribution and for those who request them by mail. Too often such papers are read aloud, the researcher failing to recognize the important difference between an effective oral presentation and the reading of written words. Such papers should always be talked through or depicted visually without reading lengthy prose, but that is not the subject of this chapter. The whole process is depicted in Exhibit 7.1 which is a useful illustration of the types of steps one goes through in any academic writing process.

Journals

Submitting a paper to a journal follows a similar procedure. In this case, there is no special invitation and anyone can submit a manuscript at any time. One submits the paper and it is generally given a quick review by the journal editor who, on deciding of its general interest, sends it to a panel of reviewers. Most often there are two or three reviewers who are themselves academics and who undertake a blind review; that is, they evaluate the paper without knowledge of its author's name. Papers recommended for publication are sent back to the author sometimes for further revisions but once accepted, the paper is scheduled for publication. This might take a year after the paper was submitted and in leading journals, the rejection rate is over 95 per cent. Research scholars are not paid for their papers but publish because of their general commitment to an academic career, the advancement of knowledge, and to enhance their personal prestige and reputation. In short, its high on ego, low on cash.

Books

Books are developed by the author and submitted to a publisher, generally first in proposal form; then sample chapters may be developed. Increasingly, publishers are

Exhibit 7.1: Flow chart for effective scholarly communication

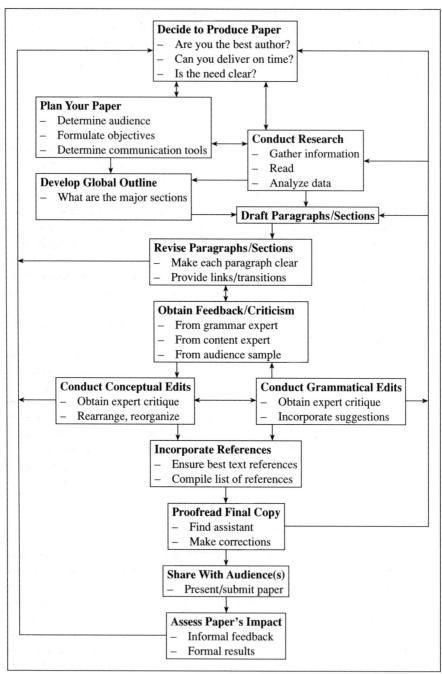

using the process of external review to assess the quality of manuscripts. Once they undertake to publish, the author works diligently with the editor of the publishing house to revise the manuscript in every detail. In this case, the author is paid a royalty, generally about 10 per cent of the retail price of the book. It is not a route to riches, however, as the press run for academic books is generally only a couple of thousand copies.

Scholarly Editorial Style

With all these various outlets for publication, authors are obliged to follow established stylistic conventions in their writing. Of all the available conventions, the one which has probably had more research and development than any other and the one I recommend is that of the American Psychological Association (APA) as summarized in its *Publication Manual* (1994). This style manual began in 1928 and has been revised periodically over the last half century. It provides a straightforward method for citing references and is generally amenable to the requirements of modern word processing. A few other style manuals are also highly developed and some are preferred by people in historical research, but the APA Manual should be learned thoroughly by every social scientist. Most authoritative journals will not accept manuscripts in any other style. It is the author's obligation to write things according to convention and a manuscript failing to do so will be returned. The same applies for theses and dissertations which are sometimes subject to criticism because they have violated these editorial rules. In extreme cases, theses have been graded unsatisfactory largely because the student was sloppy in dealing with these conventions. While conventions may seem unimportant to the new researcher, violations of conventions indicates that one is a novice. If the treatment is inconsistent and sloppy, it further suggests the possibility of sloppiness in the research itself. Therefore, serious researchers should obtain and become familiar with the manual. You can also receive valuable tips by picking up journals which follow APA style and examining the way the various articles are written, organized and referenced. If even that fails, there is now a software program that sets up the references for you.

The Use of References

Practically all research relies on, and refers to, previous research in its particular field. Reference to previous research establishes one's familiarity with the general field and places a research study in context. There are two general methods to refer to previous work. First, one can make general reference to a previous work by citing the author, followed by the date in parenthesis, e.g., Smith (1986). This is used to back-up general assertions or to acknowledge that someone else has done a study in a similar area. In one sense it is simply a genuflection to other respected researchers, but it is important in showing the links your study has with previous research. Often several studies are referred to when making an assertion. Examples of this type of referencing are shown in Exhibit 7.2.

Exhibit 7.2: Examples of general referencing in textual material

---

1 Quasi-experimental approaches (Campbell & Stanley, 1963) are an alternative . . .

2 The problem of validity has concerned many researchers (Campbell & Stanley, 1963; Fisher, 1923; Gayle, 1987).

3 Smith's study (cited in Jones, 1954) reveals . . .

Exhibit 7.3: Examples of methods for referring to direct quotes in textual material

---

1 Smith (1988) found that 'participants with higher motivation scores performed consistently higher in final tests' (p. 93).

2 'Participants with higher motivation scores performed consistently higher in final tests' (Smith, 1988, p. 93).

Note: These quotes, being short, are included in the normal format of the text. Quotes of more than 40 words are indented in a freestanding block concluding with the reference in one of the above forms.

The second referencing method incorporates direct quotes. Short quotations of fewer than 40 words can be run into a sentence in the text with quotation marks around the quoted passage, followed by parenthesis, the author, date and page number, e.g., (Smith, 1986, p. 245). Sometimes the sentence structure is varied and the page number is separated from the author. When longer passages are quoted, they should be indented in total. There are no quotation marks used and the same conventions follow for the author, date and page number. These conventions are shown in Exhibit 7.3. Where an author wrote more than one article in a given year, these are designated by placing the suffixes a, b, c, after the year of publication, e.g., (Smith, 1986a, 1986b).

References, Bibliographies and Annotated Bibliographies

In APA style, each reference cited in the text must be accompanied at the end of the publication by a full citation in a list of references. Note that this is not a bibliography as it contains only those things specifically cited. It is arranged alphabetically and multiple works of each author are listed chronologically. The accuracy and punctuation of these references is of critical importance. Furthermore, there are detailed conventions for how works with various types of author in various sources are to be cited. It is beyond the scope of this chapter to provide all the variations, but the reference sections at the end of chapters illustrate several common types of reference. For more elaborate examples, see the APA Manual.

Bibliographies are different from reference lists. Whereas a reference list includes everything *cited* in a text, a bibliography lists every source that informed and

Exhibit 7.4:   Recording literary information

APA Citation for a Reference or Bibliography:

Strunk, W. & White, E.B. (1979). *The elements of style*, (3rd ed.). New York: MacMillan.

APA Citation for an Annotated Bibliographic Reference:

Denzin, N.K. & Lincoln, Y.S. (Eds). (1994). *Handbook of qualitative research*. Thousand Oaks, CA: Sage.

> An extensive reference text containing chapters, written by leading researchers, that address and discuss history, evolution and current state of qualitative research. The book is divided into six major sections: 1) locating the field; 2) major paradigms and perspectives; 3) strategies of inquiry; 4) methods of collecting and analyzing empirical materials; 5) the art of interpretation, evaluation and presentation, and 6) the future of qualitative research.

---

influenced the written product you are producing. Thus, if you examine various text books, you will find the bibliography section substantially longer than the reference list. Serious researchers will keep an ongoing personal bibliography of all materials they use throughout their career, and it is not uncommon for this list to have thousands of entries. Fortunately, today there are computer programs which can catalogue your literary materials and produce, in a variety of publishing styles, bibliographies and reference lists. They are a tremendous time saving device for anyone who aspires to an academic or research career. Annotated bibliographies are simply a more elaborate record of a particular reference. As well as including the standard information about the author, date, title, publisher, annotated bibliographies include a brief explanatory note. Exhibit 7.4 illustrates the difference. It is important to remember that all academic writing requires a reference list; however, only certain written products require a bibliography.

Plagiarism

It is the researcher's duty to be familiar with previous work so that a new contribution builds on the past. Generally, major ideas are acknowledged by referencing, and direct quotes are cited with the appropriate page numbers indicated as well. However, professors occasionally encounter material which should be referenced but is not. This is plagiarism, and is considered one of the most serious ethical breaches of conduct. In some cultures, students are encouraged, or even forced, to memorize lengthy passages and are required to write it as memorized, however, in the research community such practices are considered plagiarism unless the reference is given and it is clear to what aspect of the writing the reference refers. It is fine to borrow and build on others' ideas, but if you do so, be sure to acknowledge the source.

Tables and Figures

Empirical research generally incorporates tables which convey a great deal of direct information more simply and understandably than prose alone. There are several examples of tables in this book which can be referred to for sample formats. In APA style, all tables have a number; they have a title which describes their content; they have only horizontal lines; and they have headings on top of columns and often notes following the table. The format for these is also prescribed by convention. Typically, tables in a quantitative study are numeric and tables in a qualitative study are in text form.

Figures are similar to tables except that they contain pictures and sometimes prose. I follow the convention of using tables when there are numerical values and calling everything else a figure. However, in the contract research paradigm where the intention is utility, I use the term *exhibit* to refer to all types of illustrative material. That is the convention followed in this book.

Other Conventions

A number of other conventions are often done incorrectly by the novice. Numbers less than 10 and those beginning a sentence are written in words. Numbers 10 and greater are written numerically. Abbreviations of titles are put in parenthesis following the first mention of the title. Underlining is used to designate italics (though with modern word processing, this is unnecessary and you might as well format it yourself in italics). Words can be combined with numbers, e.g., 3 million.

Today, sexist terms of any sort are not considered good form, so one must take great pains to exclude the use of sexist words in writing. The APA Manual includes a guide to non-sexist terms. It sometimes takes considerable pains to avoid what have become cliché conventions but once you have learned to do this, it comes easily. Avoid such terms as she/he.

Historically, all academic writing was in the third person. Today quantitative researchers, by and large, continue to follow this tradition, but qualitative researchers do not. As the purpose of qualitative research is to 'tell a story', the written form for this type of research is often in the first person. Your decision to write in the first or third person should be based on the audience that will read your work. Certain journals require third person writing, others give the author more latitude. Once the decision is made, ensure you stick with the style you have chosen. It is very difficult to read, and decreases your credibility as a writer, if you inappropriately jump between the two writing techniques in a single text.

Verb Tenses

I have found over the years that students have considerable difficulty with verb tenses. Exhibit 7.5 summarizes what you need to know to keep them as they should be.

Exhibit 7.5: Appropriate use of verb tenses in different research documents

Section	Proposal	Thesis/dissertation/report
Introduction	The purpose of this study *is* . . . (or): The study *will* . . .	The purpose of the study *was* . . . The study *showed* . . .
	The proposal *concludes with* . . .	The thesis *is divided* into five chapters Chapter three *presents* . . .
Review of Literature	Both documents have the same use of tense:	
	Smith (1997) *concludes* . . .	Use for more generalizable findings
	Smith (1997) *concluded* . . .	Use for the specific findings of a particular study
Methodology	The procedure *will* involve . . .	The procedure *involved* . . .
	The study *incorporates* a framework . . . (or): The study *will incorporate* a framework . . .	The study *incorporated* a framework . . .
	The major research questions *are* . . .	The major research questions *were* . . .
	Three sources of data *will be* used . . .	Three sources of data *were used* . . .
	The limitations of the study *are* . . .	The limitations of the study *were* . . .
Results/Conclusions	Not Applicable	The average score *was* . . .
		The findings *imply* . . .

Organization of Research Writing

Sound organization of the product of your writing conveys the message that you are a careful and effective researcher, and it facilitates scholarly communication. The conventions for organizing a research product are as doctrinaire as are other writing conventions.

Title Page

A research report requires a title page with the title of the study, the author's institutional affiliation, the sponsor and date. The title of a report must convey its content but must not be so elaborate as to obscure the message. There is a delicate balance between a title which is too long and one which is too short. A good critic is sometimes helpful in deciding what is an appropriate title.

Abstract

The abstract is one of the most important parts of a journal article or research report. It conveys in 100–200 words the substance of the study and the abstract is all that most readers will read. It is unfortunate that the abstract is often written last and in haste. In 1987, I spent six months developing an abstract system for the Canadian International Development Agency which provided a format for two-page abstracts of evaluation reports. Each abstract took an average of two full days to write and most were revised many times after the initial draft. This illustrates the difficulty of conveying in a few words the substance of a study. Interestingly, that system has been helpful in assessing the quality of evaluation reports, many of which do not contain information essential to the production of the abstract.

Table of Contents

Long research documents such as theses require a table of contents. In developing one it is important to remember that the various sections and subsections relate to one another in hierarchical ways. Thus, there are both titles and subtitles. Generally in academic writing three or four levels of headings are suitable to convey any meaning. The convention should be set up and followed throughout the research report. In this way, the reader knows what is a part of which larger section. In my writing, I have found that a decimal system of numbers is helpful in organizing thoughts and keeping track of headings.

Body of the Report

The text is organized into chapters or sections according to the table of contents. Generally, major sections such as chapters begin on a new odd-numbered page which in the case of two-sided printing may necessitate a blank page at the end of the previous section.

References

The reference list begins a new section immediately following the completed body of the report.

Appendixes

Appendixes are the last section of the report. They include other material which would break up the flow of the text if included there. Each appendix is self-contained with its own title and story. Typically, appendixes include data collection instruments and such things as lists of people interviewed. In some cases, the appendixes are included in a second volume.

Conclusion

Writing of all types is a highly creative activity. The work you produce is unique to you and did not exist before you wrote it down. In this sense, it is a good indication of your thinking, your experience and training and your attention to convention and detail. Good writing is a pleasure to produce and a pleasure to read. Poor writing is a great chore and the obligation of university professors to read; much of it is one of the more distasteful parts of the role. Hopefully, this chapter will spare you and your professors from at least some avoidable grief.

Reference

Gowers, Sir E. (1954). *The complete plain words*. Baltimore, MD: Penguin Books.

For Further Study

American Psychological Association. (1994). *Publication manual of the American Psychological Association* (4th ed.). Washington, DC: Author.

Becker, H.S. (1986). *Writing for social scientists*. Chicago, IL: University of Chicago Press.

Giltrow, J. (1991). *Academic writing: How to read and write scholarly prose*. Peterborough, ON: Broadview Press.

Miller, J.I. & Taylor, B.J. (1987). *The thesis writers handbook: A complete one-source guide for writers of research papers*. West Linn, OR: Alcove.

Strunk, W. & White, E.B. (1979). *The elements of style* (3rd ed.). New York: MacMillan.

Watson, G. (1987). *Writing a thesis: A guide to long essays and dissertations*. New York: Longman.

Williams, J.M. (1981). *Style: Ten lessons in clarity and grace*. Glenview Scott, IL: Foresman.

Zinsser, W. (1980). *On writing well: An informed guide to writing nonfiction*. New York: Harper and Row.

Chapter 8

Review of the Literature

Successful research is based on all the knowledge, thinking and research that precedes it, and for this reason a review of the literature is an essential step in the process of embarking on a research study. A review of literature is a summary, analysis and interpretation of the theoretical, conceptual and research literature related to a topic or theme. It is broader than a review of the research which only reviews research literature, and it generally provides the framework for a bridge between a piece of original research and the work which preceded it. One major exception are literature reviews for historical research where the literature review is essentially data collection because there is not a body of related literature in the same sense as for most other types of research. Thus, the historical research review looks at new sources or combines old sources in new ways. It differs considerably from the type of review described here. This chapter considers the purposes of a review of literature, it outlines the essential steps in conducting a review and it suggests ways of presenting it.

Reviewing the literature is not something that is done, completed, put aside and forgotten. Experienced researchers know that reviewing the literature is an ongoing, continuous process. A doctoral student of mine, who struggled with writing the literature review for her masters thesis, reflected on the experience this way:

> The path to understanding winds like a river. As it meanders, the river gains strength from the mountains, sources within valleys, and tributaries along the way. And like the river, our effort to understand adult learners winds a path that gains strength from the knowledge gained through previous research. By examining earlier studies, in consideration of their social context, we begin to see how the river bends and understand the forces which cause it to meander.
>
> The purpose of this chapter is to review and synthesize the literature that informs this study. Anderson (1990) writes that a literature review is designed to summarize, analyze, and interpret the conceptual and theoretical research related to a research project. When I began this study I didn't fully understand the implications of Anderson's words, I do now! It has been a struggle to develop a chapter which does justice to the available resources; resources which have helped shape the study, enrich the data collection and analysis, and strengthen my understanding of the findings. Reviewing the literature has been a continuous activity and, like emerging themes in qualitative research, it is only in reflection that I can step back from the material and fully understand how the literature has guided and informed this study. (Arsenault, 1996, p. 9)

In the beginning, one should become familiar with the basic works related to a field of research. This is generally the level of understanding most graduating masters students reach as a result of their research experience. At the doctoral level, the literature review should reveal a greater depth of understanding and demonstrate that the candidate has interacted with some of the researchers, issues, debates and criticisms. The PhD graduate will typically have a deeper knowledge of the specific fields so that, in some cases, when the dissertation is complete, the PhD graduate will be a world expert in that particular subfield which was the subject of the dissertation. The career researcher has the perspective of time. He or she will follow the literature through its six types of knowledge (see Chapter 5) and will gain the wisdom of experience. Thus, these researchers have an intimate appreciation for how the field has evolved, what research studies have been published that redirect the field, the critical debates and criticisms of the various types of research. Furthermore, such researchers will have contributed to evolution of the field and, therefore, have interacted with its evolving directions. It is typical for graduate students to review the literature early in their studies and then direct their attention to collecting and analyzing data. It is always wise, however, to continue reviewing the literature as your study unfolds. The study itself might take a year or more to complete and during that time, some significant literature may be published.

The Purpose of the Review

Reviews of literature are becoming increasingly important as the number and availability of studies in all disciplines escalates. In fact, research reviews are no longer required formalities; they have become research activities in their own right. They involve many of the same steps as doing original research. If done well, a literature review collects data, analyzes and interprets it, and writes it up with conclusions for the benefit of larger communities. In research journals, the main purpose of the review is to convey the background of a specific field and provide other interested researchers with the information required to comprehend and complete a study.

In a thesis or dissertation, the review has other important dimensions. It provides an example of your work and indicates to the reader your general level of scholarship. The quality of your work, its accuracy, its inclusions and exclusions, its method of organization and presentation, establishes your credibility as a researcher and provides a base of validity for your study. The review of the literature ensures that your research is new and indicates how it relates to and complements the overall field. Without an adequate review there is a danger that you may unknowingly replicate the work which went before. In this regard, the review provides an indication of whether a research study is warranted as well as an indication of its probability of finding something new and making a contribution. When successive studies have failed to produce positive findings it is likely that the area is sterile and does not justify further replication. A review can be very helpful because it indicates the methodologies that have been used by others in pursuit of knowledge in the discipline. A format I encourage my graduate students to use is presented in

Appendix 8.1. This type of analysis provides a framework for identifying the literature and may include a description of the major experimental designs, the instruments used to collect the data, the populations with which the research was conducted and so forth. Finally, for graduate students especially, it is an excellent way to help in the overall process of sharpening the research question and limiting it so that it is do-able and relates to past research in the field.

Reviewing Secondary Sources

Secondary source materials are those written by an author who was not a direct observer or participant in the events described. Existing summaries and reviews are one example and provide a good starting point for students attempting to learn about a field prior to zeroing in on a specific research problem.

The Review of Educational Research is a quarterly journal containing critical, integrative reviews of research literature on significant topics. Its reviews often represent exemplary models of review and pull together an area in ways that identify directions needed for research. The *Encyclopedia of Educational Research* and the *Handbook of Research on Teaching* (unfortunately now dated) are both excellent publications containing reviews by many of the world's leading scholars. They, too, suggest areas for future research.

Referring to these publications should help you define a topic, and identify the major researchers in your area of study and the range of studies conducted. By grounding your study in previous reviews you will save yourself months of work and gain an appreciation of the work which has come before yours.

Collecting the Primary Literature

Collecting literature to review involves browsing, skimming, reading and photo-copying relevant works. Good research generally has a theoretical or conceptual basis, so you need to be familiar with these aspects of the discipline if you are to assess other research studies and design your own. Two types of literature need to be distinguished: conceptual and research. The conceptual literature includes basic writings in the field as well as recent writings from key thinkers. It provides a theoretical and conceptual base that helps delimit the problem, provide a historical overview of the field, and indicates the variables and areas in which research is to be pursued. Those who have taken a graduate course in a specialty will have this background; those pursuing new areas will need to do considerably more work.

As well as to understand the theoretical and conceptual literature, a review of the literature considers previous research. That is, it reviews studies done in the field and summarizes their major conclusions. The latter are found in journals and in dissertations and research reports.

In the beginning, one tends to read generally and extensively all materials related to the field. Graduate students will have to read much more than people experienced in a discipline who are familiar with the basic works. An excellent beginning is to obtain a bibliography from a professor or other knowledgeable expert who has compiled a listing of the major works in a given field. This is especially helpful for the theoretical foundations. The *Bibliographic Index* provides the source of bibliographies published as part of articles and books. If you can locate a recent bibliography on your topic it will save immeasurable time.

Research studies present somewhat different problems. In some instances, a great number of research studies appear to bear on the problem under investigation. Generally, this occurs when the research problem is not sufficiently focused. In such instances, it is helpful to pick out studies which are most specific and which might help cast the problem in a new frame. The other extreme occurs when there are almost no studies in the problem area. In some cases, this is a result of a lack of research with the descriptors indicated; in other cases it implies that the research problem is too narrow in focus; and in others it may indicate a potential growth area for future research. If your search results in limited findings, broaden the net and seek research using a wider range of descriptors and synonyms. You might still be able to preserve these restrictions in your problem statement but within the context of a broader literature on the subject.

Collecting literature is an ongoing process. As it unfolds you are advised to begin classifying studies into the theoretical and conceptual articles; those which bear generally on the topic, and those which have a specific and direct relationship to the problem under study. Because the review of literature is a research process it becomes important to describe the methods employed to conduct it and its limits and limitations. A good research problem is grounded in one or more disciplines and these should be acknowledged. Within disciplines, there may be different theoretical perspectives with which you should be familiar, but generally one emerges as the basis for your study. Within the research literature you ideally want studies with a similar focus. The major factors in the design of studies, the instruments used, the populations involved and the recency of studies are all taken into consideration. For this reason, it becomes important to record and report on the conventions and rules used to exclude various sources of literature. In general, you will report the steps taken to define the boundaries of the literature you include. It is easy to be faulted for excluding important things but not so if you have limited the scope of your review and have thereby excluded them on rational grounds.

Analyzing the Literature

The conceptual and theoretical literature is reported on in order to demonstrate your understanding of the evolution and state of the field. It is exceedingly helpful if you can derive or borrow from the literature a conceptual framework which can form the basis of the research review and of your study (see Chapter 6). Such a framework will outline the critical factors and variables and indicate some interaction among them. It may also serve as a useful way of organizing the review of research. The various research studies selected for inclusion are then organized in some fashion either using the conceptual framework or at least by categorizing them under distinct headings.

The best and most salient works will be selected for review. Thorough studies of the quality of educational research (see, Persell, 1976) indicate that 30–40 per cent of published studies are of poor quality with poor designs, inappropriate designs and conclusions not supported by the evidence. Major categories of problems with internal and external validity have been noted by Campbell and Stanley (1963), but in addition, the reviewer should be sensitive to deliberate bias, sampling problems, the use of poor or untested instruments, non-equivalent control groups and poor conceptualization. It is important to assess the quality of the studies reviewed so that the best can be given the most weight and those with obvious mistakes can be avoided.

The review itself will weave together the studies into an interesting and informative story line out of which come useful conclusions. Reference to a given study will range from a genuflection to its importance in the evolution of research in the field to a major description and critique of the study and its methodology. You are attempting here to summarize the state of the art of research in the field. To do so, you will pay attention to *what, when, where, who* and *how* it was done. The research review indicates *what* research has already been undertaken in the field and the results achieved. This is the typical purpose of research reviews, but it is not the only one. The reviewer should be sensitive to *when* the research was conducted. Research in the social sciences is contextual and often follows cycles so that a flurry of activities for a couple of years may be followed by a period of relative inactivity. It is important to know whether the research contemplated is in vogue at the moment or whether it has been exhausted only later to be rediscovered when different approaches and issues come to the fore. The question of *where* refers to the geographic base of the study. As an example, for Canadian researchers much of the literature refers to American studies, so there may be a need for further research in the Canadian setting. *Who* was studied becomes important because a lot of research attempts to extend the work of previous researchers to new populations — different age groups, genders and so forth. Finally, the question of *how* the study was conducted is particularly important for one contemplating research. Not only should you be generally familiar with the methods employed previously, but they often provide a route which your study can follow. Instruments can sometimes be used from previous studies and you can often identify methodological weaknesses which justify a new more sophisticated piece of analysis.

Analysis of previous research used to be strictly in narrative form. Today, tabular presentations are becoming increasingly justified since there are so many studies on a given topic (see Appendix 8.1). A carefully designed table including the author, date, subjects, methodology and conclusions can be exceedingly helpful in cutting through a great mass of literature. Such tables also serve as an excellent way of summarizing the verbal narrative. In their most elaborate form, to summarize quantitative studies, these tables include statistical estimations of the size of the effects enabling different studies to be compared in a valid way. Appendix 8.1 illustrates a simple tabular presentation used in a literature review and Appendix 8.2, from the same study, provides a more detailed summary of the information used in developing the research frameworks.

The summation of all this analysis should permit you to formulate general conclusions about the state of the art of research related to the topic. Future directions should be relatively self-evident and this should set the stage for the proposed study. At the same time, the review can serve to clarify definitions, assumptions and limitations which are useful for the contemplated research. Very often, the review is concluded with a set of new research questions or hypotheses which emanate from the conceptual framework and research that has been studied. These become organizers for the problem to be investigated.

Presenting the Review

The way a review of literature is presented differs in a journal article or short research proposal from that found in a dissertation or thesis. In the former case, the audience is other researchers who are knowledgeable in the field and consequently they do not require extensive narrative. Rather, they require reference to several salient studies which set the stage for the subsequent research. Of course, some journals specialize in publishing extensive literature reviews and these help shape the field in their own right. For that purpose, and for most student thesis work, a review of literature should be treated in some respects, at least, like any other piece of research. It normally has an introduction, which lays the basis for the review. Here it is useful to include some of the theory and conceptual work or refer to previous reviews to set the framework for the review of research studies that follows. Another section should outline the major methods and procedures used, including data sources and limitations. In some cases, the criteria for relevance of studies is reported here. Finally, the introduction may describe how the studies are to be grouped in the review that follows. The section on findings will outline the discoveries from major studies and will weave them together into an integrated state of the art picture. The review normally concludes with a summary that brings together the discoveries. This section might reiterate the research problem to be investigated and outline the various research questions to be explored. As with any research paper, the review refers to a list of references. This must be scrupulously accurate and presented in acceptable publication style. Any sloppiness here will reflect the possibility of sloppiness in the study which follows. Only the references cited in the review are listed and the list of references is placed at the end of the proposal or study, but before the appendices.

Conclusion

A good literature review is a pleasure to produce and a joy to read. It gives you something concrete to do early in the study and builds your confidence that the definition and design of your study extends what has been done before. It is a good test of you and your problem as it requires diligence, care and thoroughness. It spans the range from strictly mechanical work to highly conceptual thinking. It sets the context for your research and foreshadows your probable contribution.

References

Arsenault, N. (1996). *Understanding older adults in education: Decision-making and Elderhostel*. Unpublished master's thesis, McGill University, Montreal, QC.

Campbell, D., & Stanely, J. (1973). *Experimental and quasi-experimental designs for research*. Chicago: Rand McNally.

Persell, C.H. (1976). *Quality, careers and training in educational and social research*. Bayside, NY: General Hall.

Part II

Types of Research

Chapter 9

Introduction to Types of Research

What is a research method? A research method is an approach to addressing a research question or problem. Methodology can be compared to fine cooking in that there are many approaches to each product. The French certainly do not make their bread like the Greeks or Czechoslovakians, and the taste and texture of the product differs considerably from one to the other. Which product you prefer is a matter of personal taste and perhaps relates as well to what you intend to do with the bread. No matter how you process your bread, all approaches require essential ingredients: flour, yeast and water. In the same way, research methods all need data, though its precise nature varies from one approach to another as does the method by which it is processed. What you achieve as your final product depends both on the quality of the data and on the way that it is processed.

To conclude the cooking analogy, many of the best cooks are masters of one particular approach. The same holds true of research methods, but as in the case of cooks, some people are able to combine approaches and improvise depending on the particular challenge at hand. It is useful to observe that the best cooks are often well grounded in one approach even though they may later go beyond it. For the beginner, it makes considerable sense to learn one approach thoroughly before straying too far into the unknown. Many beginning researchers mix their methods without a good understanding of any one of them. For example, graduate theses often contain some empirical results followed by one or two case studies. In many instances, neither approach is particularly well-handled and the result is merely a learning experience of no general use to anyone but the person who did it.

Until relatively recently, the verb 'research' was somewhat confined in the methods to choose among, but now the possibilities are highly varied. Contemporary educational researchers can borrow from the methodological advances in the traditional associated disciplines as well as from the newer methodologies that have gained acceptance in the field of education. Previous scepticism about the validity of methods outside the narrow domain of experimental research has given way to a more healthy respect for a wide range of methods which have contributed to the advancement of education. The beginner, however, should beware that the more eclectic approach to educational research presents risk of a decline in research standards. The best researchers are experts in the methodology they follow. Those who combine methods and appear to take more licence, normally have a sound grounding in the separate methods which they use in combinations. The best route to valid research is to learn the various methods systematically and in depth. Then, you will be in a position to select from among a wide repertoire and use them in different circumstances.

Defining the Methodology

In practice, except for historical research, the methodology section of a research report, thesis or dissertation is a separate section which describes what the researcher did. There are many ways of organizing the information. Those who do experimental research in psychology, for example, will follow the established headings used by the American Psychological Association as reflected in its journals. For general educational research, more flexibility is warranted. I advocate eight ingredients which you should at least consider including. You may not have all the sections, depending on the type of methodology you use, but, this outline of sub-parts will give you an idea of the elements that need to be covered. Normally, you should describe the general approach and/or procedure, the framework, research questions, sources of data, instruments, method of analysis and limitations. The amount of detail you include on each of these topics depends, in part, for whom you are writing. A journal article will be brief, whereas a thesis will require a full description of everything that was done. In a thesis or dissertation, even the data collection instruments are included, though normally as appendices. As you read research studies, look for these elements of the methodology and see whether you would be in a position to replicate the study from the description given.

Essential Ingredients

Whatever the approach one follows, there should be a thorough description of the key ingredients, enabling any other researcher to understand what was done and replicate it if he or she so desires. The precise nature of the information varies according to the method chosen and what follows is a generalized schema with qualifications noted when appropriate. The methodology section of a research proposal or report of a completed study should include reference to appropriate elements from those that follow.

General Approach

I like to begin the methodology section with a short description of the general approach followed. This may only be a paragraph or two but is important as a way of grounding the methodology in one or more of the traditional approaches used (e.g., experimental, case study, correlational study).

Procedure

In general, all studies should include a section on procedure. The procedure consists of a general statement of how the study was undertaken, who was contacted, when and by whom, what forms the data collection took, ethical issues, and all other matters which would permit another competent researcher to replicate the study. In essence, the procedure section gives a clear and straightforward account of what was done. In a sense, it provides a general overview of the methodology section and portrays the context for specific details which are described more fully in separate sections that follow.

Framework

In some studies there is a need to describe the framework followed (see Chapter 6). This framework often results from the review of the literature and is described in that section of the research proposal or report, but there are instances when it fits more logically in the methodology section. Wherever it fits, when a framework is used, it needs to be described fully.

Research Questions

Research questions and subquestions must always be included. In my preferred approach, these questions emerge from the literature review and are included as the conclusion to that section. This way they set the stage for the methodological discussion that follows.

Sources of Data

The sources of data should be fully described, whether they be documents, settings that were observed, people interviewed or people who completed scales, tests or questionnaires. When the study involves a sample, it, along with the sampling procedures must be described. The sample is normally described in terms of the numbers of people with the various characteristics called for in the framework of the study. These are often reported in numerical and tabular form. The sampling procedure must be carefully articulated in order for the reader to understand the relationship of the sample to the group or target population from which it was drawn.

Instruments

The data collection instruments need to be described. Instruments include tests and questionnaires, observation schedules and any other tool used to collect data. Ideally, with quantitative instruments, the reliability and validity should be reported. With qualitative studies, reporting on these issues varies (see Chapter 13). If any of the instruments were used in previous studies, that should be noted as well as a clear description of any alterations or modifications that are made. In general, the methodology section describes each instrument in two or three paragraphs and a copy of the actual instrument is included as an appendix.

Analysis

A brief description of the particular type of analysis followed should be included. It provides another level of detail to that described in the introductory section on general approach. If there are new or adapted methods of analysis used, they may require considerable technical detail to convey clearly what was done. If standard approaches were used, these are described in shorthand. For example, in a quantitative statistical study, there are generally technical terms to describe the procedures used (e.g., analysis of variance). Sometimes this section also outlines the particular decision conventions used in the statistical analysis such as the adopted level of significance. In qualitative research, the chain-of-evidence or audit trail (see Chapter 13) is often reported as it helps in understanding how the findings have been derived.

Limitations

Finally, all good studies should indicate the limitations of the research. These are the factors that may threaten the various elements such as objectivity, validity, and in quantitative research, generalizability. The limitations section includes both errors resulting from inherent design limitations and those that occur while the study evolves. In the game of conducting and reporting research, there is no harm in having limitations, but it is bad form not to admit them.

Types of Methods

Various authors use different terms and groupings to come up with different methodologies. This text lists nine methods. Some researchers are methodological experts in one specific method, others are more eclectic in their pursuits. Remember that the method that you choose will, to some degree, dictate the questions you address and the approaches you take. Whether or not you use all the various methods, you should be familiar with them so that you can be a literate consumer of educational research.

As one goes about choosing a research area, one must also consider the general method to follow. Often these decisions are interrelated. You are advised to choose a method which builds on your orientation and is supported by your training, but you must also be sensitive to the relationship of the central research question to the method for addressing it. The subsequent six chapters describe six different methods which span various levels and research orientations. Exhibit 9.1 lists

Exhibit 9.1: Example of various research methods in response to the integration of disabled children into the regular classroom

Method	Major Concerns/Research Questions
Historical	How have disabled children been treated in the past?
Descriptive	What proportion of the children are classified as disabled and in what ways are they schooled?
Experimental/ Quasi-Experimental	How does the performance and attitudes of disabled children, who are integrated, compare to those educated in a separate school?
Correlational	What are the best predictors of success for disabled children integrated into a regular classroom?
Qualitative	What happens to the culture of a regular classroom when disabled children are introduced?
Program evaluation	How successful was the school system's program of integrating disabled children?
Case study	What happened to John Smith when he was integrated into the regular classroom?
Policy research	In what ways can the school system deal effectively with its disabled pupils?
Organizational evaluation	What is required, within a school, to ensure the successful integration of disabled children?

these methods and, with the example of integrating disabled children into the regular classroom, describes how the different research designs lead to different sorts of questions.

The Historical Method

Historical research comes from deep traditions and differs from the other methodologies in the way the methodology section is written. In most historical research, the methodology is integrated into the body of the report. Sometimes it is included in the introduction and at other times, the various elements of methodology are integrated throughout. Chapter 10 of the text provides a brief description of the historical method. Even if you do not intend to conduct historical research, you will find the methodology useful in selected parts of other types of studies, such as program evaluation or policy research. In the example of Exhibit 9.1, the historian would be concerned with how we treated disabled children in the past, perhaps looking for differences across jurisdictions or for children with differing sorts of handicaps.

Descriptive Methods

Various descriptive methods are described in Chapter 11. Just as data are fundamental to research, description is an essential extension of data. There are many types of data and many ways to describe, but we need accurate and understandable description in order to communicate what we observe. The example in Exhibit 9.1 merely attempts to define how authorities define disability and to determine how many children are so classified.

Experimental and Quasi-experimental Methods

These are comparative methods in which different groups of people or organizations receive different opportunities and the researcher attempts to demonstrate the differences among the groups on some type of quantitative measure such as student examination results. These methods have dominated educational research for much of the century, though they are now being supplanted by more eclectic methods. In the example, there could be a range of comparative questions asked.

Correlational Methods

Correlational methods attempt to explore relationships between variables as described in Chapter 12. Note that you need quantitative data in order to conduct correlational research. Correlational research relies on pairs of observations, each related to an individual or other unit of analysis. Be sure you understand the fact that correlation does not mean that one variable causes another. It only means that there is a relationship. The cause may be something else entirely. Although one variable does not necessarily cause the other, knowledge of a first may allow prediction of a second. That opens up a whole field of prediction studies and the use of mathematical models and equations to predict future states. The example related to disabled children defines a typical question that attempts to predict success factors.

Qualitative Methods

Chapter 13 discusses the multi-method, interpretive and naturalistic focus qualitative researchers use to understand and bring meaning to particular phenomena in a given environment. Ethnography, phenomenology, case study, biographical, grounded theory and applied/action research are among the wide range of qualitative approaches used to study phenomena. The intent is to uncover the implicit meaning in a particular situation from one or more perspectives. The data may include dynamic interaction such as one observes or analyzes through discourse, semiotics, narrative and content analysis. In studying disabled children, one focus that may interest the qualitative researcher is the meaning various stakeholders attach to integrating disabled children into the classroom.

Program Evaluation Methods

The field of evaluation research has mushroomed in recent years and Chapter 14 examines how one evaluates educational and other types of programs. Evaluation research combines both qualitative and quantitative methods to address questions about programs generally related to an overall framework. In the disabled child example, the evaluator would examine the program and evaluate its rationale, efficiency, effectiveness, effects and impacts.

Case Study Methods

The case study examines some significant incident or series of events to clarify what happens in such situations. These methods are also eclectic, though like program evaluation, they follow models and frameworks that have become somewhat standard. The case study defined in Exhibit 9.1 considers what happened to a single child. Another approach might study educational change exemplified by the introduction of the new program.

Policy Research

Policy research is a field concerned with research about various aspects of policy. In some cases the focus is retrospective and examines the results of policy (sometimes referred to as 'policy in implementation'), while in others, the researcher is concerned with the prospective aspect (the 'what if' question). Thus, much of policy research has either an evaluative dimension or is concerned with potential futures were specific formulations of policy implemented. It is a field that typically involves a range of other research methods and normally the contributions of other disciplines such as economics. Because it is an advanced subject, this book does not include a chapter on policy research.

Organizational Evaluation

Organizational evaluation is concerned with research that helps to clarify certain dimensions of organizations such as their capacity and their performance. The whole organization is the unit of analysis in such research which can effectively produce an evaluative case study of the organization. My colleagues and I have developed a framework for assessing the motivation, capacity and performance of organizations and we have conducted extensive work on self-assessment processes. This is also an advanced topic, so is not covered in detail in this book. The reader is invited to consult Lusthaus, Anderson & Murphy (1995) for a description of the framework used in this work. The book can be downloaded from the IDRC web site at http://www.idrc.ca.

Statistics and Research

Of all the subjects that graduate students in education face, statistics is often the most troublesome. Mathematics is difficult enough, but the situation is typically complicated by texts and courses that provide rich theoretical material that stands between a learner and his or her problem. It reminds me of an African college I once visited where the students were learning to swim, but as there was no water for the pool, it was a theoretical course where students stood beside their desks and moved their arms as if they were swimming. To me, the only way to understand statistics is to apply them — preferably to the data you have collected and care most about. The problem in these terms is how you understand the underlying secrets in your data and learn the tools that help you do so.

Reducing the Field to Three Concepts

In applied statistics there are only three types of problem: descriptive, comparative and relational. All the rest merely refine, and typically the refinement gets in the way of understanding what is going on. The purpose with the *descriptive problem* is to describe the data you have. How many of the teachers in your sample are female? What is their age distribution? How did respondents answer each of the questions on your questionnaire? All the statistics do is give you shortcuts to describing these types of questions. See Chapter 11 for a more in-depth discussion on descriptive research.

The *comparative problem* determines whether groups are the same or different, and if different, how. There may be two groups (i.e. males and females) or many groups (i.e. states or provinces in a country). What statistics do is use descriptive statistics for each group to determine whether they are the same or different. Technically, statistics determine whether the differences observed are what one would expect by chance alone. This is the concept of statistically significant differences, and two conventions: whether the differences would be as large as those observed less than 5 per cent of the time or less than 1 per cent of the time. Refer to Chapter 11 for further detail.

The *relational problem* considers how variables relate to one another. For example, are people's heights related to their weights? This is answered by a simple correlation between height and weight. In more complex cases, the relational question asks whether a whole battery of variables are related to a second battery of different variables. For example, are a person's background characteristics (such as IQ, standard achievement test scores, socioeconomic status) related to their college success (measured by annual grade point average)? In the refined analyzes, the statistics can pick out the variables with the strongest relationship and determine how many of the variables are significantly related when the effects of others are accounted for. More about this later in Chapter 12.

The issue in statistical analysis is to choose which of the three problems you wish to address. This is clearly another instance that demonstrates why your research problem statement has to match the intended analysis. If your research question is descriptive, then descriptive statistics are called for. If you want to explore how variables interrelate, then use a correlational approach. In practice, the several research questions that define the crux of your problem (see Chapter 4) may each call for a different type of statistical analysis.

Conclusion

Through these examples you should begin to understand the inherent differences in the various methods and realize that they focus on different sorts of concerns. Obviously, historical research is concerned with the past, differentiating it from all other methods, but every method has a particular focus and concern. If your research questions suggest one of these concerns then they also suggest which method is appropriate for pursuing them. Thus if you want to predict, you need to use a correlational method, if you want to evaluate, then use a program evaluation model, and if you want to understand how people feel and gain insight into the underlying phenomena, then a qualitative method would be best. Once you become familiar with each approach, you should be in a position to identify how questions link logically to approaches. Bear in mind also, that these methods are not pure and researchers often combine approaches. For example, you might do historical or descriptive work to identify an issue or problem and then follow it up using predictive approaches. Success at prediction might suggest applications in the realm of educational policy.

Research method is an approach to examining a research question. There are a number of approaches to research; this text reviews six. As you attempt to define and refine your particular research problem, you should consider its methodological implications. Make sure that the problem you wish to pursue is suited to the method you intend to apply. Make sure also that you have the background and strengths required in that method to be able to apply it successfully to your research problem.

Reference

Lusthaus, C., Anderson, G., & Murphy, E. (1995). *Institutional assessment: A framework for strengthening organizational capacity for IDRC's research partners*. Ottawa: IDRC.

Chapter 10

Historical Research

Most of us are interested in the past and curious about the way things were in former eras. Those whose curiosity reaches the stage of commitment to do something about it will be interested in historical research. Historical research is past-oriented research which seeks to illuminate a question of current interest by an intensive study of material that already exists. Historiography refers to the systematic collection and objective evaluation of data related to past occurrences in order to explore research questions or test hypotheses concerning causes, effects or trends of those events that may help explain present events and anticipate future events. Since history deals with the past, the purpose of historical research cannot be to control phenomena. Instead, the research is intended to help understand or explain what went on and perhaps to predict into the future. Such journals as the *History of Education Quarterly*, published by the History of Education Society and the School of Education of New York University provide good examples of the types of historical studies that are currently under way.

Description

Historical research shares a great deal with qualitative research in education even though it may make use of quantitative material. Like other forms of qualitative research, the concern is with natural behavior in a real situation and the focus is on interpretation of what it means in the context. Unlike other forms of educational research, the historical researcher does not create data. Rather, the historian attempts to discover data that exists already in some form.

Problem Definition

Historical research problems arise from personal interests which are often kindled by exposure to a person, event or logical source of unused original data. In a review of historical topics, Beach (1969) identified five generic types of topic common in the history of education.

Biographies, institutional histories and histories of particular educational movements are prevalent examples of descriptive research. In such works the historian seeks to describe what happened. There need not be elaborate hypotheses or startling new issues; the motivation is to describe something that has not been fully described before. There are countless local opportunities for such research and these make good problems for the beginner. Note that with institutional history, the historian tends to approach the task from a social and historical point of view, whereas the same subject can be studied by researchers in institutional development or organizational evaluation.

Current social issues form another generic topic type. Such issues as the privatization of schooling, the accountability movement, gender and civil rights beg the question of how such issues were viewed in previous eras. These topics are also descriptive, though explanation typically follows. For example, Bayley (1987), in an analytic study, examined why modern languages were introduced into the curriculum in England a century ago. Her study addressed the issue of resistance to the teaching of practical subjects in secondary schools and related as well to important gender differences which suggest new historical perspectives on gender equity.

A third type of historical inquiry involves attempts to interpret ideas or events that had previously seemed unrelated, for example, the relationship of educational opportunities for youth aged 16–20 and problems of youth unemployment. Another example would be the flows of Hispanic immigrants into the United States and the teaching of Spanish in American schools. A related type is the synthesis of old data or the combination of such data with new historical facts or interpretations. For example, new facts about the life of an influential educator could be used to reinterpret his contributions to education.

The fifth type of historical problem is called revisionist history. It is an attempt to reinterpret events that other historians have already studied. Very often, with the passage of time, we know more about the context in which events have taken place and are then able to revisit our earlier interpretations. As might be expected, this is the most advanced type of historical research and is the one requiring most experience.

These five types of issues provide a good starting point for the problem definition process. You must go on, however, to determine whether a sufficient data base exists to permit a successful study. If there are reams of data you may need to confine the topic by limiting the time span of a personal or institutional history. In so doing, there are often definable eras which suggest logical breakpoints. As with all types of research problem, the definition process should continue as you begin collecting and analyzing the data. You may uncover unthought-of issues or possibilities which may raise the conceptual level of the study. For example, in studying an educator you could find evidence of the introduction of an educational innovation or method years earlier than previously believed.

Procedure

Basic Steps

Unlike most research procedures, historical research tends to be idiosyncratic depending both on the individual doing the research and on the nature of the topic. In general, however, historians tend to go through the following six steps:

1 Specification of the universe of data required to address the problem adequately.
2 Initial determination that sufficient data are available.
3 Data collection through:
   (a) consideration of known data;
   (b) seeking known data from primary and secondary sources;
   (c) seeking new and previously unknown data.
4 Initial writing of report and descriptive phase of research.
5 Interaction of writing and additional data search and examination.
6 Completion of interpretative phase.

Sources of Data

Educational historians typically make use of four types of historical data sources: documents, oral records, quantitative records and artifacts. Documents are by far the most common data source, but there are many categories of documents ranging from print materials like newspapers, committee reports and yearbooks to informal handwritten documents such as letters, diaries and memoirs. Historians distinguish between intentional documents, produced for public consumption, and unpremeditated documents written for personal use. The intended purpose of the different sorts is different, which affects the validity of the information they contain. For example, oral records include not only oral histories recorded to illuminate the past, but also songs, tales and ballads passed from one generation to another. Quantitative records are important sources of historical data. Tax roles, class lists, birth registries, school report results and other quantitative records can give useful information about participation in education, performance and so forth. Artifacts and relics include objects and sometimes documents which have antiquarian significance. Old school texts, report card forms, corporal punishment devices and old photographs are examples.

It is important to distinguish between primary and secondary data sources. Primary sources refer to documents written by a witness to the events, whereas secondary sources render a second-hand version of what happened.

Data Collection

One difference between historical research and most other types is that the researcher has no ability to create new data. He or she must work with what already exists. Occasionally, it is possible to incorporate interviews and other such techniques as part of historical research. Much of it, to be sure, is conducted in detective-like fashion whereby information is traced as to source, and those knowledgeable about the event or situation are contacted and used as informants and also sources of written data. In general, quality historical research relies on primary data sources and one should ensure that sufficient sources of this type exist in order to address the problem.

The particular research topic or problem will suggest the logical types of data that may possibly exist. So, for example, a study of a person will attempt to locate biographies, photographs, letters, diaries and newspaper references, whereas a study of attendance patterns in a school will focus on other types of historical records. The researcher brainstorms a universe of possibilities and then develops a search plan. Three types of sources need to be identified. Preliminary sources such as bibliographies, atlases and other such standard references will need to be consulted merely to see what general descriptive information exists about the people, places or events being researched. These general references should lead to secondary sources such as books, theses, articles about the topic. Third, one needs to identify potential primary sources and their probable location. These may be found in archives, museums or personal collections. A search plan should proceed from the general secondary sources to the specific primary sources and should be explicit if it is to aid the process. The researcher can then pursue the plan and be sure that relevant sources of data are covered.

As the data collection process begins, the researcher has to record the information gathered. Previously, this had to be painstakingly copied by hand on cards for later analysis, but today, photocopying is the norm. One difficulty, however, is the nature of historical material. Much of it is fragile and must be handled with extreme care. Sometimes it cannot be copied either because people will not give permission, it cannot be removed from a location without copying facilities, or it is in faded condition and can only be copied by using elaborate photographic techniques.

Occasionally, historians collect data using sampling or other statistical techniques. In this case, the standard quantitative procedures would be used. Be sure that you accurately label and classify the data. If voluminous, historical data can be overwhelming and useable classification systems are a big help. Systems from file folders to computer data bases can be used for the purpose.

Data Analysis

An important issue in the analysis of historical data is to realize that data in historical research were not developed in the first place for use in research. The data had a life of their own and were recorded and filed to fulfill someone else's purpose. For this reason, much information is distorted, biased, or otherwise invalid. The researcher must evaluate the data, a process generally referred to as historical criticism. Two aspects need to be considered: the source and the content. Thus, historical criticism includes external criticism, establishment of the authenticity of the source including its date, author and legitimacy, and internal criticism, evaluating the accuracy and worth of the statements contained in an historical document. This implies evaluating and weighing data according to the extent to which the primary source observer was a credible witness. Information recorded at the time of an event is given more credibility than that reported a long time afterwards.

The central role of the historian is the interpretation of the data in the light of historical criticism. Each fact and supposition must be carefully weighed and added to the case leading to the research conclusion. One challenge for the researcher is the development of a framework for organizing and interpreting the data. Many can be used, but two are worth noting here: organization by date and according to concept. The latter implies identifying key issues or themes then organizing and interpreting the data on that basis.

The historian must carefully weigh the extent to which causality can be inferred and generalization is justified. Historical evidence, like a one-shot case study, cannot be repeated. Furthermore, there is no control group so one can never be sure if one event caused another. The best that can be done is to establish a plausible connection between the presumed cause and effect. Similarly, historians must assess the extent to which the situation of one educator or school was reflective of the general pattern at that time.

Writing the Report

As the data collection and analysis procedure progresses, the historical researcher synthesizes the data and writes it up. This is quite analogous to the creation of a review of research as there are no set formulas, nor are there prescriptions for how to do it. It is a case of constantly revising and reflecting, and obtaining criticism and advice from others in order to develop the most defensible resolution of the problem. If a framework can be developed, that may suggest a logical organization, but that, too, is idiosyncratic.

In historical research, the review of literature tends not to be a separate section, nor is it done independently from the research itself. Rather, it is integrated as part of the data collection, analysis and reporting. Furthermore, the literature tends to be much broader in historical study than in other forms of research. It may include all forms of written communication including primary sources like letters, minutes, legal documents as well as the typical secondary sources found in books and journals.

Thus, historical books and dissertations are of infinite variety. The development of a suitable outline goes a long way towards solving the research problem.

Limitations

A major limitation of historical research is that there is limited opportunity to test the conclusions in a new situation. It might be possible to validate a general conclusion, but much of it is specific to the situation researched, and unless new data are discovered it may not be profitably researched again.

A second limitation is that the data are always incomplete. You do not have the luxury of collecting more data since you presumably have all that exists. So, you are drawing conclusions from partial, if not fragmentary, evidence. A third general limitation is the validity of the data themselves. Since they were not created to aid the research, they had another purpose and risk being biased. When there are divergent sources of data converging on a similar conclusion, this limitation is reduced.

All researchers bring their own perspective and personal baggage to the problem. The difference with qualitative researchers in general is that there are few conventions about the form of data collection and reporting requirements. The historian, therefore, like the novelist, can create a storyline and text which is only incidentally shaped by the available data. You or I might do it differently and we might relate a different history.

Conclusion

Historical research has its special rewards. People who own or control historical records are often keen to have researchers use them. It is fun to discover things about the past that give shape to present ideas and patterns of thought and it is rewarding to make a contribution to people and institutions which care about the past which affects them. Historical research is also something which can generally be pursued alone with no rigid timetables or artificial constraints. It is a labour of love limited only by your energy and imagination.

References

Bayley, S. (1987). *Modern languages as emerging curriculum subjects in England, 1864– 1918*. Unpublished Ph.D. Dissertation, McGill University, Montreal.
Beach, M. (1969). History of education. *Review of Educational Research, 39*, pp. 561–576.

Chapter 11

Descriptive Research

Descriptive methods are introduced here because accurate description is fundamental to all research, although description is not really a method by itself. For this reason this chapter does not include all the elements normally associated with other research methods.

Description is important because we often do not know the state of the thing being described. For example, we may be interested in the opinions of the population concerning some issue. In such cases a poll is typically taken by which the percentage for, against and undecided can be determined (note that the poll merely describes the result). Its interpretation is another matter. Sometimes researchers want to know the instance of some behavior such as the amount of time a teacher spends talking, the number of decisions a school principal makes in a day or the number of school windows broken in a year. Such descriptive data may be an end in themselves, or they might be necessary to formulate more detailed research questions or to structure a more precise data collection instrument.

Description may be quantitative or qualitative. Quantitative description is based on counts or measurements which are generally reduced to statistical indicators such as frequencies, means, standard deviations and ranges. Qualitative data can be presented in prose, or through audio tape, photographs or film. New technologies are enabling the use of CD-ROM to record data from interviews and focus groups.

Description

Any approach that attempts to describe data might be referred to as a descriptive method. There is a range of sophistication possible in any description whether quantitative or qualitative. The simplest quantitative description reports the data in raw form. As the description gets more sophisticated, the researcher groups the data and presents it in tables and figures. The use of descriptive statistics is merely a convenient way of description. Data are reported in tables organized to give a suitable overall picture at a glance. These simplify the description and lend meaning to data which in raw form is hard to interpret. The most complete and useful descriptions present data in matrices or frameworks (see Chapter 6) which convey data characteristics for sub-groups or different cells in the framework. Often summary statistics such as means, standard deviations, measures of normalcy and so forth are also provided.

Basic Statistical Concepts

Quantitative description requires familiarity with basic statistical concepts including:

Frequency	Counting the number who respond that way
Mean	Average numerical score of a group
Standard deviation	Measure of spread in scores
Normal distribution	The Bell-shaped curve
Skewed distribution	Scores are bunched at one extreme

Types of Variables

It is also important to understand how different types of variables can be used to clarify understanding and make the description most meaningful:

Nominal variable	The number used is just a label; it has no quantitative meaning
Ordinal variable	The number used represents a quantity or amount
Rank order variable	The number represents where something stands in relation to others on a list
Interval variable	Data are grouped into ranges of values (e.g., age: 35–45)

Qualitative description ranges from brief narrative passages to whole books devoted to the description of a phenomena or setting. Contemporary researchers are also using modern technology to facilitate such description. One of my doctoral students is considering the use of CD-ROM technology keyed to the text in his dissertation and enabling the reader to pull up an actual interview or view a meeting in progress. In their most complete form qualitative descriptions lead to interpretations which are the basis of ethnography as a method. In general, most studies include such description to some degree, though it may be a minor part of the whole.

Specific Types of Descriptive Methods

There are several uses of descriptive methods which are sufficiently common to be methods in their own right.

Content Analysis

Content analysis is applied to the analysis of data in documents and refers to the systematic description of the contents of documents. Four common uses for content analysis are:

- to describe the relative frequency and importance of certain topics;
- to evaluate bias, prejudice or propaganda in print materials;
- to assess the level of difficulty in reading materials; and
- to analyze types of errors in students' work.

At its simplest level, content analysis involves counting concepts, words or occurrences in documents and reporting them in tabular form. One generally structures a measure which lists the topics to be counted. In this way, one can analyze bias in materials. The treatment of women in text books, for example, can be assessed by counting the number of positive references, the number of negative or gender stereotypical responses, and so forth.

This example illustrates one major limitation of content analysis: it counts as data only what is there and rarely what is missing! In such applications, one must guard against the fallacy of unbiased omissions. Often, the problem is that the target group of interest is not mentioned in the text at all, rather than being mentioned in negative terms. Thus, if one were considering the stereotyping of women, it might be advisable to compare the references to men to those implicating women and to assess the extent of equal treatment (See Chapter 16 on benchmarking).

The other approach to content analysis involves the development or use of a formula or scale with which to analyze such things as the reading level of materials. A number of standard scales for this purpose are based on such variables as the numbers of words per sentence, the occurrence of selected words from a standard list and so forth. These scales can be applied to any text and will indicate the reading level, which is most commonly expressed as a grade level equivalent. In the same way researchers can develop scales to measure the occurrence of concepts, types of arithmetic problems or anything else of interest.

Tracer Studies

Tracer studies involve the tracking down of people who were participants in prior educational experiences (World Bank, 1983). In this sense, tracer studies are longitudinal methods which involve tracking people from one point in time to another. Some people erroneously use such methods to attempt to show that the educational experience caused the present state of former participants. The assumption is that by finding out where people are and what they are doing, we can attribute what they have done to their prior training and experience. Chapter 10 describes the fallacy of attributing cause-and-effect in such studies. If inappropriately used, tracer studies are invalid, but they are effective for studying such phenomena as attrition or brain drain. In one study (Universalia, 1982), my colleagues and I were able to trace 93 per cent of Caribbean scholarship trainees previously supported by the Canadian International Development Agency and found that 76 per cent were residing in their country of origin, with 70 per cent in jobs directly related to their training (p. 51). This study provided considerable support for the cost-effectiveness of a program which was suspected of encouraging a substantial brain drain. Tracer studies incorporate the use of telephone directories, mailing lists and personal networks to track people whose whereabouts may have been lost.

Sociometry

Sociometry attempts to assess the social structure within a group of individuals by ascertaining the status of each individual in the group. Various tools are used for this purpose but they generally share a common procedure. They ask people to identify those with whom they have most affinity. This is generally done by asking members to indicate persons with whom they would most like to do an assignment or share other responsibilities. The whole group may thus pick first and second choices and these are analyzed to find the patterns of inter-personal relationships in the group. Persons who are most popular are called stars, and those whom no-one selects are referred to as isolates. Sociograms are special types of figures which report the findings of sociometry.

Problem Definition

The challenge in problem definition with descriptive methods is to be clear in advance what data are needed for the description. Indeed this is what separates the accomplished researcher from the casual observer. A trained researcher will define the data needs and the form of data before it is collected.

In some types of research *indicators* are defined. These are predetermined measures which are considered critical to monitor for the problem under study. For example, the number of students who drop out of school in a year would be an indicator. Another quantitative example would be the number of teachers who agree with a statement. Indicators might also be qualitative, for example, the extent to which a teacher is teaching the prescribed curriculum. Proper indicators provide a good index of what descriptive data are important. The major issue with indicators is to focus on the right issues. This is just a variation of defining the right research problem. Unless you can focus on exactly the right issue, the description may be of limited use. It is also possible to be highly creative in defining indicators, to the point that the definition itself becomes a statement of interest. For example, in an evaluation I conducted of the Office of the United Nations High Commissioner for Refugees (UNHCR), my colleagues and I dealt with issues of organizational performance using such variables as the share of the total world resources available for humanitarian agencies accessed by UNHCR (a ratio variable), and the available money per refugee described over time. Description of the former variable showed that UNHCR had declined its share of the market over a five year period; the latter showed a tremendous escalation in cost coinciding with the conflict in the former Yugoslavia.

Defining dynamic indicators of performance can be a major endeavour in research and organizational development. Some recent research on the performance of research organizations indicates the challenges. In attempting to assess the worth of a researcher, how does one weigh research grants — which are inputs — and publications — which are outputs? Does a book have more worth than a scholarly research article? How do one's peers value the various journals in a field? What weight is placed on the various types of co-authorship? How does one compare the worth of one publication that changed the direction of a whole field of research to numerous articles that made incremental differences? The process of clarifying the values underlying these variables becomes a vital exercise in organizational development.

One good way of focusing descriptive data is to plan the study in sufficient detail that blank charts and tables are prepared in advance. This effectively indicates how the data will be organized and presented and makes it perfectly clear what data need to be collected. The data collection procedure then becomes filling up the empty tables. In qualitative research, techniques commonly used in making films can be applied. In that case, a story board is prepared indicating how the film flows from scene to scene and how the visuals match the narrative. In qualitative description the researcher can similarly define the problem by projecting forward to the particular perspectives and viewpoints that need to be portrayed.

Procedure

Instruments

The most commonly used instruments for descriptive research are reports, texts, questionnaires, scales and observation schedules; however, film and video also have their place. Reports refer to all kinds of existing material from historical data to statistics. Sometimes people complete tests as part of their research permitting the researcher to describe performance of individuals or groups. Questionnaires may be used to collect self-report data on attitudes, preferences or background information. Research scales are instruments developed to measure attitudes, personality, preferences and so forth. Finally, observational schedules are often used by trained observers to observe a situation (Croll, 1986). Some of these can be highly detailed. For example, 25 years ago, one researcher (Flanders, 1970) developed a scale to record what a teacher did every three seconds. As with all good instruments, the researcher should determine the reliability and validity of observation scales. In the case of Flanders' interaction analysis, trained observers yielded highly reliable data on 10 teacher activities, but despite many adherents the results never were shown to be related to the effectiveness of instruction, so the scale had questionable validity.

Data Collection

Valid data collection requires clearly developed procedures and the involvement of researchers or data collection personnel who can follow the procedures consistently and who will not themselves influence the data collected. Most tests, questionnaires and scales contain explicit instructions on how they are to be administered. Observation schedules are often developed to collect systematic observation on educational settings. They are preferred by some to self-reports which tend to reflect socially acceptable responses rather than what might actually occur. For example, observations of classrooms suggests that many teachers talk 80 per cent of the available class time. If those teachers were asked, they would report talking much less, perhaps only 20 per cent (see Edwards and Westgate, 1987). Observation is necessary to collect valid data on this type of phenomenon. The difficulty with observational data is the relevance of what can be observed. Often the underlying motivations may not be revealed through observation alone.

The question for the researcher is to determine the best data collection technique for what is being pursued. For example, if one were studying inter-race relations, you could give students a questionnaire to report their attitudes. Alternatively, you could observe the interactions among students of different races and have observational data on the extent of interracial contacts. In collecting observational data, four approaches can be used; the duration of behavior, frequency counting, interval sampling and continuous sampling. Duration recording examines the time that something occurs. For example, the time a student spends out of his or her seat. Frequency counts refer to the number of times the student would leave his or her seat. Interval sampling refers to what is happening to a particular individual at predetermined intervals. For example, what a teacher is doing every fifth minute. Continuous recording collects a narrative record of data in diary type form. It reconstructs events as completely as possible. In some observational situations recording devices are used and the tapes are analyzed in order to have accurate measures of who was doing what when.

Qualitative Data Analysis

Qualitative data are analyzed in interpretative ways whereby the researcher makes judgments about what the data say. The data reported describes the situation and the researcher seeks to interpret their meaning within a particular context. Sometimes the interpretation is bounded by the data under study, but more typically it is interpreted in the light of theory.

Quantitative Data Analysis: Describing Your Data Using Descriptive Statistics

Descriptive statistics are not rocket science. This is what six year-olds do when they report on how many crayons of each color they have in their box! The essence of description is the frequency distribution: how many subjects got each score. The best way to understand the description is to see it represented in a picture, typically

Exhibit 11.1:   Typical histogram

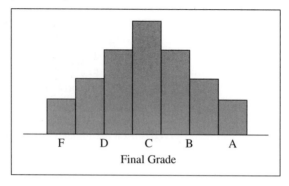

F   D   C   B   A
Final Grade

in a frequency distribution. The easiest picture to understand is a histogram that uses graphic bars of different lengths to represent how many (on the Y or vertical axis) got each value (on the X or horizontal axis). In practice, histograms often group a range of values for this representation (e.g., by grouping the ages of teachers in five-year intervals). The advantage of the histogram is its commonness which means that most people seeing a histogram can readily understand it. Note, however, that it is possible to distort the meaning by choosing the intervals in certain ways. Many narrow bars will give the impression of a jagged and uneven distribution; whereas, grouping them in wider bands will convey an impression of orderliness.

Exhibit 11.1 shows a typical histogram. This is a symmetrical distribution that resembles a 'normal' curve. The normal curve is the theoretical shape that is most common in nature. For example, if we were to show the distribution of a physical variable such as people's heights, the curve would be normal. With such a normal curve, it is possible to generalize in such a way that one can say the proportion of people who are say more than two metres in height. This property of being able to generalize is essential to comparative statistics as described later. An alternative to the histogram is a smooth curve (also called a frequency polygon) that simply uses a line to connect the number of subjects obtaining each score. This is particularly useful for continuous variables where the intervals between the scores are relatively small. For example, if we were describing school marks on a 0–100 per cent continuum, then a smooth curve would be the most complete image. If we expressed the marks as A, B, C, D, E and F then a histogram would do the data justice.

Not all distributions are normal. Exhibit 11.2 shows a distribution in which the majority of the scores are at one end of the scale. It is not symmetrical and consequently does not have the properties of the normal curve. This is a typical distribution for Likert Scale questionnaire items in which there is a 'ceiling' effect (see p. 174). It is caused by having items that most people 'strongly agree' with (and is corrected by having a wording that is not so conducive to semi-unanimous agreement). Here, too, it is possible to use a statistic that describes the asymmetrical distribution. It is called the 'skewness' of the distribution.

Exhibit 11.2:   Histogram showing skewed distribution

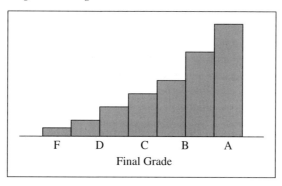

Exhibit 11.3:   Histogram with a bimodal distribution

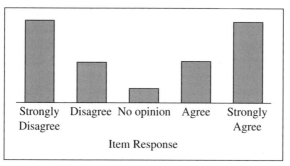

Exhibit 11.3 shows a 'bimodal' distribution in which people score at the extremes. On a Likert Scale item, this implies that people either 'strongly disagree' or 'strongly agree' with few holding neutral views. It is the result one might get on questionnaire items about socially controversial policies such as capital punishment or abortion.

Of course, one can show the same thing as any of these distributions in tabular form. In that case, one could use one column to show how many received each score or band of scores. This is a useful way to depict data, because it permits the use of more than one column in what are called 'cross-tabulations'. For example, two columns might show the distribution for males and females separately. You can also have more than two columns. The columns typically represent nominal variables that define different groups. If more than one column is of this type, the logical question is whether the distributions in one column (say for males) is the same as that in another column (females). This crosses into the second type of research question: comparison among groups. This begins to enter the field of experimental research methods, but we will consider one type of such a comparison here. The case I refer to is when we describe the number or proportion of cases that have some characteristic (such as agreeing with a statement) and we want to find out whether the groups are equivalent. For example, if one were to compare the percentage of males 'in favour' of a social issue to the percentage of females so inclined, then there is a 2×2 table (for or against vs. male or female). Thus, we might find that 40 per cent of males are in favour, but that 60 per cent of females are in favour. The real comparative issue is whether the views of the two groups are sufficiently disparate to be considered different. Theoretical projections can tell us what percentage of times the result we achieved would be expected by chance alone. This is expressed as a probability (convention dictates that we accept that the groups have different distributions if $p < 0.05$; or $p < 0.01$). To do this the computer program computes a statistic called *Chi Square* that permits the program to compare the results we obtain with the theoretical results for an infinite number of cross-tabulations of the same nature. For simple practical purposes, we need to determine whether the *Chi Square* value is what would be expected by chance alone, or not, and with what probability. The *Chi Square* really tells us whether the frequency distributions in the various columns are similar in shape, or are different. When the probability of a chance relationship is sufficiently low, we then need to examine the distributions for each group to see where the differences are. In the simple example, it would be reasonable to conclude that females are more inclined to be in favour than males.

Of course, we need not restrict the analysis to two categories as in the previous example. If we were to compare school classes in terms of grade distributions (the number of As, Bs, Cs, Ds, Es, and Fs) then cross-tabulations and *Chi Square* will apply just as in the simple case. The only difference is the potential difficulty of interpreting the observed differences among the various classes. In practice, we might find that some of the classes were similar, but that the significant difference is a result of one or two classes that are very different from the norm. It would also be possible to have differences that are not so defined and are much more difficult to interpret.

Writing the Report

Writing the results of qualitative description takes a great variety of forms. They range from elaborate verbal descriptions including actual quotations of speech to a wide variety of tabular and statistical summaries of what is being described. With quantitative data, one generally arranges the results in tables. These should be arranged in conventional format with appropriate title, headings, labels and footnotes. In most research reporting, the tables are an integral part of the text. If they are factual and totally descriptive, they often stand on their own merits, such as a table describing the sample. More typically, explanation or interpretation is provided in the text and one refers in prose to the general results in the accompanying table. In a sense you direct the reader to the significant features shown in the descriptive table. For example, you might say: 'As shown in Table 1, 90 per cent of the male respondents agreed or strongly agreed with the statement.' This type of prose complements the tabular display and provides continuity in the text. This convention applies to all data reporting and analysis, whether descriptive or more complex.

Modern computer software has made the production of figures and graphics commonplace. Often a pie chart or bar charts comparing groups are far more helpful to the reader than tables and prose. The caution here is that the proportions used in the graphics can easily distort the perceived meaning. If one looks at the daily newspaper graphs of the Dow-Jones it appears that stock market swings are much more dramatic than they really are, simply because only the top fraction of the curve is presented, and the scale is distorted relative to the total value of the market. A graph of percentage change would tell a different story. As with tables, any graphics need to be accurately and completely labelled to enable the reader to know exactly what you want to describe.

Limitations

Descriptive data are subject to two general types of limitations, those related to reliability and validity. To maximize reliability, one needs to use procedures and measures which will lead to consistent results no matter who is involved in collecting the data. The issue in quantitative description is to define indicators precisely and to structure data collection instruments which lead to reliable results. In qualitative methods, the problem is largely in the training and experience of the researcher who records and reports the data.

A more common problem is that of validity, having the data relate to what you think you are describing. One problem is choosing inappropriate indicators and focusing on the description of things which are not relevant to your intention. You may focus, for example, on behaviors as an indicator of attitudes but might not uncover important attitudes that do not manifest themselves in overt behavior. There are a wide variety of limitations caused by intentional or unintended biases in the researcher. In using quantitative data, the researcher must be careful to present results in a fair and unbiased way. It is easy to group and present statistics in ways which emphasize a particular point of view. Similarly, descriptive data can easily be presented to mislead. The researcher therefore must constantly struggle to eliminate these tendencies. A fourth problem is the sampling problem and the generalizability of results, or external validity. The problem is that the descriptive data reported refer to a specific sample or set of observations which may not relate to the general pattern. This limitation is often a limitation of reporting and is caused by the tendency of some researchers to talk about their observations in ways which suggest that they apply in general rather than to a specific sample or set of circumstances. It is all right to have limitations, but only if they are acknowledged openly and taken seriously in data interpretation.

References

Croll, Paul (1986). *Systematic classroom observation*. London: Falmer Press.

Edwards, A.D., & Westgate, D.P.G. (1987). *Investigating classroom talk*. London: Falmer Press.

Flanders, N. (1970). *Analyzing teacher behaviors, reading*. MA: Addison-Wesley.

Universalia Management Group Ltd. (1982). *Canada training awards: Mid-project evaluation*. Montreal: Author.

World Bank. (1983). *Tracer study guidelines*. Washington, DC: Author.

Chapter 12

Correlational Research

Researchers often collect data on several variables and want to know about the relationships among them. In one sense this is a next level of description, an explanatory level that describes how one variable relates to another. Thus, description in educational research need not be limited to description using variables taken one at a time. Description gains added depth when it includes relationships among variables. In describing a group of teachers, for example, we could describe their leadership ability by listing scores they obtain on a leadership scale. We might also describe how well their pupils do on their final exams. We now have two different variables with scores on both pertaining to each teacher. The obvious question is whether these two variables are related. That is, do the pupils of teachers with high leadership scores perform any differently on final exams than those with low leadership scores? Research problems of this type are the subject of correlational research.

Description

Correlational research involves the calculation of a *correlation coefficient* which is a measure of the extent to which variables vary in the same way. Correlation coefficients range from -1.0 to $+1.0$ with 0 meaning no relationship between the variables, and 1.0 meaning a perfect relationship, one to the other. A positive correlation is one in which a higher score on one variable is related to a higher score on the other. This is expressed by a positive value for the correlation coefficient. When there is a negative sign, as one variable increases, scores on the other decrease.

There are a number of specific types of correlation coefficient such as the 'rank-order' and 'Pearson Product-Moment' correlation. Each type is used for a specific purpose and type of data and it is beyond the present treatment to explain these differences. However, all types tend to work the same way conceptually, so if you understand the concept the rest is a matter of technical detail.

Correlation research is one way of describing in quantitative terms the degree to which variables are related. Typically, correlational studies investigate a number of variables believed to be related to an important variable such as academic achievement. The former are referred to as *independent variables* or *predictor variables* while the latter is known as the *dependent* or *criterion* variable. If two or more different predictors are both correlated with the same dependent variable, then in combination they can be made to correlate higher than either one by itself. This principle

Exhibit 12.1: Contributions of variance of two variables with a third

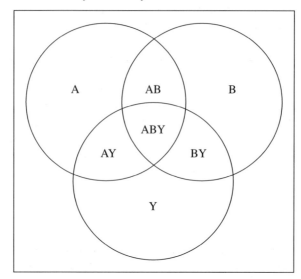

leads to a mathematical formulation known as *multiple correlation*. Multiple correlation combines two or more independent variables to enhance the relationship to a dependent variable.

Without going into elaborate statistics, it is important to understand that the square of the correlation is more important than its absolute value. The square of the correlation indicates the proportion of variance held in common between the two variables. The value of r does not directly correspond to the strength of the relationship; it is the square of r, r^2, that indicates the amount of variance that the two variables share. If r = 0.5, then r^2 = 0.25, so the two variables share 25 per cent common variance. In other words, you can explain 25 per cent of the variation in value of one variable by knowing the other. For example, if one knows a man's height, one can predict his weight. Prediction is not guaranteed, but if you wished to bet, you would be better off predicting that the taller man would be heavier.

If variable A shares 25 per cent common variance with variable Y and variable B shares 25 per cent common variance with variable Y, then how much variance do A and B share collectively with variable Y? The answer is that it depends on how much variance A and B share with one another. If they are totally independent, then together they would share 50 per cent collectively. More typically, they will inter-correlate at 0.50 and share 25 per cent variance in common. The collective contribution of A and B to variance in Y will be as shown in Exhibit 12.1. The common variance is AY plus ABY plus BY. A *multiple correlation*, R, combines variables to predict the value of another. A multiple correlation might have 8 or 10 predictors and one criterion variable. In a Step-Wise R, the computer program begins with the variable that predicts the greatest amount of variance, then adds the one that contributes the most additional variance, and so on until all the predictable variance is accounted for. At each stage, there is a test of statistical significance that determines whether the addition is what one would predict by chance alone. In this way, a list of 10 predictors might be reduced to two or three that give all the significant information.

The correlation coefficient thus described refers to a linear relationship between variables. Beginning some 30 years ago, researchers have found curvilinear relationships (Anderson, 1968). For example, motivation level is related to performance in a curvilinear manner. If you have too little motivation or too much, you will receive lower performance scores than those with some optimum mid-level of motivation. If one wants to be sure what is going on, it is a good idea to plot the scores on a graph and undertake a visual inspection of how the pairs of variables interrelate. The sure way to understand any data is to graph them — good pictures do not lie.

Problem Definition

There are two major approaches to addressing research questions using correlational methods: *looking*, and *looking for*. In general, the looking approach is utilitarian; whereas the looking for approach is more theoretical. Often one generates as many as 50 or more variables with corresponding scores on each variable for every person or element for which data have been collected. For example, a battery of tests might lead to a whole series of scores for the people taking it. In the looking approach the researcher generates correlation coefficients among all variables and then examines them to see which ones are related. One then generally seeks explanations for why these relationships exist. This is an easy way to find significant relationships as the odds are stacked in favour of finding something and what is found can generally be explained. It is a sort of astrological approach to research in which natural and unnatural happenings add credence to a theory of generalities. Thus, this is a useful approach only for preliminary exploration which should be followed by more rigorous research approaches.

One useful application of the looking approach is *factor analysis*. This procedure uses the intercorrelations among a whole collection of variables to determine underlying factors to which the involved variables relate. For example, several questionnaire items might all relate to a 'satisfaction' factor assumed to be the underlying variable to which they all relate. In practice, one often has 10–20 variables or more which are analyzed to determine 5 or 6 underlying factors. This is a useful thing to do with attitude scales and certain types of questionnaires to develop scales that describe a more generalized conception of what is going on among the variables. It helps avoid the problem of many similar relationships appearing as if there is a lot happening when in reality, it is a small number of underlying factors which can more parsimoniously explain it all.

Another applied use of correlational research is for prediction. If two variables are correlated, then the scores on one can be used to predict the scores on the other. If one variable relates to a different time, then prediction may be useful. As one would expect, if many variables are correlated with another, then in combination better predictions can be obtained. As noted earlier, multiple correlation is the technique used for combining independent variables and relating them to a dependent variable. *Multiple regression* is the term used for predicting scores from such multiple correlations. Such multiple regressions can often lead to relatively accurate predictions and are important tools for the researcher interested in understanding how the predictors interrelate.

The researcher can analyze the multiple regression equation to see how the various predictors combine and interact to predict scores on the criterion variable. For example, a list of characteristics of teaching procedures and methods could be used to predict student success on final examinations and the equation would lead to understanding how these teaching methods combine to relate to exam results. In this case the problem definition would be in terms of understanding how the various predictors lead to performance results.

A similar principle enables us to predict whether a person will exceed or fail to reach a given score. Thus, we can separate people into distinct groups in this way such as those who pass and those who fail. The term for predicting group membership is *discriminant analysis*. Like other procedures based on multiple correlation, it develops an equation, but the equation predicts a position of each subject in space in a way that predicts group membership. For example, one could use a battery of variables to predict people who later commit suicide or become convicted criminals, or who are homosexual, etc. In practice, the procedure is rather powerful and can be very useful in determining variables that relate to group membership. The intention in doing so is to generalize beyond the data at hand in an attempt to predict the future based on knowledge of the past.

The looking for approach is more aligned with theoretical application as it involves making a prediction of significant correlations based on theory or prior research. The data are then examined to test the theory or principle in a new or applied situation. This is akin to the hypothesis-testing approach used by some researchers: If the theory is correct, then variable A should be related to variable B. Of course, researchers use inductive techniques as well in an attempt to understand theory.

Procedure

Sources of Data and Instruments

As the problem is defined so too are the sources of data and instruments. Data might already exist in a suitable form and may be able to be used for the purpose at hand. Alternatively, original data can be collected using any suitable test or data collection instrument. One caution pertaining to data is the need for a normal distribution in order to make appropriate use of the required statistics.

Appendix 12.1 provides an example of existing data which can be used to examine relationships among variables using correlation techniques. The table lists national statistics for the 50 countries with the highest under 5-year-old infant mortality rates together with data on the number of radio sets, school completion rates and male adult literacy. In this case the unit of analysis is the country and the statistics used are country averages on each of these variables. Note that in most developing countries, national statistics are not reliable or valid so one might question the overall utility of these indicators. This is one problem with correlational methods — they can capitalize on the errors and limitations in the data to produce statistically significant data which might be meaningless.

Researchers most often collect their own data using all sorts of instruments, such as attitude scales, results from surveys, statistics on file or measures of performance. Any instrument can be used as long as the data collected are approximately normally distributed. Of course, you also need paired data, which is to say, corresponding scores on different measure for each individual. In other words, if Mary Jane received 106 on an IQ test and 32 on a geometry test the scores 106 and 32 are paired as they both apply to the same individual, Mary Jane.

Data Collection

There is not much that is unique to data collection for correlational methods. The normal cautions and conventions apply. One useful rule of thumb, however, is that data collected from the same sources are more likely to correlate (and often spuriously) than are data sets from different sources. Thus, if you ask an individual different things on the same questionnaire you are likely to have them correlated. Validity of your findings are enhanced if you use different data sources. For example, if you were correlating student personality and performance it would be better to measure personality on one scale and performance using another method such as how well the student performs in class.

Data Analysis

The data are analyzed using appropriate correlational techniques and the results are put into a correlation matrix. Exhibit 12.2 provides an example for the 50 countries listed in Appendix 12.1. Correlation matrices have the same variables on the

Exhibit 12.2: Correlation matrix for country indicators

Indicator	1	2	3	4
1 Under-5 mortality	1.0			
2 Number of radios per 1000	−0.236	1.0		
3 Per cent Grade 1 completing pre-school	−0.397	0.128	1.0	
4 Male adult literacy	−0.542	0.229	0.265	1.0

Exhibit 12.3:   Scattergram of literacy correlates

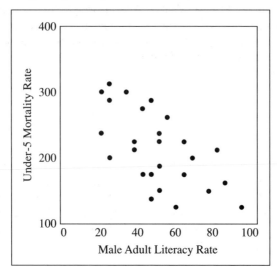

vertical and horizontal axes and each cell in the table indicates the correlation between the pair of variables corresponding to the cell. The diagonal always contains 1.0s since the diagonal cells represent the correlation of each variable with itself. In the example, the correlation between variable 1 (under-5 mortality) and variable 3 (per cent primary school completion) is −0.397. This signifies that the higher the under-5 mortality, the lower the primary school completion rate. Exhibit 12.3 shows the plot of paired data points for the relationship between under-5 mortality and adult literacy. You can see a general but slight negative relationship. There is also a slight curvilinear tendency. It is not very strong when seen visually. Remember that the square of the correlation is the most important numerical data and the square of 0.542 is only 0.294 meaning that these two variables share only 29.4 per cent common variance. Thus, this result by itself is not very useful for prediction.

The relationship does not imply that the scores on one variable are causing the scores on the other. They are related, but not necessarily in a causal way. What, then, does this result mean? In words, the higher a country's infant mortality, the lower its primary school completion rate. In reality, both variables are probably related to an important third variable such as poverty. It may be responsible for a causal relationship. This is called the *third-variable problem* and is always a possibility with correlational research. It is always possible that some third underlying variable is responsible for the relationship between the first two.

Report Preparation

Reports based on correlational research generally follow a traditional research report format. The focus tends to be the correlation matrix and its interpretation. These days most published studies will go beyond a simple correlation matrix in interpreting the data. Computers make further analysis a straight-forward matter and such techniques as multiple correlation offer possibilities for more complete understanding of the relationships among many variables, so they are now routine. For example, a multiple correlation approach to the data in Exhibit 12.3 leads to the following regression equation:

$$\text{Adult literacy} = -0.196 \text{ (under-5 mortality)} + 0.036 \text{ (number of radios)}$$
$$+ 0.049 \text{ (primary school completion)} + 85.94$$

Without going into detail, the equation shows that under-5 mortality (with its high coefficient of −0.196) is the only significant predictor of adult literacy, when all predictors are considered together, even though the other variables also correlate with it. The resulting multiple correlation is 0.572, not much higher than the 0.542 of under-5 mortality alone. Thus, in this case, the battery of three predictors is little better than the best predictor by itself.

Limitations

The correlational approach has a number of important limitations.

1   Loose associations — Often variables are loosely associated and the correlational approach does little more than give evidence for these loose associations. Because the resulting correlations are low, they may not be helpful except in suggesting additional more rigorous forms of research.
2   Simplicity of linear model — Traditional correlation methods assume linear relationships between variables. The world does not always operate in such a simple fashion and application of correlational methods alone may miss important underlying relationships.
3   Unit of analysis problems — Researchers must be conscious of the true unit of analysis which is often the classroom or school rather than the number of students. Thus, one may in actuality have far fewer cases than presumed.
4   Significance problems — With a large number of cases, you do not need high values of the correlation coefficient to produce statistical significance. However, such correlations may have little or no practical significance even though they represent more than a chance relationship.
5   Causality problems — Correlation does not establish cause-and-effect relationships and it is less rigorous than the experimental approach because variables are not controlled by the experimenter. There is also the ever-present possibility of third variables acting as underlying factors responsible for the relationships.

Conclusion

Correlational approaches are useful for initial exploration of relationships, particularly when there are a large number of variables. They also offer powerful tools for developing simplified data analysis instruments from large masses of data, and they provide efficient ways to predict based on a battery of variables. Another strength of these methods is that they use data obtained in naturalistic settings and they facilitate exploration of a large number of relationships simultaneously. Thus, correlational methods respond to the ambiguity and complexity of the real world. They uncover degrees of relationship rather than the all-or-nothing question posed by experimental designs which often focus on whether or not a relationship exists rather than its degree. Used appropriately, correlational methods also are useful for testing theory dealing with relationships. The weaknesses of these methods are that powerful computers able to use procedures that capitalize on minuscule variations — even error — may show strong relationships in small samples which do not generalize well.

Reference

Anderson, G. (1968). *Effects of classroom social climate on individual learning*. Unpublished Ed.D. doctoral dissertation, Harvard University, Cambridge, MA.

Chapter 13

Qualitative Research

Nancy Arsenault and Gary Anderson

Qualitative research is a form of inquiry that explores phenomena in their natural settings and uses multi-methods to interpret, understand, explain and bring meaning to them. Like the mountain lake, qualitative research has many sources that contribute to its shape and substance. Just as the rain, snow and small mountain streams blend together uniting into one body of water, the multiple perspectives, differing theoretical positions, diverse methods of collecting, analyzing and interpreting data blend together to reveal a deep and rich form of research. Qualitative research is an inductive form of inquiry whose results are a blend of research skill, luck and a particular perspective. Like the fisherman on uncharted waters, you may have an idea of what lies beneath the surface, but you cannot always be sure. As the fisherman knows, where you happen to anchor your boat, the particular lure you choose and the skill you demonstrate in fishing has a great deal to do with what you catch. Similarly, the qualitative researcher soon learns that being in the right place at the right time is all important. Moreover, the researcher's perspective also influences what might be found. A researcher with an avowed feminist perspective will not view a situation through the same lens as a phenomenologist, ethnographer or constructivist, yet their methodological approaches and techniques may be similar. They might all be extraordinarily skilled, yet they could end up with differing interpretations.

As a field of inquiry in the human sciences, qualitative research has a long and distinguished history (Denzin & Lincoln, 1994). However, through much of this century qualitative research paradigms and methodologies have taken a back seat to the positivist view of the world, a view that believes in an objective reality that can be studied, captured and understood (see Chapter 1). A fundamental assumption of the qualitative research paradigm is that a profound understanding of the world can be gained through conversation and observation in natural settings rather than through experimental manipulation under artificial conditions. While the positivists, or scientific research community, seeks to prove or disprove hypotheses in search for the 'truth', the qualitative research community seeks an understanding of phenomena from multiple perspectives, within a real world context. Leading qualitative research experts Yvonna Lincoln and Norman Denzin, offer this generic definition:

> Qualitative research is multi-method in focus, involving an interpretive, naturalistic approach to its subject matter. This means that qualitative researchers study

things in their natural settings, attempting to make sense of, or interpret, phenomena in terms of the meanings people bring to them. Qualitative research involves the studied use and collection of a variety of empirical materials — case study, personal experience, introspective, life story, interview, observational, historical, interactional, and visual texts — that describe routine and problematic moments and meanings in individuals' lives. (Denzin & Lincoln, 1994, p. 2)

For much of this century, the field of psychology had a dominant influence on educational research. But it was the failure of the psychological approach to facilitate understanding of how classroom learning occurred that gave rise to an alternative, qualitative methodology for educational research known as ethnography. Psychological research did an imperfect job predicting why some people learned and others did not, so researchers began to explore the setting and culture in which learning took place. This line of research was also much better adapted to some of the concerns of the 1960s. For example, when a busload of black children went, for the first time, to a previously all-white school, Robert Rist (1978), an ethnographer, was there to observe how they would relate to this new situation. This was an important political event and the researcher's concerns were for the *entire context* of the situation, a vital aspect of all forms of qualitative research. This one example alone helps demonstrate the limitations of the behavioral science and psychology approaches that do not lend themselves to investigating certain phenomenon.

One of the greatest difficulties for the novice researcher interested in qualitative research is differentiating the various research paradigms. To date, we have compared, in broad terms, the qualitative and quantitative paradigms, but the distinctions do not end there. Think of the qualitative research paradigm as an umbrella with each spoke representing another view of the world, another paradigm. For example, cultural studies are concerned with the social inequalities that exist in societies and the need to emancipate members of a community from oppression. Feminism is also concerned with emancipation; however, the focus here is on gender issues and the long-standing marginalization or abuse of women. Constructivism, yet another perspective, aims at understanding and reconstructing knowledge with the goal of moving toward consensus and more informed ways of knowing. Each qualitative research tradition adopts its own assumptions, criteria and methods of inquiry. Each paradigm represents a different view of the world, not better, not worse, just different. It is beyond the scope of this book to elaborate in any detail on these multiple perspectives, therefore references for more detailed readings are provided at the end of this chapter (see Guba & Lincoln, 1994).

Qualitative Research Methods

Just as the quantitative scientist has at his or her disposal a variety of methods of inquiry, so too does the qualitative researcher. Exhibit 13.1 lists five types of qualitative research methods, often used in educational research and identifies the primary research interest of that approach.

Exhibit 13.1: Qualitative research methods

Method	Research Interest
Applied	Research that aims to assess, describe, document or inform problems from the stakeholder's perspective
Case study	Examines a specific phenomenon
Ethnography	Concerned with the culture of people and organizations
Grounded theory	An inductive approach to deriving theory
Phenomenology	Aimed at understanding the meaning of experiences in our everyday lives

Applied

Applied research is concerned with addressing problems of the world as they are perceived by participants, organizations or groups of people. Applied research is action-oriented and aims to assess, describe, document or inform people concerned about the phenomena under investigation. Findings are intended to have an immediate and practical value, as contrasted with basic research aimed at adding to existing knowledge bases. In the field of education, policy, evaluation and contract are all examples of applied research.

Case Study

A case study is an investigation defined by an interest in a specific phenomenon within its real-life context. It is a qualitative form of inquiry that relies on multiple sources of information. Its distinctive feature is the case that may be an event or process considered worthy of study. Chapter 15 is devoted to detailing this type of research.

Ethnography

The term ethnography generally refers to research which has one or more of the following features: a strong emphasis on exploring phenomena within their natural setting; a tendency to work with data which is not pre-coded in terms of its analytic categories; investigation of a small number of cases; and a form of analysis which emphasizes description and explanation rather than quantification and statistical analysis (Atkinson & Hammersley, 1994). While ethnography is relatively new in the field of education, it has a long and respected history in the fields of anthropology and sociology (see Bogdan & Biklen, 1992). The first department of sociology was founded at the University of Chicago in 1892. One of the leading early figures in the department was Robert Park who went there in 1916, after having worked as a newspaper reporter. He applied the techniques of journalism to the social issues of the day and encouraged students to go forth into society and observe how people lived, a revolutionary idea in education at the time. Out of that tradition emerged such classic studies as the *Sociology of Teaching* (Waller, 1932), *Street-Corner Society*, a study of life among poor Italian men in Boston (Whyte, 1955) and Becker's study of schoolteachers (Becker, 1951). Even the anthropologist Margaret Mead, after returning from Samoa, turned her attention to schools as organizations and the role of teachers in them (Mead, 1942). All these researchers used their previous background and training in qualitative methods and fieldwork to investigate educational phenomenon. Hammersley & Atkinson (1995) provide a detailed discussion of this methodology.

Grounded Theory

"Grounded theory is a general methodology for developing theory that is grounded in data systematically gathered and analyzed" (Strauss & Corbin, 1994, p. 273). It is an inductive approach to theory development that can be thought of as two funnels joined where they narrow, at the center. At the top, new data are collected in multiple stages, emergent themes are identified, interpreted, compared and refined. This process creates a funnel of new information from which constructs and theories are developed (the middle). These theories are then cast out into various sampling groups to determine the strength of the similarities and differences of the theoretical constructs with different populations. The stronger the support for the theoretical propositions, the wider the base at the bottom. What differentiates this research method from its qualitative counterparts is the emphasis on theory development. For a detailed discussion of this method see Glasner & Strauss (1967) or Strauss & Corbin (1990).

Phenomenology

German philosopher Edmund Husserl (1859–1935) spent his life developing and refining the phenomenological approach to studying human science. "His guiding belief was that to understand human phenomena we need to put aside our established views and assumptions and learn to "see" things as they present themselves in our experiences and to "describe" them in their own terms" (Priebe, 1993, p. 50). Phenomenology asks the question, 'What is this experience like?' or 'What is the meaning of something?' It is a type of research that attempts to illuminate and explain phenomena rather than classify, taxonomize or abstract it (Van Manen, 1990). It is also inter-subjective, which means the researcher must develop a dialogic relationship with the phenomenon to validate what is being described. There is no hidden political agenda nor any attempt to persuade the reader towards one belief or another. It is purely an attempt to represent the experiences of the observed accurately. Phenomenological research also relies on retrospective reflection — thinking about the experience and what it means, after the fact. It is less concerned with facts (e.g., How did you learn to do research?) but rather with understanding the nature of human activity (e.g., What was the nature of your learning experience?). Informative readings for people interested in this research methodology include those of Moustakas (1994) and Eisner (1991).

Open and Focused Problem Definition

There are two basic approaches to defining qualitative research problems, open and focused. An inquiry with an open problem is used when little is known about the subject under consideration. It entails collecting a broad spectrum of data and is typically used to discover the nature of the phenomenon, often leading to hypotheses as well as conclusions. For example, Wolcott (1973) did a detailed case study on one school principal, for at that time no one really knew what principals did. Focused inquiries, in contrast, are used to study areas in which a great deal is already known and problems, questions or hypotheses already exist. Focused studies consequently rely on built-in boundaries. For example, a researcher might study the classroom of a teacher with a long reputation for having her graduates do well in subsequent schooling. We know a great deal about effective teaching and teachers, so the study in question would use this as background and interpret the classroom of the high performing teacher in light of this knowledge.

The Research Population/Sample Size

"There are no rules for sample size in qualitative inquiry. Sample size depends on what you want to know, the purpose of the inquiry, what's at stake, what will be useful, what will have credibility, and what can be done with available time and resources" (Patton, 1990, p. 184). Exhibit 13.2 identifies, describes and provides an example of a range of purposeful sampling techniques that can be used in educational settings.

The Qualitative Researcher

Qualitative and quantitative researchers alike define problems, select research designs, develop methodologies, collect, analyze and interpret data, and report findings. There is, however, one significant difference between the two. In qualitative research, the researcher is the principal data collection instrument; whereas in quantitative research, scientifically designed data collection tools are developed (e.g. attitude survey, IQ test). As we have stated earlier, this is a vital element of this research paradigm, one which is embraced and accepted. Regardless of the way you choose to collect data (e.g. interviews, observation) it is imperative that the researcher try to understand phenomena and interpret the social reality from two perspectives,

Exhibit 13.2: Purposeful samples

Type	Description	Example
Convenience	Quick, easy, available	Volunteers at your school
Typical	People who fit the expected norm	An average kindergarten classroom of students
Criterion	Cases which meet a set of predetermined conditions	All 12–16-year-old, female gymnasts who have competed in at least one regional competition, in the past 2 years
Deviant cases	Cases which knowingly go against the norm	Highschool dropouts
Homogenous	As many similar characteristics as possible within a group of people	All gifted children in a special music program
Snowball	A technique used to locate key informants on a referral basis	One university president recommends another, who in turn recommends the president of their professional association, who then suggests a specific program director, and so on
Confirming or disconfirming cases	Specific people or scenarios the researcher identifies to validate, strengthen or cast out emerging themes	Requesting to meet with a group of students who display a certain attitude or behavior towards their peers
Opportunistic	On-the-spot opportunities that become available while in the field	While researching the educational policies of a province, you cross paths with the Minister of Education who is giving a keynote speech at a conference you are attending. You ask for a 15-minute interview and are granted permission
Maximum variation	Purposefully selecting as diverse a population as possible	A group of 30 executive MBA students all with different professional qualifications and backgrounds
Critical case	A case which can yield the greatest results when resources are limited	Evaluating a private school with a consistent track record of student satisfaction and effective resource management
Politically correct	One which satisfies the political climate of the day	A school that has embraced a new policy on integration

emic and etic. Understanding how the world looks from an *etic perspective* requires that the researcher constantly look at phenomena and ask, 'What does this event or interaction mean to the individual?' The goal is to try and understand how participants view their world, what it looks like through their eyes. Concurrently, the qualitative researcher also must be cognizant of his or her own *emic perspective*, acknowledging conceptual and theoretical understanding of the participants' social reality. While these perspectives can sound confusing to the novice, a mnemonic we use to remember these two perspectives is: e**mic–m**ine, e**tic–t**heirs. First, try and understand phenomena through the participants' eyes, then place that understanding within your theoretical and conceptual framework of the phenomena and reconsider the participants' perspective with the goal of trying to define, unravel, reveal or explain their world.

Field Work

Field work, entering the field, field notes, field, field, field! Where is the field? What do you do in the field? The term *field* is used generically in qualitative research and quite simply refers to where the phenomenon exists. Think of the field as a construction site. As an outsider, to enter the site you need permission (entering the field). Once at the site there are a variety of construction activities taking place (data collection activities in the field) and there are blueprints, workplans and activity logs that guide and record activities (detailed field notes kept by the researcher). Field work is an essential component of qualitative research and depending on the research design you select, you may spend a great deal of time doing field work. For example, ethnographers can spend years in the field attempting to understand the culture of a people; whereas a graduate student may take a phenomenological approach and spend a mere few weeks interviewing a group of university professors to understand why academic freedom is deemed an important factor in university life.

Access and Entry Issues

One of the major preoccupations of qualitative researchers is how to enter the field setting. Depending on the nature of your research, you may enter a setting covertly or overtly, the latter being recommended for the novice. Whichever approach you select, you will first need permission and this exists in two forms, formal and informal. Formal permission is granted from a person with authority in the organization, for example, the principal of a school or the superintendent of a school district. Informal access is granted from people referred to as gatekeepers, people who do not hold formal authority to approve or deny you access to a research setting, but people who nevertheless have informal influence, authority or respect. Examples of gatekeepers include the principal's secretary, an influential member of a parents' committee, a student council leader, the informal leaders on a teaching staff, and the list goes on. Knowing who the gatekeepers are in an organization, and bringing them on-stream, can be vital to your survival.

Beyond learning the rules and regulations of your particular research site, gaining formal approval, and identifying the gatekeepers, you will also want to address the following access and entry issues prior to entering a site:

- know the hierarchical structures of the organization or community;
- learn as much as you can about the setting, how, why, where and what people do;
- gain an understanding of the formal and informal political dynamics;
- learn the names of key people;
- identify the most appropriate way to communicate with people;
- know how to fit in with both your appearance and behavior.

After you have entered your research setting it is imperative that you gain and keep the respect and trust of the people you will work with, the people who will grant you permission to observe, question and/or participate in select activities. This must be done without appreciably altering the situation. In schools you must also be introduced to other participants such as children and their parents. It is generally sufficient to explain that you are a researcher studying how the school functions or how children learn or how decisions are made. Be prepared to answer questions; however, you must avoid becoming too specific for an awareness of the exact focus of your study could change people's behavior in the setting. It is obvious that if you blow your entry you may jeopardize the entire purpose of your research.

Building rapport

Building rapport with people in the research setting is extremely important. Because qualitative research seeks to understand the world through the eyes of the participant, the people with whom you interact must feel comfortable enough to speak with you. Sharing the details of one's life or talking to a stranger does not come easily to all people and, therefore, it is well worth the scheduling effort to factor in time to get to know the participants.

In a recent study we were involved with, focus groups were one of three techniques used to collect primary data and they served their purpose well (see Chapter 20 for a more detailed discussion on this technique). An unanticipated spin-off benefit was that the focus group also served as an ice-breaker to the community, gave participants an understanding of why a researcher would remain in their midst for their entire program of study, and opened the door to building a rapport with these individuals. As time progressed and the participants became more comfortable with the researcher, they began to open up, share their feelings, clarify statements they had made in the focus group, and offer new information they had been initially reluctant to share. This information, which came as a result of building rapport, proved to be some of the most valuable data collected.

Exhibit 13.3: Potential human issues in qualitative research

1 Building a rapport with individuals for the purpose of collecting data, only to leave the research setting and have the participants feeling void after your departure.

2 Occasionally, participants will share with you information of a personal or confidential nature which may influence the way you think or feel about the situation. It may also pose difficulties with issues of confidentiality and anonymity.

3 Asking people to share personal stories may result in an unexpected and overwhelming emotional response from the participant. Good judgment must be used to decide if it is appropriate to continue with the interview, or in extreme cases, of using this subject in your study.

4 You may inadvertently become involved in the politics of the setting. Certain people may try to use you as a pawn in their personal or organizational struggles. Information is power and what you do with the information you gather, who and how you share it, can have powerful, positive and negative consequences.

5 Aspects of the cultural setting may surprise you and require you to make moral judgments about the direction the research will take and/or the way you behave as a researcher.

6 The degree to which you reveal personal aspects of your life, to build rapport, must be weighed carefully against what may be gained or lost by this disclosure.

7 Mending bridges may be required if you err during the research process. As with friends and family members, apologies and corrective actions can go a long way to rebuilding and strengthening relationships that have soured due to an inadvertent error.

8 Be careful of making promises to participants: for example, offering to get back to a person on an issue, sending information or offering help with an activity. Your purpose is to do research and this must remain at the forefront. If you promise something to someone, do it. Your personal reputation and the reputation of those who granted you permission to enter the setting are at risk if you fail to come through.

Human Issues

People engaged in human science research actively and purposefully interact with people, and consequently must be aware that it is natural to encounter a variety of unique human issues. Exhibit 13.3 highlights a sample of the range of delicate situations you may encounter.

Informants or 'Others'

Informants are people within the research setting who can shed light on the phenomena under investigation. Many informants are approached informally and information is gathered by asking them a specific question or two, which helps interpret what you have observed and validates or clarifies emerging themes and ideas. It gives the researcher an insider's view of the situation and clarifies value patterns, concepts and beliefs which cannot be directly observed. Informants also fill in a lot of gaps, since the researcher cannot be in all places at all times. Data from these people is collected from interviews and focus groups.

Observation

Observational data bring to the analysis and interpretation of a setting a type of information which cannot be garnered any other way. Typically, there are three ways a researcher observes within a research setting. The first is as a *complete observer*, whereby you enter the setting and remain physically detached from the activities and social interactions. The inverse to being a complete observer is the *complete participant*. This strategy may be useful in a covert investigation where it has been agreed that the identity of the researcher and the purpose for being there would best serve the purpose by being concealed. More commonly, however, qualitative researchers find middle ground and enter a setting to collect data as a *participant observer*. In this role the researcher engages in the regular activities of the community to a degree, then periodically withdraws from the setting to check perceptions, record field notes and analyze data. After a period of reflection and perhaps recasting certain issues, the researcher re-enters the setting to validate findings and gather new evidence.

The challenge with collecting observational data is ensuring that your presence does not alter the behavior of the people in the setting. This is known as the *Hawthorne Effect*, and every effort must be made to avoid this from occurring. When collecting observational data it is also important that you remember that some participants within the research setting may forget why you are there and share personal details of their private or professional lives without particular regard to the consequences. Receiving this type of unexpected information can pose ethical, moral and political issues, so be forewarned.

Field Notes

Field notes are an indispensable data source. Patton (1990) writes that field notes should contain a written comment of everything the researcher finds worthwhile; do not leave it to recall. Field notes are the researcher's detailed and descriptive record of the research experience, including observations, a reconstruction of dialogue, personal reflections, a physical description of the setting, and decisions made that alter or direct the research process. Often notes are written on a small note pad the researcher carries; other times a laptop computer may be appropriate, and on other occasions, field notes must be written after an event because it is inappropriate to take notes in certain settings. If notes are taken during a session, it is important to review them as soon after the event as possible to fill in any blanks, fix up any 'scribbles', and add any detail you may not have had time to note. Be sure to include your immediate thoughts. Often it takes three times longer to write good field notes than to do an actual observation.

Communications

Diaries, personal and professional correspondence, lyrics, things-to-do lists, and e-mail messages are examples of the way we communicate beyond everyday speech and body language. Depending on the nature of your research project, your data base may be enriched by gathering information about how people in your study communicate. For example, if you were interested in understanding why some parent committees are effective and others are not, you may examine how different committee chairs organize their meeting agendas, learn how messages are transmitted between members, or follow-up on 'bring forward' lists to see if items are actually dealt with rather than perpetually deferred. Or, if you were interested in understanding how the personality of several successful musicians manifests itself in their music, you may examine the lyrics of their compositions, or listen to the music and try to feel how their passion for their art is symbolized in the notes placed on a music staff. Because communication is so central in our lives as individuals and social beings, gathering data on the way people communicate can be extremely insightful in certain instances.

Physical Items

Physical artifacts tell us a great deal about people, organizations and cultures. A photo album, for example, gives us insight about what people like to do, with whom they like to do it, and where they go to do it! A home with a refrigerator covered with family photos tells you something very different than a manicured home filled with contemporary art sculptures or a grass hut with no furniture. Noting the physical setting of an environment has the potential to enhance your understanding of the phenomena under study. Imagine that you have received funding to study the satisfaction of parents and children in day care centres with a high staff turnover versus those with low staff turnovers. Significant insights may be gained by noting the presence or absence of available arts and crafts materials, the type, quality and condition of the toys and play equipment, the cleanliness of bathrooms or pictures on the wall. These are all clues that help the qualitative researcher understand the larger picture.

Use of Quantitative Data in Qualitative Research

The use of quantitative data in qualitative research is not only useful, and often unavoidable, it provides yet another perspective. Continuing with the day care example, making a mental count of the number of broken toys may be useful, knowing the rate of staff turnover is important, comparing pay scales may shed light on employment variables, and the ratio of children to care givers could be significant. These are quantitative data, things with numeric values (e.g. 75 broken toys, a 1:10 vs 1:5 teacher/child ratio). While qualitative researchers may not always actively seek this type of information, it is often readily present and provides another source of insight. Most qualitative researchers do not statistically manipulate these numeric values; rather, they will use their general descriptive properties (e.g. counts, frequencies). If, on the other hand, you have selected a research methodology that purposefully blends qualitative research techniques with collecting data to be statistically analyzed, then your approach to data collection will be very different and you will have to concern yourself with various protocols relevant to the quantitative researcher.

Data Management

Managing the masses of qualitative data you collect during a study can be a nightmare, even for the most organized researcher on the planet. Between field notes, transcripts of interviews, records of physical artifacts, photographs, brochures, maps and souvenirs collected in the field, you can easily become lost in your own data. Fortunately, this can be minimized through careful planning before you enter the field. When managing qualitative data consider how a computer can be of use to you, think about a storage box for cassettes to be transcribed and another for those that are complete. Develop a filing system for raw data, keep back-up files and copies of vital information, and most of all, do not let your research materials collect in a 'to-do' pile in your office. Like field notes, do not wait to organize your data — you will regret it and your study will suffer.

Ending Data Collection

There are numerous factors that will influence the decision to end the data collection phase of your research. The two most obvious are usually *time* and *money*. If on the other hand you have sufficient resources at your disposal, there still comes a time to stop collecting data. Lincoln and Guba (1985) offer four criteria that can help you make this decision. *Exhausting your sources* is the first criterion. Basically you are tapped out, you have spoken with the necessary people and have recorded sufficient observations to complete the study. A second reason to stop collecting data is because you are only receiving tiny bits of new information, you have *saturated your categories*. The third reason, *emergence of regularities*, refers to you observing consistency or regularity in the themes, categories or constructs you have developed. Finally, you may start to sense that the new information you are receiving is not really relevant, it is removed from your line of inquiry. This is known as *overextension* and another reason to stop collecting data.

Qualitative Data Analysis and Interpretation

Analyzing qualitative data is a systematic process that organizes the data into manageable units, combines and synthesizes ideas, develops constructs, themes, patterns or theories and illuminates the important discoveries of your research. It is a monumental task that begins as soon as data are received. Unlike quantitative researchers who will wait until all surveys arrive, input the results into the computer then punch out the statistical analyzes, qualitative researchers begin to organize and interpret their data in the field and never really finish until the last computer print-out of the research report!

Qualitative data analysis is a continuous activity that constantly evolves. It also follows a pattern. Moustakas (1990) identifies five basic phases of analysis: 1) *immersion* with the experience; 2) *incubation*, a time of quiet contemplation; 3) *illumination*, a time of increased awareness, expanded meaning and new clarity; 4) *explication*, new connections are made and one prepares to communicate findings; and 5) *creative synthesis*, the research findings and experience are wound together, written and communicated. Finally, it is important to note that qualitative analysis relies heavily on a process known as *triangulation*; the use of multiple data sources, data collection methods and theories to validate research findings. Triangulation also helps eliminate bias and can help detect errors or anomalies in your discoveries.

Field Analysis

Qualitative research is an inductive form of inquiry, and consequently, when you enter the field you may feel like an astronaut who has just entered outer space and is experiencing no gravity for the first time! It will take some time to interpret and learn how to function in this new environment. As soon as you begin to interview people, observe activities or analyze documents, you intuitively begin to try and place the new information you are receiving into your research framework. You also start developing analytic questions, questions that help clarify your initial findings and help focus your study. Sometimes these questions are recast to participants and informants in the field, other times they are used to define your research framework. Exhibit 13.4 lists 12 activities to help guide you through the field analysis.

Exhibit 13.4:   Activities to help guide the field analysis

---

1 Allocate time for analysis and reflection while in the field.

2 Where time permits, begin to organize your data and create initial coding schemes (e.g. the setting, acts, activities, perspectives, participation, relationships, methods).

3 Make decisions in the field that force you to focus your study.

4 Review field notes and listen to, or transcribe, cassettes.

5 Make a list of any themes, patterns, ideas or gut intuitions that emerge.

6 Develop analytic questions and further define the problem or scenario.

7 Generate a list of questions or issues you wish to validate or clarify with respondents.

8 Make notes of your personal reflections and the decisions made; why they are made at this time, what is important.

9 Re-examine relevant theoretical literature.

10 Try to develop metaphors or analogies that help enhance your understanding.

11 Try to create a concept map that depicts preliminary constructs or relationships.

12 Remind yourself to keep looking and listening for what is NOT being said or witnessed.

Post-Field Analysis

After the data collection is complete, a period which may take many months, accepted wisdom suggests that you rest and distance yourself from the situation. When you return, you will have a fresh perspective and be mentally prepared to tackle the post-field analysis. Your goal now is to produce findings; to do this you must first find your focus then get organized. It's just like moving into a new apartment, you arrive with a bunch of boxes and must decide what goes where and why!

In other words, you have to take the mass of raw data and make sense of it within the themes, patterns or categories you identified in the field analysis. It is perfectly normal if these groupings change, for the mere act of describing data often brings new insights and thoughts about your data. This is the time of illumination and explication. Analyzing the content comes next. Whether you choose to analyze the content using typologies (groupings based on similar characteristics), structural analysis (e.g. searching for patterns), logical analysis (e.g. cross classification matrices) to name a few, this is a time of creative synthesis. Once you are comfortable with your discoveries, it is time to look back at your data for negative cases (cases which go against what you have found). You will also want to reflect on the lessons learned along the way that can be shared with the research community and sponsoring organization. Finally, you will want to start planning your final written product (Chapter 7).

Reporting

What good is doing research if you cannot share your discoveries? Writing qualitative research papers, reports, articles, theses or dissertations can be a challenge, but the mere act of writing helps to refine your thinking, crystalize your ideas, internalize the data and forces you to begin working with language suited to your anticipated reading audience. When you think about writing a qualitative research report, think of Beethoven, who took the music he heard in his head and transferred it to paper in a way which captivated the listening audience and displayed the passion he felt for his music. Just as Beethoven did not write his famous Fifth Symphony flawlessly in one sitting, you do not have to write your qualitative research report at one time. In fact, that approach could be disastrous!

Start writing early, revise, reconceptualize, and rewrite! When you get stuck expressing an idea, bounce it off a colleague or a friend. Often by discussing a difficult or challenging aspect of your research with someone else, you find new ways to express yourself and can return to your computer later and put it in print. Unlike a statistical report of numeric findings, a primary goal when writing a qualitative report is to engage the reader in your study. You must bring alive your findings through the voices and examples of the people who provided you with your information. You must convey accurately, yet succinctly, the fine details, the nuances and the exciting discoveries of your research.

Regardless of your audience (e.g. editor of journal or course professor), research writing must be well-organized, use appropriate language, and include an introduction, a body and a conclusion (refer to Chapter 7). You must also decide if you should write an analytic or reflective report. *Analytic reports* use an objective writing style where the researcher's voice is subdued or silent (third person). This is a traditional form of academic writing and still required in certain circles. *Reflective reports*, in contrast, are characterized by the presence of the researcher's voice (first person) and more literary freedom of expression. Reflective reporting is more common in qualitative research; however, it is not your personal preference which guides the decision, it is the needs and requirements of your reading audience.

Limitations

As with all forms of research, qualitative research has its limitations. One of the questions most often asked is, 'Will different observers get the same results?' We all know that there is always more than one valid view of any social situation. People might agree on the facts of the situation but not on what they mean. The qualitative researchers' defense is that the work they do is much more systematic and focused than that of teachers, artists or journalists. It involves rigorous record-keeping and they have no personal stake in the results.

The reliability of informants' information can be another source of concern. The informant's social position in the group, his or her particular personality and the relationship of the informant to the researcher all tend to color the interpretation of data. In practice, researchers triangulate their data, develop levels of confidence in their informants, and treat their information accordingly.

The quality of the research is highly contingent on the skills of the individual researcher and his or her ability to understand, record, gain insight and interpret the dearth of data collected. The researcher is the data collection instrument, and the quality of the product is directly related to the researcher's skill. This form of inquiry is both expensive and time-consuming, a shortage of either vital resource could render a study of lower quality or of limited value, through no fault of the researcher.

The question of internal validity often pops up from members of the scientific community who quantify phenomena by validating instruments such as surveys and test measurements. The internal validity of qualitative research, in contrast, comes from keeping meticulous records of all sources of information used, using detailed transcripts, and taking field notes of all communications and reflective thinking activities during the research process. This is known as an *audit trail*. A concurrent activity qualitative researchers employ is maintaining a *chain-of-evidence*. This chain takes the information recorded in the audit trail and records the decisions made concerning all aspects of the research process as they unfold and demonstrates how the links and conclusions between the data and analysis were derived. Finally, qualitative researchers declare any personal bias which may impact on their role as a researcher and make known the theoretical and conceptual perspectives on which the study is based.

Finally, the inability of qualitative research findings to be generalized to other communities has also been argued as a limitation. However, as generalization is not a fundamental component of this type of research, qualitative researchers are not bothered by this limitation.

Conclusion

Qualitative research accepts that people know themselves best and can describe, interpret and talk about their own environment. It is an inductive form of inquiry that accepts the researcher as the main data collection instrument and acknowledges that he or she is attached to a set of 'baggage' that shapes and informs the researcher's opinions, attitudes and ways of looking at phenomena and interpreting findings. It is also a form of research concerned with the context. Understanding the research environment and all its political, social, psychological, economic and cultural dynamics is vital to producing rich, useful, valid findings.

To conclude, let us return to the lake and the fisherman. To know what forms of marine life exist at varying depths in the lake, we must search below the surface of the water. To succeed in catching different types of fish, we must fish from different locations, at different times of the day, using different types of bait and varied fishing methods. Similarly, to get the underlying meaning of social phenomena, qualitative researchers must look beyond the obvious, hear what is not actually stated, interpret behaviors within their natural context, and try to understand what people tell us from their perspective, through their lens. Only then, after quiet periods of incubation, reflection and synthesis, can we write a rich, descriptive account of the research experience, share the discoveries, the lessons learned and identify new places on the lake for the next researcher to place a boat, select equipment and look beneath the surface.

References

Atkinson, P., & Hammersley, M. (1994). Ethnography and participant observation. In N.K. Denzin & Y.S. Lincoln, (1994). *Handbook of qualitative research,* pp. 248–261. Thousand Oaks, CA: Sage.

Becker, H.S. (1951). *Role and career problems of the Chicago school teacher.* Ph.D. Dissertation, University of Chicago. Published in 1980, New York: Arno Press.

Bogdan, R.C., & Biklen, S.K. (1992). *Qualitative research for education: An introduction to theory and methods* (2nd ed.). Boston, MA: Allyn and Bacon.

Denzin, N.K., & Lincoln, Y.S. (1994). *Handbook of qualitative research.* Thousand Oaks, CA: Sage.

Eisner, E. (1991). *The enlightened eye.* MacMillan: New York.

Glasner, B., & Strauss, A. (1967). *The discovery of grounded theory.* Chicago: Aldine.

Hammersley, M., & Atkinson, P. (1995). *Ethnography: Principles in practice.* New York: Travistock.

Lincoln, Y.S., & Guba, E.G. (1985). *Naturalistic inquiry.* Beverly Hills, CA: Sage.

Mead, M. (1942). An anthropologist looks at the teacher's role. *Educational Method,* pp. 219–223.

Patton, M.Q. (1990). *Qualitative evaluation and research methods* (2nd ed.). Newbury Park, CA: Sage.

Priebe, R.M. (1993). *Voc talk: Stories from the back of the school.* Unpublished doctoral dissertation, University of Alberta, Edmonton.

Rist, R. (1978). *The invisible children.* Cambridge, MA: Harvard University.

Strauss, A., & Corbin, J. (1994). Ground theory methodology: An overview. In N.K. Denzin, & Y.S. Lincoln, (1994). *Handbook of qualitative research,* pp. 273–285. Thousand Oaks, CA: Sage.

Van Manen, M. (1990). *Researching lived experience.* Ann Arbor, MI: Althouse Press.

Waller, W. (1932). *Sociology of teaching.* New York: John Wiley.

Whyte, W.F. (1955). *Street corner society.* Chicago, IL: University of Chicago Press.

Wolcott, H. (1973). *The man in the principal's office.* New York: Holt, Rinehart & Winston.

For Further Study

Guba, E.G., & Lincoln, Y.S. (1994). Competing paradigms in qualitative research. In N.K. Denzin, & Y.S. Lincoln, (1994). *Handbook of qualitative research.* pp. 105–117. Thousand Oaks, CA: Sage.

Miles, M.B., & Huberman, M.A. (1994). *Qualitative data analysis* (2nd ed.). Thousand Oaks, CA: Sage.

Moustakas, C. (1994). *Phenomenological research methods.* Thousand Oaks, CA: Sage.

Strauss, A.L., & Corbin, J. (1990). *Basics of qualitative research: Grounded theory procedures and technique.* Newbury Parks, CA: Sage.

Chapter 14

Evaluation Research

Evaluation is a prevalent activity in contemporary society. We evaluate people; we evaluate products; and increasingly, we evaluate educational programs and projects. Evaluation is one good way of assessing whether or not what we are doing is achieving what it is intended to achieve. It also can be used to examine whether the approach being followed is the best way to achieve the desired result, and sometimes evaluation is intended to question whether what we are doing is appropriate to do at all. Sometimes the major purpose of evaluation is to improve a new program or activity. This is generally referred to as *formative evaluation, monitoring* or *performance review* as its results are intended to feed back and improve on-going practice. *Summative evaluation, auditing, ex-post evaluation,* or *compliance evaluation*, on the other hand, are terms that apply to evaluations directed at determining whether the program conformed to standards or did what its funders paid for. These types of evaluations also seek to determine the consequences of a program, what it might teach for subsequent programs of this type, and they are often seen as the principal mechanism for making crucial resource allocation decisions about a program, including its continuance or termination.

People often raise the question of whether evaluation is indeed research. Evaluation is best thought of within the contract research approach (See Chapter 1). Building on that paradigm, ten of the differences between academic research and evaluation are summarized in Exhibit 14.1. Evaluation generally relates to practice and the specific project being examined. Rarely is its purpose generalization but rather an understanding of the particular circumstances which affect the outcomes being examined. Thus, evaluation is not analogous with academic research, but it does incorporate many of the techniques of research, though for a much more limited purpose. One major difference is that contract research relies not on the researcher's agenda but on the concerns of an external sponsor. The sponsor is the client of the evaluation and the sponsor sets the major agenda, agrees to the methodology and effectively controls dissemination of the results. In this chapter, we will assume a contract research model and examine evaluation using its assumptions. However, in the absence of a contractual sponsor, similar issues and methods can also be used.

For the student conducting research as part of a graduate program, evaluation may have insufficient generalizability to satisfy the research requirements of some universities, though this is not necessarily the case. The use of the case study method may be more satisfactory in such instances. In any event, I caution students on the dangers inherent in evaluating programs or organizations that employ them

Exhibit 14.1:   A comparison between academic research and program evaluation

Academic Research	Evaluation
1 Relates to theory.	1 Relates to practice.
2 Is built upon previous literature.	2 Literature reviews are often not pertinent to the evaluation issues, though lessons learned in previous evaluations are crucial.
3 Builds upon previous research activities.	3 Tends to be viewed as an isolated case study though the methodologies may be transferable.
4 Has methodological roots in positivist or post-positivist paradigms.	4 Uses an eclectic assortment of methodologies which are increasingly of the post-positivistic genre.
5 Research is ongoing often in phases that relate to academic funding.	5 Conforms to time-frames of decision-makers and often occurs within a 3–4 month period.
6 Tries to be objective and value free.	6 Is rooted in values and politics.
7 Has limited concern with practical application.	7 The major concern is practical application.
8 Prescription occurs when prediction becomes precise and/or theory becomes law.	8 Is immediately prescriptive based upon logic and experience.
9 Reports are written for other academic researchers.	9 Reports are written for implementors, users and other interested people.
10 Is intended to be published and publicly disseminated.	10 The extent of dissemination is controlled by the sponsor.

because of the conflict of interest inherent in mixing management and evaluation (unless it is conceived of as participatory or self-evaluation).

Description

The most basic form of evaluation is simply to measure what is happening. This is a variant of the descriptive method of research described in Chapter 11. While it is useful to measure what is happening, the full power of measurement is only realized when comparison is involved. In evaluation, two types of comparison are typically employed. *Baseline* data describes the condition prior to an intervention, and *periodic measurement* enables comparisons to the baseline state, thus determining progress. Benchmarking compares to a standard.

Experimental Approaches

Evaluation is a diverse field including models and traditions as varied as those in all of social science research. The early forms of evaluation came out of the experimental tradition, and good evaluations of a decade or two ago attempted to reflect sound experimental designs. To do so, researchers took elaborate pains to randomly assign students to experimental or control situations and often incorporated placebos to make those in the control group feel that they were also getting something special. Such approaches must be thought of as more than pale approximations to the true experiment. Indeed, they have evolved to provide dimensions of information that go far beyond what the typical experiment can yield. True experiments certainly have their place in situations such as computerized learning which enable the tight control of extraneous variables, but in classroom and school-based applications, more eclectic methods are generally superior. As we all know, in education it is difficult to arrange the lives of people so that they conform to the essentials of experimental design. For this reason, new evaluation approaches have emerged which do not build in the essential ingredients of an experiment and which are proving to be even more powerful in contributing to our understanding of how programs work.

Quasi-Experimental Approaches

Quasi-experimental research approaches, being much more flexible, have been used for years in evaluation projects (see Chapter 9). Since they do not require that individuals be randomly assigned to programs, they are easier to apply than true experimental methods. They have been used generally to address the question of what people learned or, more recently, what was learned by various types of individuals in various circumstances (aptitude-treatment interaction). Stated in that way, such evaluation becomes indistinguishable from academic research as it is intended to explore understanding of differences which might be generalizable. A good example of the quasi-experimental research approach to evaluation was the Lennoxville District French teaching program described in Chapter 6. In that example, a new teaching method was introduced and it was compared to alternative methods. In such experiments the line between evaluation and research is blurred.

Too often in the past, educational evaluation has been characterized by the use of elaborate methodologies to answer questions which should never have been asked in the first place. Unfortunately, most quasi-experimental methods have a track record of mixed or non-significant findings, educationally or statistically. Another limitation of quasi-experimental methods is that they rely on statistical group comparisons: does the average child perform better under treatment A or treatment B? Parents will be the first to tell the researcher that they care little for the statistical differences between average children. Their child is unique with a distinct personality and set of values, a preference for certain ways of learning and a set of individual idiosyncrasies that defy such broad-stroke group comparisons. A parent is much more interested in knowing about many softer, non-comparative dimensions:

Will the new educational method break up my child's friendship groups? Will it suit his social maturity? Will it help him get into college? These are not the typical questions of experimental comparisons. Notwithstanding their research contributions, they, therefore, have not been particularly helpful in addressing broader evaluation issues or in guiding educational policies or practices.

Value Added Evaluation

Experimental approaches are comparative. Correlational methodologies are also used in evaluation through the value added approach. Simply put, if a regression analysis says students should be achieving level X, then those that achieve above that level have 'value added'. This is the difference in performance between what is predicted and what is actually observed. If we were to forecast the performance of students based on our best quantitative methods, then those who achieve more (those who were once labelled 'over-achievers') have benefited from their educational experience. Recently, researchers have found whole schools that have performed much better than one would expect by such prediction. Researchers can then explore the causes for these differences.

Evaluation According to Standards

The previous paradigms were relativistic as opposed to absolute. Some models of evaluation used established standards and benchmarks with which to compare the program being evaluated. *Benchmarks* can be defined as best practices (e.g. the proportion of the age cohort that complete secondary schooling in the best school districts); as conforming to a professional standard (e.g. all school principals require a master's degree in administration); or as a scientific standard (e.g. school water can have no more than 1 part per million of contaminants).

Fourth Generation Approaches

In response to such limitations, in recent years the whole field of educational and public policy evaluation has blossomed. Guba and Lincoln (1989) have coined the term 'fourth generation evaluation' to describe an approach that involves the evaluation stakeholders and their perspectives as fundamental to understanding what a program has done. These new approaches are not intended to emphasize comparisons but rather have as their central concern an emphasis on gaining in-depth understanding of the program and all its effects, both planned and unplanned. Such evaluation approaches combine the strengths of quantitative and qualitative methods and have much in common with case study methodology. Like case study, their focus is on understanding, but they emphasize program effects rather than analysis of a case which is not necessarily a program.

Exhibit 14.2:   Johari's window as a means to understand fourth generation evaluation

Evaluator	Other Stakeholders	
	Known	**Unknown**
Known	A	B
Unknown	C	D

This type of evaluation is laden with the values of stakeholders who are involved in framing central questions and methodologies. As in qualitative methods in general, they impute their meaning in interpreting the findings, so the approach focuses on meaning rather than compliance, which is the agenda of most external evaluation sponsors. In recent years, participatory evaluation has been a favoured methodology for involving stakeholders in assessing projects in which they were involved either as deliverers or as beneficiaries.

Fourth generation evaluation looks at the world as consisting of multiple realities, with multiple constructions. It is a sociopolitical activity, utilizing the constructivist view of evaluation which requires the involvement, empowerment and consideration of all stakeholders' views and values. New constructions are created through a hermeneutic dialectic process reminiscent of the Johari Window depicted in Exhibit 14.2.

In this framework, the various stakeholders know many things about the program which the evaluator does not (C in the framework). Over the course of the evaluation the evaluator learns things that the other stakeholders do not know (B in the framework) as well as things that no one knew (D in the framework). The successful evaluation moves knowledge to the A cell where everyone knows it. Transparency is essential in processes that attempt to increase what is known. This has recently been referred to as *empowerment evaluation* as it empowers those involved by giving them new knowledge of the performance of their endeavour (Fetterman, Kaftarian & Wandersman, 1996).

The Logical Framework Approach

The Logical Framework Approach described in Chapter 6 shows how one can specify indicators and means of verification. This is what can be referred to as a blueprint model for evaluation as the intentions are prescribed at the outset. One knows what is expected, and by monitoring and evaluation, one can observe whether these expectations are achieved. It is a particularly effective mode for inanimate programs such as a construction project. In that case, it is clear what is to happen and when, and the evaluator merely reports on progress.

An example might clarify the approach when it is applied to educational programs. The example I will use involves an evaluation of the East/West Enterprise Exchange, an exchange program being conducted by the Schulich School of

Exhibit 14.3:   Abbreviated logical framework for the east/west enterprise exchange

Levels/Summary	Indicators	Assumptions
Goal:		
Increase trade with region. Assist Eastern Europe with transition to market economy.	Increased imports and exports between Canada and Eastern Europe.	Canada continues to have relatively free access to markets in the region.
Purpose:		
Facilitate new business ventures. Strengthen management capacities in Eastern Europe.	Number of Canadian businesses that conclude joint venture agreements with businesses in Eastern Europe.	The Eastern European business context is sufficiently supportive to permit Canadian business expansion into the region.
Output:		
Trained participants in business management. Business plans.	Number of participants who complete the program. Number of business plans.	Training is a significant impediment to business development.
Inputs:		
6-week exchange program. Program management. Business internships.	Number of Canadian businesses sponsoring participants.	There are sufficient numbers of potential participants competent in English.

Management of York University, one of Canada's leading management schools. The program selects business entrepreneurs in Central and Eastern Europe and Russia and matches them with Canadian companies who provide partial sponsorship. Participants spend six weeks in Canada of which four are at the university learning about business management and two are in an internship with the sponsoring firm. The program is designed to teach business concepts and skills, to benefit the businesses in Europe and to generate trade relationships through joint business ventures and other means. Since the Canadian government is a major sponsor, they asked me to lead a team of my associates in Universalia to conduct a program evaluation. Exhibit 14.3 outlines the logic of the program and shows the types of indicators that were used to evaluate it.

It is clear that one could collect data on the indicators and then report on progress over time. On the surface the logical framework approach is attractive, but not if it is treated as a static prescription. In human processes many intervening forces typically come into play, and people often then abandon the framework rather than adapting it dynamically. The principles of strategic management suggest that such frameworks require frequent updating which gives them much more utility in educational evaluation. Furthermore, the questions that fall from the logical framework are not the questions of most concern to program stakeholders. They want to know other things that relate better to an alternative framework.

Exhibit 14.4:   Summary of major issues of a logical approach to program evaluation

Major Issues	Essential Questions	Comments
Rationale	• Does the program make sense? • Will achievement of the program's objectives ensure attainment of its goal?	The evaluator must understand the program and its environmental context.
Effectiveness	• Has the program achieved its objectives?	The program must have explicit objectives on which everyone agrees.
Efficiency	• How well has the program been managed? • Were there better ways of achieving the same results at less cost? • Were the most cost-effective alternatives used in managing the program?	In Canadian government usage, the major concern with efficiency is project administration.
Relevance	• Are the objectives still relevant? • Is the program supported by stakeholders?	Is it sustainable?
Effects and Impacts	• What has happened as a result of the program? • What are the unplanned effects? • What are the probable long term program consequences?	The evaluator must be sensitive to both planned and unplanned program effects.

Universalia's Framework for Rationale, Effectiveness, Efficiency, Relevance, and Effects and Impact

One framework that has proven to be of great utility over the past two decades is the logical approach developed initially by the Office of the Controller General of Canada (OCG, 1981) and it is the basis for most mandatory evaluations of federal programs in Canada, and increasingly in many international agencies in other parts of the world. My colleagues and I have developed this framework with a number of Canadian and international agencies leading to a refined model that appears to have fairly general applicability in program evaluation. The approach we use includes five major issues to be addressed in program and project evaluations. These are summarized in Exhibit 14.4 and expanded into a full question tree in Exhibit 14.5. The major contributions of this model are its emphasis of project rationale and project effects and impacts. I consider these essential areas for exploration in any evaluation. Let us now consider the specific evaluation questions emanating from the framework. To do so, the illustration in Exhibit 14.5 has to do with a decision about whether or not to continue to fund the program.

Exhibit 14.5: Decision tree for evaluating whether to continue funding a project

1.0 Should we continue to fund the project?

1.1 Is there a sound rationale for continued funding?	1.2 How effective is the project? Is it achieving its objectives?	1.3 How efficient is the project in objectives achievement?	1.4 How sustainable is the project? Does it continue to be relevant?	1.5 What impact is the project having on its stakeholders and their context?
1.1.1 Does the project continue to fit within the funder's policy?	1.2.1 To what degree is objective A being achieved?	1.3.1 What is the cost – effectiveness of objectives achievement?	1.4.1 What revenue does it generate relative to the total cost?	1.5.1 Planned effects and impact?
1.1.2 If effective and efficient, will continuation of the project help ensure attainment of the funders' purpose and goal for this endeavour?	1.2.2 To what degree is objective B being achieved?	1.3.2 What is the efficiency in terms of time to achieve objectives?	1.4.2 What degree of stakeholder support does it have for its mission?	1.5.2 Unplanned effects and impact?
1.1.3 What are the comparative advantages of alternatives that reflect our values for this area of endeavour?	1.2.3 To what degree is objective C being achieved?	1.3.3 Were there better ways of achieving the same results at less cost or in lesser time?	1.4.3 How is the context changing that might affect sustainability?	1.5.3 What is the cost-benefit of the project?
1.1.4 What are the stakeholder/political pressures to continue?		1.3.4 Were resources allocated as contracted?		1.5.4 What were anticipated effects not achieved?
1.1.5 Does the project work at cross-purposes with other funding priorities?		1.3.5 Were the most cost-effective alternatives used in managing the project?		1.5.5 What lessons can be learned from this project experience?

Program *rationale* (or continuing rationale) is the type of fundamental issue which typically remains overlooked. However, it is often the crux of whether or not a program makes sense. For example, a recent evaluation of a series of training and other projects in support of the Tanzanian Railway Corporation suggested that the railway made less and less sense since the cost of trucking had decreased to levels lower than could be expected from the railway even at optimum performance. This is a classic rationale question in that one questions what is being done or why effort is being expended when failure is practically guaranteed. Another example is a training evaluation in a major corporation which showed that the training was effective in teaching new skills, but over a third of those trained were laid off within six months of receiving the training due to overall corporate downsizing. Thus, the rationale question considers whether the program makes sense to continue given alternatives, the status of observed program performance and so forth. Note that the rationale questions often derive from the assumptions column in the logical framework.

Program *effectiveness* is the extent to which the program has achieved its objectives. That is, the extent to which planned outputs were achieved. For example, if the objective is to obtain 100 school graduates, the evaluator counts the number who actually graduated. Of course, this matches the output indicators of the logical framework. Graduation may be the objective, but it is not the whole story. It is possible that though the participants graduate, they become introverted or resort to a life of crime, or leave the profession for which they were trained, a common problem with teachers. That raises the issue of effects and impact discussed later.

Program *efficiency* is another issue which too few evaluations consider. The program may be achieving appropriate things, but not in the most efficient way. In practice, the whole program management function is assessed as part of the study of efficiency. Thus, in a non-comparative way the evaluator examines the various management functions such as coordination, control, planning and decision-making and assesses how well these functions are performed. This can be done using standards of the field (e.g. management costs should not exceed 25 per cent of the cost of total programming), by considering the cost-effectiveness of alternatives, or by examining the unit costs of achieving program objectives (e.g. the cost of producing one graduate).

Program *relevance* is a concern closely related to rationale: 'Does anyone care about the existence of a program?' It is taken care of automatically in private sector programs which need purchasers to sustain a program. Unfortunately, in the public sector, it can go unaddressed. For example, in universities, there are many program areas that cannot be sustained on utilitarian grounds alone. The evaluator needs to inform the program funders and other stakeholders about this reality. It is often evaluated through consideration of demand for an educational program both by students and by employers of the graduates.

Program *effects* and *impacts* refer to the totality of what the program is doing. Effects are short term while impact relates to the lasting contributions of the program. For example, programs which train teachers in developing countries generally produce the teachers, but often fail to improve education in the country. Largely because of their low status and poor wages, many teachers leave the profession once they have sufficient qualifications to find a better job. In several projects I have evaluated that support faculty development in university faculties of business in Southeast Asia and Eastern Europe, the salary differential between what a professor earns and wages in the private sector may be ten-fold. The evaluation question is that of finding out what the program is doing to the education system. Such effects go beyond the project or program outputs and concerns of effectiveness. Naturally, both planned and unplanned consequences should be studied.

Steps in Conducting a Program Evaluation

Problem Definition

The first question that needs to be asked is why the evaluation is being undertaken. There are a number of general reasons for evaluating programs and projects, the most important of which are:

- To determine whether to continue or discontinue a project or program.
- To improve the program's practices and procedures.
- To adjust specific program strategies and techniques.
- To learn lessons for use when instituting similar programs elsewhere.
- To help decide how to allocate resources among competing programs.
- To validate program results to outside funders.
- To determine if the program is meeting its stated objectives.
- To measure a program's effects and impact.

These general reasons give some guidance as to the purpose of an evaluation. In practice, the purpose must be worked out much more specifically for the program being evaluated. The first step is for the person sponsoring the evaluation to develop *Terms of Reference* (TORs). Terms of Reference are the specific issues and concerns which the evaluation is to address. They generally reflect the five issues in the general framework, however, they normally also provide much more detailed descriptions of what the evaluation is to include and any particular questions or concerns of the evaluation sponsor. Terms of reference usually include the evaluation objective, evaluation issues and questions, a definition of who the evaluation is for, the evaluation schedule and available resources for it. In the case of the East/ West Enterprise Exchange, the normal issues as stated in Exhibit 14.5 were to be included, but the major issue of the evaluation was to examine the effects and impact of the program.

By its nature, evaluation is a political activity and in conducting any evaluation one needs to be fully aware of what one is getting into. Increasingly, the federal government and other sponsors are incorporating mandatory evaluation for all programs. In such cases, evaluation is expected and the political problems are minimized. In public education, on the other hand, evaluation tends to be the exception, reserved for new programs or those about which questions have been raised. Too frequently, evaluations are commissioned merely to get rid of program managers who have fallen out of favour. One must constantly ask why the evaluation is really being commissioned, whether there is commitment to follow through with the results, and whether the evaluation is a genuine activity or the evaluator is merely being used to fulfill someone else's agenda. Be sure you can live within these parameters before you agree to proceed.

One of the first jobs of the evaluator is to go over the TORs to clarify the meaning of the questions, to make sure that the specifics are well understood, that any hidden agendas are uncovered and to find out who is to use the evaluation results. Part of the challenge is to ensure that the issues in the TORs are understood by all stakeholders and in keeping with fourth generation approaches, reflect all the concerns, not just those of the program funder. In practice, sometimes funders have serious constraints on what is considered and how their concerns are phrased while program managers and consumers sometimes have different concerns. If all stakeholders are to cooperate and find the evaluation relevant they need a role in clarifying the evaluation agenda.

The objectives for the evaluation help in defining the problem. They foreshadow some of the important questions, but in themselves they do not adequately define the problem. For this purpose, one must understand the program and its functioning. Then the TORs can be translated into more specific questions and subquestions in a workplan that responds to the TORs.

The Workplan

One of the first tasks of the evaluators is to develop a workplan which is a document describing in detail the methodology to be used in conducting the evaluation. The advantage of the workplan is that once approved by the client it constitutes agreement on how the evaluation will take place. Evaluations offer unlimited opportunities for misunderstanding and the workplan helps clarify things in advance. Typically, the workplan will include a statement of the objectives and purposes, of the major issues and questions together with a description of how each issue is to be addressed, any instruments to be used in data collection, a breakdown of the tasks and activities to be completed, the responsibilities of team members for the various tasks, the time each task will take and an indication of the format of the evaluation report. The next four sections outline some of the elements of the workplan.

The Evaluation Team

Some evaluations are done by an individual, others involve a whole team. It is important that whoever does the evaluation has the background of knowledge, experience and credibility to be in a position to do the job. Occasionally, participatory evaluation is undertaken in which people who have been involved with the project or program participate directly as members of the evaluation team. This is particularly valuable in formative evaluations, where the purpose is to gain understanding of what is going on and how to improve it. One major advantage of participatory evaluation is that it is easier to communicate and implement its results than when the evaluation is done externally. However, such participatory evaluation sacrifices credibility as it is generally not perceived as independent. Whenever there is a team of evaluators, the management of the team raises additional complications. There should always be a team leader and the roles and responsibilities of each team member should be clearly specified in advance. Invariably, the leader is responsible for preparation of the final report which can be difficult to prepare when it involves integrating work of several team members.

Sources of Data

Evaluations generally include numerous sources of data. People are one of the most important sources. The evaluator must obtain information from those most knowledgeable and involved in the program. These will include staff as well as senior managers who may have initiated the program and, in the case of many education programs, the evaluation may also include students. A second source of information are the documents which describe the program. The program proposal and any progress reports will be exceedingly helpful in the evaluation analysis. Most federal projects involve a logical framework analysis or equivalent, an inception report or management plan and often quarterly and annual reports. All these are essential project documents. Project files also contain important information for evaluations. Finally, visits to the site of the project are often indispensable as they show the dynamic and often provide incidental data available in no other way.

Evaluation Framework

In my experience, in conducting numerous project and program evaluations, one of the most useful tools is that of an evaluation framework. The framework is a concrete translation of the terms of reference into key issues of the evaluation, the questions and subquestions that must be addressed and the indicators and methods used to collect the data. Appendix 14.1 is a reduced version of such an evaluation framework for the East/West Enterprise Exchange evaluation. Typically, I develop such a framework from the terms of reference and then go over it in great depth with those sponsoring the evaluation. We agree not only on the issues and questions but also on the method and data sources to be used to address them. The framework is also very useful in allocating responsibility for activities and in planning the exercise so that sufficient time is allocated to each issue and question.

Instruments

Once the preferred methods of data collection and the indicators for each subquestion have been decided, sources of data need to be considered and data collection instruments need to be developed. One of the most common instruments used in evaluations is the interview protocol. In practice evaluators develop a series of protocols for various categories of respondents. Generally, the most significant and politically-important respondents are interviewed while more routinized data is collected with questionnaires. The importance of well-planned interviews cannot be over-stressed since they provide a means of building trust and confidence in the process of those who will be called upon to implement any recommendations. Besides interview protocols and questionnaires, evaluations should normally include such instruments as blank tables into which quantitative data can be recorded. This is particularly useful for effectiveness questions where planned and actual outputs can be listed. Observation schedules, frameworks for content analysis and diagrams are also often useful. In the latter category, it is sometimes useful to construct from documents a planned or presumed organization chart which is modified and updated during the data collection.

Data Collection

Many program evaluations involve case study methodologies and incorporate all types of quantitative and qualitative data. Major methodologies include: observation, interviewing, questionnaires, unobtrusive measures and sometimes diaries, meetings and the use of knowledgeable informants. One of the major concerns of the evaluator is the validity of the data obtained. The major safeguard on validity is to obtain confirmation from as many data sources as possible. The method is referred to as *triangulation*, whereby various sources of data point in the same direction relative to a given conclusion. It is important throughout the study, but particularly during the data collection, that one be sensitive to the personal and ethical issues involved in evaluation research. The evaluator naturally has a position of power over those being evaluated and, therefore, he or she must be sensitive to the concerns and real lives of people who might be affected by the results.

In practice, the collection of data begins when the evaluation is first proposed. The first step involves a review of all program documentation. This precedes development of the workplan and is indispensable in developing the right questions, the best procedures and methods of data collection. As soon as the evaluator is on board, he or she begins receiving reactions and information from those involved. However, the public and formal data collection begins after the workplan is developed. Though there are generally many phases to the data collection reflecting the various instruments and sources of data, formal visits to the project site are of particular importance. Meetings should be prearranged and one must be sure to give all stakeholders an opportunity to express their views fully and privately. It is generally poor on ethical grounds to report who said what about others, but it is acceptable to provide generalized perceptions or quantify them by indicating the number of respondents holding a particular view. In my work, data collection is not complete until the whole evaluation is put to rest. Reactions to a draft evaluation report are often insightful new perspectives and these are a crucial aspect of data collection.

Data Analysis

As with most forms of research, the analysis of data is seldom a linear didactic process, but with evaluations it can be especially eclectic. Good evaluations will often involve all types of data and many forms of analysis and the challenge for the evaluator is to cut through any statistics or particular biases and personal points of view to come to the core of understanding about the project or program being evaluated. Increasingly, in today's evaluations, all stakeholders are engaged in participating in data analysis. In objective terms, is it effective? What unplanned effects is it having? Does it make sense to continue such a project? Are the benefits sufficient to justify the costs incurred? In general, a compatible evaluation team is most helpful in going through this stage of the analysis. Once consensus is reached, the challenge becomes to write the report.

Writing the Report

An evaluation report differs from most research in that it is an action-oriented document and the users differ considerably from academic researchers. The readers have a stake in the results and, as with any human evaluation process, program leaders will take all comments personally. The final report should have no factual errors and there should always be a phase of report preparation in which program leaders can correct factual errors in the draft. Of course, there are also areas of judgment which may result in disagreement. These are areas where the evaluator's expertise takes precedence and for better or for worse, the evaluator's judgment will generally carry the most weight.

Most evaluation reports are overly long. The best reports cover the essence in not more than 20 to 30 pages, though they may have extensive appendices. The best evaluation reports have an executive summary which might be as little as two pages and should not be more than five or six. The question that needs to be asked is who are the major audiences for the report. Sometimes there are different audiences with different information needs yielding conflicting messages about the nature of the report. A typical report includes an executive summary, an introductory chapter describing the purpose and methodology followed. The results and finding are then organized according to the major issues of the evaluation. Generally, it should conclude with a summary of recommendations.

Limitations

A general limitation of program evaluation is that like many forms of research, it could be started much better after it is complete. That is, it is often not until the culmination of an evaluation that one fully understands the questions or best procedures to address them. One particular constraint that evaluations suffer is a timeline geared to the demands of decision-makers. They need information in time to make decisions and it is not always possible to have as thorough a piece of research as one would have liked. With academic research there are no decision-makers awaiting the results, so if necessary, one can begin again and re-analyze the problem and its solution.

It is easy to be critical of many evaluations as their validity is often suspect. The major reason is that few evaluations follow sound principles and research procedures. Perhaps the most common limitation is that they are not grounded in reliable and valid data. In fact, many reports use an expert posture which takes the form of a critique rather than a piece of research. We cannot escape our values, but we have an obligation to present data on which we base our conclusions. Then, in proper academic fashion, those who disagree with the conclusions will have all the data and the argument can be appropriately focused on interpretation.

Sometimes, of course, the data itself is suspect, often because the instruments were poorly developed, important sources of data were ignored in the workplan or the data were not collected with care. Validity is much improved through the use of multiple sources of data for each question. With proper triangulation it will be difficult to refute conclusions which follow logically from multiple data sources. Interpretation of data is also improved when multiple stakeholders are involved in reviewing its meaning.

Another serious limitation of evaluation research are the moral and ethical issues that evaluation presents. Sometimes you must decide not to evaluate because of the limits and restrictions. On other occasions you may be subject to influence or recommendations, or you may discover things such as impropriety or fraud.

Unlike some other forms of research, the true test of the validity of an evaluation is its application and effects on the program being evaluated. A good evaluation will address the objectives of its sponsor and will lead to positive changes in the program under study.

Conclusion

Many evaluation reports sit on shelves and nothing much happens as a result. Good evaluation reports are only one step in the overall evaluation process which involves people and probes them to action. Sometimes the results are implemented because of the power and authority of the evaluator and the terms of reference calling for a program audit or a concrete decision on continuance. More often, the results of the evaluation will filter down to the project in a variety of ways. Research on the effects of evaluations indicate that they are often most effective when there is someone within the project who is convinced of the merits of the evaluation and champions its dissemination.

References

Fetterman, D., Kaftarian, S., & Wandersman, A. (Eds.). (1996). *Empowerment evaluation: Knowledge and tools for self-assessment and accountability*. Thousand Oaks, CA: Sage.

Guba, E. & Lincoln, Y. (1989) *Fourth generation evaluation*. Newbury Park, CA: Sage Publications.

For Further Study

Office of the Controller General Canada. (1981). *Principles for the evaluation of programs by federal departments and agencies*. Ottawa: Minister of Supply and Services.
Rossi, P.H., & Freeman, H.E. (1989). *Evaluation: A systematic approach*. (4th ed.). Thousand Oaks, CA: Sage.
Shadish, W.R., Jr., Cook, T.D., & Leviton, L.C. (1996). *Foundations of program evaluation*. Thousand Oaks, CA: Sage.

Chapter 15

Case Study

Case study is a familiar term to many people, but there is little agreement on what exactly constitutes a case study (Merriam, 1988). A case study is a holistic research method that uses multiple sources of evidence to analyze or evaluate a specific phenomenon or instance. Most case study research is interpretive and seeks to bring to life a case. It often, but not exclusively, occurs in a natural setting and it may employ qualitative and/or quantitative methods and measures.

Many of the traditional methods of educational research (experimental, quasi-experimental, correlational) have emerged from academic disciplines that do not lend themselves well to a wide array of educational situations. The integration of disabled children into regular classrooms, the introduction of computers in education, and the adoption of a new strategy for university management are just a few examples which do not readily allow tight control or experimental manipulation. Education is a process and, at times, requires a research method which is process-oriented, flexible and adaptable to changing circumstances and a dynamic context. Given these boundaries, case study method is often appropriate.

Generally speaking, case studies are a useful way to systematically look at a specific case, collect data, analyze and interpret findings within their context and report results. The emphasis is on understanding and no value stance is assumed. The case study research method is not to be confused with the use of case studies as a teaching tool. In such fields as law and business, real cases are summarized, or pseudo cases created, then given to students to analyze and dissect. In this application, the data base is generally weak and the case is subject to various interpretations and various applications of theory. Case study research, on the other hand, is highly data-based and strives for the same degree of reliability and validity as any good research.

Followers of more traditional research methods sometimes look down on case study on the grounds that it lacks rigor. It incorporates no statistical tests and it does not readily permit generalization. None of these half truths need to apply to the case study method, which, in its best form, is valid, rigorous and often generalizable. It is true to say, however, that the case study is one of the most difficult methods to do well and the poor examples sometimes reported do not enhance its reputation, but neither do they represent inherent characteristics of the method.

Description

Case study has been confused with other types of research such as historical or evaluation research, however there are distinct differences. Historical research, as discussed in Chapter 10, deals with the past, whereas case study deals with contemporary events in their natural context. Evaluation research seeks to find out what happened and compare it to what was planned. Case study, on the other hand, is concerned with how things happen and why. Both evaluation research and case study often try to accommodate the varied perspectives of those involved, a key factor in their popularity and relevance.

Several case study definitions exist and they vary in their degree of detail. Robert Stake (1996), an education evaluation expert, succinctly stated that "as a form of research, case study is defined by interest in individual cases, not by the methods of inquiry used" (p. 236). The United States General Accounting Office (GAO), who have used case studies to research a wide range of topics from urban housing to weapon systems testing, defines case study as, "a method for learning about a complex instance, based on a comprehensive understanding of that instance, obtained by extensive description and analysis of that instance taken as a whole" (GAO, 1990, p. 14). The most elaborate definition of case study comes from Yin (1994), an experimental psychologist. His two part technical definition reads as follows:

1. A case study is an empirical inquiry that
   - investigates a contemporary phenomenon within its real-life context, especially when
   - the boundaries between phenomenon and context are not clearly evident.
2. The case study inquiry
   - copes with the technically distinctive situation in which there will be many more variables of interest than data points, and as one result
   - relies on multiple sources of evidence, with data needing to converge in a triangulating fashion, and as another result
   - benefits from the prior development of theoretical propositions to guide data collection and analysis (p. 13).

As one reads these definitions it becomes clear why the case study method is a challenge, especially for the novice researcher, for it requires: 1) selecting a type of case study; 2) establishing boundaries for the case; 3) the knowledge and ability to collect data skillfully from multiple sources; 4) the capacity to interpret, synthesize and recast information during data collection, and; 5) expertise to triangulate multiple sources of information and place the findings into a context, supported by prior theoretical knowledge, which will enhance understanding.

Problem Definition

One difficulty in case study research is actually defining the case. While this might appear to be trivial, it can be profound. A case study might focus on a particular decision and how it was implemented. It might involve the adoption of policy or it might consider the deliberations of a committee or other group of people and their interaction. The famous Watergate case study by Bernstein and Woodword, for example, focused not on the Watergate burglary or Richard Nixon but on the cover-up which was the focus that led to the unfolding case study. In any case study, the researcher should have a clear vision of what the case is and what unit of analysis will be examined.

The choice of a case implies a knowledge of some interesting issue or feature and that sets the general parameters for the important 'why' question and identifies the unit of analysis. For example, one might ask why one developing nation prospered while its neighbors fell to ruin or why an individual with overwhelming physical disabilities is able to rise above great handicaps and excel in life. Whatever unit of analysis you choose, it is important to make this distinction up front, for it will not only influence the focus of the investigation and help you understand the dynamics, it will permit you to set the boundaries for the investigation, define subquestions, and narrow data collection options.

The first major issue in case study research is to focus on the problem — what issue or issues are being investigated? This, of course, relates clearly to the unit of analysis. In case study research, data collection and data analysis are concurrent activities, so one must be clear on the issue being investigated. The issue gives rise to critical questions which can be summarized in an issues and questions matrix, as described in Chapter 14 on evaluation research. Typically, questions occur at two levels. There are questions asked of specific individuals when they are interviewed or when they fill out questionnaires, and there are questions asked of the case itself. Remember to keep in mind that the major themes relate to how things are taking place and why. The emphasis in case study is to explain and these types of questions help to do that.

It is important to reiterate that the decision to use a case study generally relates to your interest in describing, explaining or evaluating a specific case. Prior to confirming the use of a case study design, it is imperative that you first ensure the problem or topic is worthy of study. If it is, you can then select a suitable type of case study design, identify your unit of analysis, then you are free to move on to other decisions such as the role of the researcher, use of research teams, gaining access, data sources and collection, analysis and reporting. The planning process presented in Chapter 3 provides a useful guide.

Procedure

Selecting a Case Study

A case study is difficult to do well, therefore the researcher contemplating a case study should be experienced in all the separate requisite methods. He or she should have a deep understanding of the relevant literature, be flexible, be able to ask good questions, listen, observe, and have an inquiring open mind. The novice researcher is cautioned about using case study methods prematurely. The successful case study often uses a team of researchers and benefits from the diverse and complementary strengths of each member. In conducting a case study, especially with a research team, planning is essential.

When selecting a case the researcher may first want to consider if the case is intrinsic, instrumental, or collective (Stake, 1996). Intrinsic studies are used to gain a better understanding of a specific case, whereas instrumental case study helps refine theory or provide insight into an issue. Finally, collective case studies examine a number of cases jointly to seek understanding into a population or general condition.

The GAO (1990) identifies six types of case studies which provide a useful starting point for researchers ready to select a specific type of case study.

- *Illustrative:* descriptive in character and intended to add realism and in-depth examples to other information about a program or policy;
- *Exploratory*: also a descriptive case study but is aimed at generating hypotheses for later investigation rather than illustrating;
- *Critical instance*: examines a single instance of unique interest or serves as a critical test of an assertion about a program, problem or strategy;
- *Program implementation*: investigates operations, often at several sites and often normatively;
- *Program effects*: examines causality and usually involves multi-site, multi-method assessments;
- *Cumulative*: brings together many case studies to answer an evaluation question, whether descriptive, normative, or cause-and-effect (p. 9).

This list of case study types is not intended to be exhaustive, but it does help provide focus. It is important at this stage to consider what it is that you hope the case will say. Naturally, other factors will impact on the type of case study selected including resources, time-lines, depth of the investigation and consideration of the end users; but these considerations are common to all research endeavors.

Sources of Data

In conducting case studies, one typically uses seven sources of evidence: documentation, file data, interviews, site visits, direct observation, participant observation and physical artifacts. For most case study topics *documentation*, in the form of articles, letters, memoranda, agendas, previous studies and newspaper articles, is generally available. Relevant *file data or archives* may also exist in the form of service or performance records, staff rosters, computer data bases or internal reports and studies. The *interview* is a prime source of case study data. Typically a case study researcher will interview a wide range of respondents which serves two purposes. The first purpose is to add greater depth of understanding to issues that relate to the case at hand. The second purpose is to use the interview to identify key informants who are part of the case. Often key informants have inside knowledge which is critical to the case and these individuals can enhance the validity of the conclusions drawn. Field work is common in case study and consists of two elements, *site visitations*, which permit the researcher to access the phenomena under study, and direct or participant observation. *Direct observation* data can be very helpful for understanding the context, why things are the way they are, based on an accumulation of information garnered from several sources. An alternative or complement to direct observation is participant observation, a role anthropological researchers often assume. *Participant observers* are researchers who join in the regular activities of a community. The value added from this perspective is associated with the opportunity to get closer to people in the study and share a common experience. This can enhance the researcher's insight into interpersonal behaviors and motivations, and build relationships. Finally, *physical artifacts* such as a student's art work or contents of display cases can provide an interesting view about what people, organizations, communities or cultures value.

As with all research methods, the case study researcher must maintain meticulous field notes and record all types of data collected. One of the challenges for researchers, once in the field, is an expansion or alteration of the data sources. This aspect of researching in the real world or life-world may be unavoidable and unplanned, but it is not necessarily negative. Understanding the context of a phenomenon or instance is central to case study research. Therefore, having the researcher immersed into the dynamics of the case study world may in fact bring many benefits such as exposing new data sources, creating opportunities to corroborate findings, and strengthen findings. Because of the unknown dynamic of field research, coupled with the need to allow your sources to be retraced, it is essential that a detailed record be kept of all document sources, including the identities of persons interviewed. This record is often called a *chain-of-evidence*, *data trail*, or *audit trail*.

Instruments

One strength of the case study is its use of multiple data sources; however, it is because of this factor that case studies are not recommended for the novice researcher. To maximize the findings in a case study, researchers will need to incorporate a full range of formal and informal instruments, from questionnaires to observation schedules, hence the requirement for experience and expertise.

Data Collection

As in any methodology, one should have a work-plan that defines what will be done, who will do it, when it will be done and how. However, as case study research often involves extensive field work, one must remain flexible and be prepared to add or alter opportunities to collect data from new sources. As the case study is a part of a contemporary phenomenon, the data collection should be ideally phased

so that the researcher is present as major events occur. This is of particular importance when working with a research team. Because data collection and data analysis
are concurrent activities, it is critical that the primary researcher be involved in
all aspects of collecting data, interpreting and analyzing findings and recasting the
issues as the study unfolds. Think of the detective who must solve a murder after it
is committed — it would be far easier to do if he or she observed the events leading
up to the killing! Of course, like the detective, the researcher can reconstruct some
of the history in order to pick up certain case details, but this is a less desirable
path. If key informants are no longer available, attempting a case may become
questionable.

An important aspect of data collection is the data base you build that will form
the foundation for your required chain-of-evidence. Weak case studies generally
confuse the data with its reporting, whereas the best case studies maintain a separate inventory of data with transcripts, charts, tables, numbers and other evidence
which may not be reported in the case study report but are included as appendices
or can be retrieved by other interested researchers. When I conclude a case study, I
generally finish with a full cardboard box of documents and other evidence which
is archived for possible future reference. This brings us to the next consideration.
When do you stop collecting data in a case study?

Lincoln and Guba (1985) address the issue of when to stop collecting data.
Four simple points guide this decision: 1) stop when you have exhausted all sources of
information; 2) stop when it appears the categories you have identified are defined;
3) stop when you develop a sense that each construct you develop is a regular
occurrence or an anomaly, and 4) stop when the new information being gathered
stretches beyond the boundaries of the study.

A final consideration, associated with collecting data, concerns the extent to
which researchers disclose their personal feelings, values or opinions when engaged
in interviews or participant observation. This type of personal sharing often occurs
in the spirit of building trust, developing relationships or encouraging dialogue; however, researchers are cautioned to think carefully about the possible impact of their
personal disclosures. The effects may be positive or negative, and it would be naïve
to believe that there will be no impact. We are, however, human, as are the people
we study, so ultimately like any ethical decision the choice becomes a subjective
decision of the researcher based on a careful analysis and weighing of the possible
consequences.

Data Analysis

Analyzing data is like walking through a maze. There are many routes available,
some lead you quickly to the end, others force you to choose one path over another,
and some routes lead to a dead end causing you to retrace your steps and try again.
The mass of case study data can present insurmountable problems unless one knows
how to approach the task. Basically data analysis involves four elements: interpreting your findings while in the field, coding and organizing the data into themes and

constructs, searching for disproving themes or evidence, and testing alternative interpretations of the data to see if your understanding of the information changes. As well, analysis involves a great deal of contemplation, reflection, imagination and experience.

Generally, there are two approaches to analyzing the data. One approach is to use an analytical strategy which takes the literature and theoretical background of the case and uses it as an organizational framework. The second approach, the qualitative research approach, organizes the data into descriptive themes that emerged during the data collection and preliminary analysis. The decision to choose the analytic or qualitative approach will depend largely on the type of case study selected and the requirements of the audience who will read and use the information. It is also possible to merge these approaches by first organizing your analysis according to emergent themes, then extending the analysis to examine the findings in consideration of existing literature and theory.

As we have mentioned, the preliminary phase of data analysis occurs while collecting the data and is considered a distinct advantage for case study research. As you learn about the case, new questions may surface, your investigation may be guided in a certain direction, you may begin to develop explanations of causal links between events, or hypotheses may emerge. The information gathered starts shaping the analysis, for the researcher engages in a substantial amount of reflection and interpretation of information and events. This process is a natural element of qualitative research for it is accepted that you, as a researcher, are unable to separate yourself from the research experience. The important thing to remember is to record your ongoing thoughts, ideas for analysis and early themes, for this extends your audit trail from collection to the analysis and strengthens your final discoveries. By having a trail to look back on, even if it is somewhat informal, you are in a better position to: 1) defend choices you made; 2) take a macro-view of why your analysis veered in a particular direction; and 3) guide future researchers who wish to replicate your study.

One useful technique for doing so is called *pattern matching*, where the patterns of relationships observed in one instance are predicted in another. When the two patterns of interaction match, then validity is added to the conclusion. When I conduct case studies, I like to maintain a list of general conclusions learned about the data as they are collected. I then test these conclusions with informants and in my future data collection. They help direct the types of questions to be asked in interviews or the types of statistics to be located and checked and they keep me on track by helping prevent me from returning home without a crucial piece of information. In case study research, the analysis phase takes place as the data are being collected. The opportunity to test them in the field is an advantage of this methodology.

Reporting

"Many a researcher would like to tell the whole story but of course cannot; the whole story exceeds anyone's knowing, and anyone's telling" (Stake, 1996, p. 240).

The choice about what to include, and of equal importance, what not to include is a major decision. I find it useful to think of the professional photographer who takes hundreds of photographs of an historic event. Only two pictures will be published. To get two pictures 'which say it all', it is imperative that the photographer take several rolls of film and take shots from different angles, all the while remaining focused on his goal — the type of photo which says it all. Only once the photographer has developed all the films and analyzed them for clarity, color, lighting, and of course content, can two negatives be selected.

Case study reporting is the same. A great deal of multiple source evidence must be organized, reduced and only the most salient, descriptive examples reported. The content of the report and the presentation format will depend largely on the purpose of the study and the intended audience. Analytic reports may follow a traditional format that subdues the voice of the researcher and presents a rather factual account which includes an introduction, literature review, methodology, findings, discussion and conclusion. An alternative reporting format is reflective — the researcher's voice is heard throughout the report and data are woven into the story. This is typical of case studies that are published as books and not written for academic journals. Here researchers often take license and replace the dry deductive research style with lively narrative, sometimes incorporating suspense and intrigue. Typical formats can be linear, analytic, chronological, theory-building or suspenseful. I organized one case study into various themes suggested by the participants and in this way used the verbatim comments of parents, teachers and students to describe the complexities of an alternative school.

Limitations

Many critics of the case study method argue that it lacks reliability and that another researcher might come to a differing conclusion. In defense of this charge, good case studies create a data base which incorporates multiple data sources and go beyond a single questionnaire or set of interviews. Triangulation is used to interpret findings, test alternative ideas, identify negative cases and point the analysis towards a clear conclusion based on the evidence collected. Findings based on conclusions suggested by different data sources are far stronger than those suggested by one alone.

With respect to internal validity, the strongest argument in favor of the case study is that it incorporates a chain-of-evidence, a tight and interconnected path of recording evidence so that the reader who was not present to observe the case can follow the analysis and come to the stated conclusion. Thus, the case study itself strives for internal validity, trying to understand what is going on in the studied situation.

The extent to which generalizability or external validity is possible will relate to the extent to which a case is typical or involves typical phenomena. It is very difficult to generalize on the basis of one case. Very often, however, multiple cases can be studied, analyzed and conclusions drawn. For example, in looking at case studies of university development in Third World countries, I have been able to observe a number of similarities and common occurrences. These have been turned into what are referred to as 'Lessons Learned'. A lesson is something derived from a given case but which has potential generalizability to other situations and settings. By analyzing a variety of evaluation and case study reports, many international development agencies are developing a corporate memory of lessons learned which can be used in the planning of development projects. Most studies for such agencies now incorporate a section on lessons learned.

Conclusion

Case studies can be extremely illuminating, fun to do and particularly useful in certain fields such as education. Remember, however, that they pose many challenges to the novice who is still apprenticing as a researcher. As a form of research, case studies can also be difficult in terms of theses, publication and academic kudos. They take a long time, often have scant theoretical underpinnings and can be voluminous in their written form. Be sure if you set out on a case study that you know what you are getting into and be clear on why you are doing it.

For Further Study

Lincoln, Y.S., & Guba, E.D. (1985). *Naturalistic inquiry.* Beverly Hills, CA: Sage.

Merriam, S. (1988). *Case study research in education: A qualitative approach.* San Francisco, CA: Jossey-Bass.

Stake, R.E. (1996). Case Studies. In N.K. Denzin & Y.S. Lincoln (Eds.), *Handbook of qualitative research*, pp. 236–47. Thousand Oaks, CA: Sage.

United States, General Accounting Office. (1990). *Case study evaluations.* Transfer Paper 10. 1. 9, Washington, DC: GAO.

Yin, R.K. (1994). *Case study research: Design and methods* (2nd ed.). Beverly Hills, CA: Sage.

Part III

Data Collection

Chapter 16

Data Collection

A major distinguishing feature of research as compared to philosophy, for example, is that it is based on observable and measurable data. Research collects information about the world, processes it, and then through analysis draws conclusions. There is much information to be collected, and many ways of collecting it, but before discussing that it is important to acknowledge that, as researchers, we must be in a position of observing and recording. The great psychologist, Thorndike, argued that if a thing existed, it existed in some amount, and if it existed in some amount, it could be measured. Today, of course, we have a much wider spectrum of what is considered data and valid ways of measuring, but the point still holds.

Recall the distinction between primary and secondary data noted in Chapter 1. Most primary data comes from artifacts, historical documents, observations or directly from people; whereas secondary data normally comes from other people's accounts. Observational data may be recorded electronically, but is then typically converted into some other classification system; the recording is primary data, but the classification or edited version may be secondary. Data from people includes that collected through interviews, various group method discussion techniques, questionnaires, attitude scales, tests and other such measures.

This text has referred to the unit of analysis on several occasions, and this is an essential concept for data collection. You have to understand what your data applies to; you need to understand the intended unit of analysis. If you study a learning problem, your unit of analysis could be a behavior; it could also conceivably be a child. In the former instance you may collect data on different behaviors of a single child; in the latter, you would want to collect data on many children. If we wish to analyze teaching, we are probably interested in teachers and what they do, so the unit of analysis is the teacher. However, if we study learning behaviors, the unit of analysis might be the learner. There are two reasons to be concerned with the unit of analysis. First, we need to employ data collection procedures and instruments that are appropriate for the unit being studied. For example, if we want to study the performance of different schools, it is important to focus on the school as the unit. An example of the type of data that would be appropriate to collect, could relate to the school's performance on such proxy indicators as the proportion who complete 12 years, the proportion who receive a diploma and so forth. While these indicators depend on individual pupils, the data we want is school-level data. Second, if we collect quantitative data and employ tests of statistical significance, we depend on using the correct number of degrees of freedom (generally one less than the number of units being analyzed). If the unit of analysis is classes, we must not confuse this with the total number of pupils or we will get an inflated number of degrees of freedom and the statistical tests may erroneously indicate that the results are significant when they actually are not because the degrees of freedom were smaller.

However we observe and record data, our record has to be both reliable and valid (review definitions of reliability and validity in Chapter 1). The data we collect requires both these properties if they are to support sound research. Reliable, or consistent, data records depend on the instrument used to collect them and the approach used to gather the data. Whether it is a questionnaire, interview protocol, observation schedule, or whatever, it needs to give consistent information every time it is used. That is, it needs to be reliable. The information generated also must be worthwhile information for the purpose at hand — that is, it must be valid. It must inform us about the knowledge, skill or attitude of an individual, the dynamics of a group, the size of a school system or the gross national product of a nation. It is easy to find someone who will offer a number, but that is pointless unless the number means something in the real world.

Collecting the data can be one of the most enjoyable aspects of doing research, but unless you know what you are doing, it can lead to research of poor quality. The urge to get on with it must be tempered with a clear sense of what you want to achieve and skill in how to get the information you need. This part of the book prescribes the basics that you need to collect data that will stand up to scrutiny in its reliability and validity. Of course, only experience and actual practice will polish basic skills and make you a flexible and competent researcher.

Basically, there are four general approaches to data collection: non-personal interaction with a subject (person) who provides data, personal interaction, observation of a setting and examination of documents and artifacts. The data collection itself requires some sort of instrument such as a test, questionnaire or the researcher. Some of the major tools are covered in subsequent chapters. Every approach and data collection instrument has strengths and limitations, as well as reliability and validity considerations. These are summarized in Exhibit 16.1.

The Basic Tools and Techniques

The tools and techniques reviewed in subsequent chapters include:

Sample Survey

Much educational research involves a sample survey from which the results can be generalized to the whole group or target population of interest. A sample survey is a method for collecting data from a sub-sample of the whole group. The intent and purpose is to sample a sufficient number, with the desired characteristics, to permit

Exhibit 16.1:   Approaches to data collection

Approach	Reliability	Validity
Non-personal interaction with a subject who provides data		
Questionnaire	Reliability is a concern when the questionnaire incorporates scales that are sensitive to the subject's moods, etc. Most straightforward multiple-choice questions are answered consistently.	Generally, face validity is the only form used, sometimes with confirmation from a pilot test with a small group. There is no guarantee that people understand the questions or are truthful.
Attitude or personality scale	Scales are typically subjected to statistical checks such as split-half reliability coefficients which equate with the correlation of results between two halves of the scale.	Good scales relate to theory and have years of use and validation with earlier types of instruments presumed to measure the same thing, or they are found to be valid in prediction or use.
Written test	Objectively-scored tests such as multiple choice tests of math ability can have statistical reliability checks. For tests that use essay answers, scoring grids and multiple readers help reliability.	These can be valid measuring instruments, particularly with benchmarking against a known pool of standardized items. Objectively-scored test items can be screened for validity statistically and invalid items can be discarded.
Behavior performance test	Reliability is typically safeguarded by multiple trials (e.g. run the race three times; play the computer simulation again) or a panel of judges (as in international diving competitions).	There is often a close connection between what is being measured and the question being addressed (e.g. How fast the subject can run 100 m).
Personal interaction with a subject who provides data		
Interview	In normative interviews, reliability varies greatly according to interviewer's skill, fatigue, training, etc. The challenge in key informant interviews is to ensure that the subject is consistent over time. Multiple sessions can help.	People typically provide socially acceptable responses which are not valid. About 5 per cent may lie in response to factual questions: 'Do you own a car?'
Focus group	Multiple groups are used to get convergence which takes care of reliability problems.	The group process and multiple groups enable a skilled facilitator to get a valid picture.

Approach	Reliability	Validity
Observation of a setting such as a classroom, meeting, schoolyard		
Expert opinion and criticism	Can be unreliable because it is not guided by an explicit structure; the better experts use an implicit structure which helps.	Highly variable depending on the expert and field. Experts can produce great insights when the quest is one instance of behavior rather than the group norm.
Observation schedule	The most reliable procedures test the schedule and train observers for consistency of ratings.	Given reliable procedures, they are a factual indication of what happened, but not necessarily a record of what is important.
Participant observation	This is always a question, but years of training in qualitative methodology helps participant observers to ensure reliability.	The advantage is that observation takes place in a natural setting, but the interpretation of meaning may not be valid. While it can be checked with informants, it cannot be replicated in another setting.
Examination of documents and artifacts		
Physical/ chemical testing	Can be highly reliable.	Can be valid for dating, analysis of substance composition, etc.
Content analysis	Quantitative data such as word counts are highly reliable; 'soft' aspects of content less so.	Validity relates to the purpose the writer had for producing the document and the researcher's question in studying it.

valid generalization to all cases in the group. This is a well known procedure in polling, and its main purpose is efficiency — to minimize the time and expense of collecting data while preserving the intention of finding out what the whole population is like. Like other data collection techniques, you have to be concerned with reliability and validity.

Questionnaire

Most of us are all too familiar with questionnaires which have come into disrepute due to poorly constructed and executed questionnaire surveys. Chapter 17 describes how to eliminate most of the common problems with the method. A questionnaire survey is:

- a printed or electronic list of questions;
- distributed to a predetermined selection of individuals;
- individuals complete and return questionnaire.

Face-to-Face Interview

Interviews are also familiar to all of us, but unlike everyday interviews, the interview used for research purposes is a highly disciplined endeavour. A face-to-face interview involves:

- personal interaction between an interviewer and an interviewee;
- a dynamic process in which the interviewer asks questions, normally according to a guide or protocol;
- a mechanical or electronic process through which the interviewer records answers.

Telephone Interview

The telephone interview:

- is like a face-to-face interview, but conducted over the telephone;
- involves recording of responses as with a face-to-face interview.

Focus Group

The focus group is another technique that has come into vogue in recent years. A focus group is a group process in which:

- there is group discussion of a predetermined issue or topic;
- group members share certain common characteristics;
- the group is led by a facilitator or moderator;
- the responses are usually recorded by an assistant moderator.

How to Select a Method

With so many methods, how does one select the most appropriate one for the purpose? The four methods described here have both strengths and weaknesses that are listed in Exhibit 16.2.

Consider these strengths and weaknesses when selecting a method. The following chapters provide more detail on the methods, but unless you are able to consider all alternatives you may risk efficiency in your study, or worse, you may employ a method that is inappropriate for your purpose. Remember that the results you get are often a product of the method you use to get them. Some research questions cannot be effectively addressed with some methods, and the question you wish to explore can often be sharpened by your attempts to apply a suitable method with which to explore it.

Exhibit 16.2:   Strengths and weaknesses of four methods of data collection

Strengths	**Weaknesses**
Questionnaire survey	
• highly efficient for routine data collection with a large number of respondents; • lends itself to quantitative analysis and the use of powerful descriptive and inferential statistics; • enables use of large number of questions; • can provide for individual comments and perspectives in the respondent's own words.	• people will not respond due to 'questionnaire fatigue' (leads to non-response bias); • depends on extensive planning and pre-testing of instrument; • always a danger of people not understanding the question — leading to response bias; • conversion of questionnaire answers to computer can result in data entry errors.
Face-to-face interview	
• shows value placed on individual subject; • allows for in-depth analysis and pursuit of details geared to each respondent; • few respondents refuse to be interviewed, leading to 100 per cent response and good validity for the sample interviewed.	• personal nature may lead to people saying things to please, rather than truthfully; • requires careful planning of questions, training if multiple interviewers used; • validity relies on skilled interviewers; • logistically difficult to arrange for efficient interviews; • time-consuming for all parties; expensive; • often difficult to analyze in ways which give clear messages.
Telephone interview	
• has many of the advantages of face-to-face at considerably lower cost; • telephone medium permits rapid coding of responses, on paper or computer; • protocol and answers can be computer-driven.	• Some respondents consider it intrusive, but it can be convenient to respondents if pre-arranged; • the interviewer often cannot maintain the respondent's attention for an extended period.
Focus group	
• uses group synergy to maximize recall and highlight the diversity of perspectives; • provides rich qualitative perspectives; • group process can uncover underlying attitudes.	• requires extensive question-planning and logistics planning; • depends on a skilled group facilitator; • does not lend itself to quantification.

Exhibit 16.3: How to select a method

How to select a method when you use:

Questionnaire Surveys	**Interviews**	**Focus Groups**
• the target population is large (i.e. greater than 200);	• you need to incorporate the views of key people (key informant interview);	• you need rich description to portray underlying attitudes;
• you require a large amount of categorical data;	• the target population is small (e.g. 50), use key informant interviews;	• you believe that group synergy is necessary to uncover underlying feelings;
• your interest in needs assessment requires quantitative data;	• your information needs are for depth rather than breadth;	• it is feasible to assemble a group while avoiding intact groups;
• you want to see the different responses of designated sub-groups, such as male: female;	• you have reason to believe that people will not return a questionnaire;	• you have access to a skilled focus group leader and data recorder;
• you want to clarify your team's objectives by involving them in a questionnaire development exercise;	• the target population is geographically dispersed and telephone interviews are feasible (This method can be used with large groups through normative interviews and quantified responses).	• you want to teach suppliers what the consumer wants through the power of group observation (one-way mirror or video).
• the target population is geographically dispersed;		
• you have access to people who can process and analyze this type of data accurately.		

Summary

The three approaches to data collection from human subjects are compared in Exhibit 16.3.

Chapter 17

Questionnaires

The questionnaire has become one of the most used and abused means of collecting information. If well constructed, a questionnaire permits the collection of reliable and reasonably valid data in a simple, cheap and timely manner. However, there are many sloppy questionnaires and these yield unreliable data of limited validity and utility. The decision to use a questionnaire is often motivated by a need to collect routine data from a large number of respondents who may be in one or several locations, for example, schools within a district. In this situation a questionnaire can be administered to a group at one school or it may be widely dispersed throughout the district. Questionnaires can be efficiently administered by mail; however, unless sufficient care is taken, the rate of return can be a gamble. Researchers who elect to use this form of data collection are cautioned to think carefully before they use questionnaires to gather information which could be gathered in another more efficient or valid way.

A good questionnaire is difficult to construct, and to do the job well it will probably take 10 to 50 hours, including pilot-testing, revision and formatting. While time-consuming, constructing a questionnaire is a good way to sharpen what you really need to know, and if done thoroughly, it will greatly facilitate the data analysis phase of the research. The task of developing and implementing a questionnaire can be accomplished by following the six essential steps outlined in this chapter: determine your questions, draft the questionnaire items, sequence the items, design the questionnaire, pilot-test and revise the instrument, and develop a strategy for data collection and analysis.

Step 1: Determine Your Questions

To develop valid questionnaires, you must first clearly identify your general information needs. What types of information do you require and from whom? Accurately defining your needs is critical and will make it easier to write questions that will answer your research questions and achieve your goals. Different target groups may provide different types of information and a clear understanding of the purpose of the research will help you limit your questions to the relevant information and no more. In a busy world there is no place for questions which might be interesting to ask but are not related to the central theme.

Developing sharp general research questions (see Chapter 4) is an essential step in constructing a questionnaire. As noted in Chapter 14 and illustrated in

Exhibit 14.5, the general questions or issues can be organized into an evaluation or research framework. This framework helps define the overall topic categories for the questionnaire and provides a funnel for developing subquestions. To illustrate, consider the specific, yet broad question, 'Who are the program participants?' This question gives rise to immediate subquestions such as, 'What are the demographic characteristics of the participants?' This in turn can lead to even more specific questions: 'What is the highest level of formal education held by the participants?' 'What is their gender?' 'What is the age distribution of the participants?' These questions themselves are not questions for the questionnaire; rather, they indicate what you want to know.

Every broad research question asked should generate a number of subquestions. If your research relates to a research framework, it will be relatively easy to list many subquestions which are necessary to fill out your understanding of each main issue. Of course, not every subquestion will be addressed in the questionnaire, for certain subquestions may be better answered using another technique such as studying files and documents or interviewing a key informant.

Finally, before drafting the questionnaire items, you should highlight, underline or place a check-mark beside each subquestion that will be addressed through the questionnaire. This will save you time later and help crystalize your thinking. Asking yourself whether each question is absolutely necessary is a challenging task for it is easy to have a lot of questions. It is much harder, yet essential, to restrict yourself to a manageable number of important questions.

Step 2: Draft the Items

Once you have written your research questions and subquestions, questionnaire items will become immediately apparent. Brainstorm as many items for each subquestion as possible to help you gain a full understanding of the breadth and depth of each question. This task complete, you can move on and select the format(s) for the questions. There is an infinite range of question types and many beginners waste time trying to generate creative approaches to questionnaire wording and format. My advice is to master six basic question formats before you attempt alternatives which may get you into trouble. Years of experience have taught me that fill-in-the-blank, multiple choice, comment on, list, Likert scales, and rank order questions will serve most needs and achieve reliable and valid responses. Also, these question formats are familiar to respondents and they should understand how to complete the items. Thus, these six common question formats should serve as models for your work:

Fill-in-the-blank

This common format asks a question and leaves a blank for the response. The stem should be a complete sentence rather than just a phrase. Normally, the answer should not be more than a word, number or phrase (see Exhibit 17.1).

Exhibit 17.1: Sample fill-in-the-blank item

How many management courses have you completed in the past two years?_____

Note that the answer blank follows the question. I prefer it to be on the same print line as the last phrase of the question and of a length appropriate to the length of response expected.

Multiple Choice

Multiple choice questions are similar to fill-in-the-blank questions, except the respondent is given a choice of answers and must check one. Sometimes there are discrete response options (e.g. sex: male or female) in other instances a range of values is presented (e.g. annual income: $10,000–$50,000).

It is preferable to provide the response choices and this requires that you understand and be aware of the range of possible responses. Normally four to eight defined response choices are provided. Distinct choices may make the analysis easier and they provide natural groupings for comparing respondents of various types. Occasionally, a blank response option is included if you feel that the range of responses may be larger than you have identified (Exhibit 17.2). Remember though, blank options in a multiple choice question increase the analytic challenge.

The visual presentation of the multiple choice question is also important. Many people use a line instead of a box, but this confuses some respondents for, in a long list of response options, it is not readily apparent which line corresponds to which choice. When using the box, it should *follow* the answer choice rather than precede it and when possible, answer choices should be listed in a single column. In practice this often consumes too much space, so two columns are used. The danger with more than one column is that people will miss the second column and choose only from the first. The problem is not serious when the choices are in numerical sequence or refer to a defined and inclusive set of options such as one's district of residence.

Exhibit 17.2: Sample multiple choice items

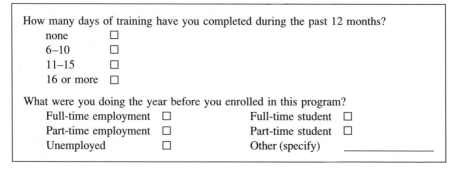

How many days of training have you completed during the past 12 months?
- none ☐
- 6–10 ☐
- 11–15 ☐
- 16 or more ☐

What were you doing the year before you enrolled in this program?
- Full-time employment ☐
- Part-time employment ☐
- Unemployed ☐
- Full-time student ☐
- Part-time student ☐
- Other (specify) _____

Exhibit 17.3:   Sample comment-on item

To what extent did the training session relate to your job needs?

_____

_____

_____

Comment-on

The comment-on question is similar in format to the fill-in-the-blank question, except for one critical difference. The comment-on question attempts to elicit an extensive answer by posing a question and leaving enough space for the respondent to write a short paragraph. While this format is essential for in-depth understanding, such questions should not be overused. They tend to bias the results by giving a greater weight to those who are verbally expressive and tend to evoke responses only from those with extreme views. Furthermore, the information is difficult to analyze and can often be obtained in other ways. Extensive use of these items is a sign that the questionnaire writer has taken an easy route. Thoughtful use of the comment-on question will pay dividends later on if used appropriately. The example in Exhibit 17.3 illustrates this type of question.

As with all questions that require a narrative response, the amount of space you provide will generally indicate the degree of detail you expect. Sometimes a parenthetical note is added instructing the respondent to add extra sheets as necessary.

List

Asking the respondent to list things is a good way to find out views in an unbiased way. This open format forces the respondent to think up answers without having a list of 'acceptable' options from which to choose. In my experience it is best to encourage the respondent to list a specified number of views, say three or five. Otherwise, the responses of a few vocal individuals may outweigh the majority who list very little. If each respondent lists three, then it is easy to conduct a content analysis by counting the number of times each theme is mentioned. Exhibit 17.4 illustrates this approach.

A useful variation on this type of question is to ask for the list *in order of importance*. This provides additional information on the potency of each suggestion and enables you to weight the order during the analysis. Using the modified statement, 'List, in order of importance, the three most important skills you acquired during this training session', the most important skill can be assigned a weight of 3, the second 2, and the third, 1. Thus, in this example, first choices are three times as potent as third choices. Another variation on the list question is to ask the respondent in a subsequent question to pick the one from the list which is most important.

Exhibit 17.4:   Sample list item

List three most important skills you acquired during this training session.

1 _____

2 _____

3 _____

Exhibit 17.5:   Sample Likert scale item

	Strongly Disagree	Disagree	Not Sure	Agree	Strongly Agree
I use research methods in my job	☐	☐	☐	☐	☐

Likert Scales

The Likert Scale is one of the most useful question forms. The scale is named after Rensis Likert who developed this format in 1932. In its most popular form, the respondent is presented a sentence and is asked to agree or disagree on a three, five or seven-point scale, as shown in Exhibit 17.5.

Note that a question is not asked. Rather, a clear statement is made and the respondent is asked to indicate whether the statement reflects his or her views. One secret to having effective Likert scales is to observe the following rules for sentencing:

- Use single sentences containing only one complete thought;
- statements should be short, rarely exceeding 20 words;
- statements should not be in the past tense;
- statements should cover the entire range of expected responses. Those which are likely to be endorsed by almost everyone or by almost no one should be avoided;
- avoid statements that are factual or capable of being interpreted as factual;
- avoid statements that may be interpreted in more than one way;
- avoid the use of universals such as all, always, none and never;
- words such as only, just, merely should be used with care and moderation;
- avoid the use of words that may not be understood by the intended respondents; and
- do not use double negatives.

While Likert scales can have many response points (three to seven being most common), a 5-point scale is the most practical for most common purposes. It is easy to respond to, straightforward to analyze, and sufficient for most needs. Young children, however, are more comfortable with a 3-point or even 2-point scale. The issue of whether or not to have a neutral mid-point is often debated. I lean to having

Exhibit 17.6:   Alternate examples of Likert scales

Strongly approve . . .	Approve . . .	Undecided . . .	Disapprove . . .	Strongly disapprove . . .
Probably right . . .	Right . . .	Doubtful . . .	Probably wrong . . .	Certainly wrong . . .
Much greater . . .	Somewhat greater . . .	Equal . . .	Somewhat less . . .	Not at all . . .
Very high . . .	A little above average . . .	Average . . .	A little below average . . .	Very low . . .
Practically all . . .	Many . . .	About half . . .	A few . . .	Practically none . . .
Like very much . . .	Like somewhat . . .	Neutral . . .	Dislike somewhat . . .	Dislike very much . . .
Everyone . . .	The majority . . .	Quite a few . . .	A few . . .	None . . .
Strongly urge . . .	Approve . . .	Neutral . . .	Slightly disapprove . . .	Strongly disapprove . . .
Favour in all aspects . . .	Favour in most aspects . . .	Neutral . . .	Favour in a few aspects . . .	Do not favour at all . . .
Absolutely true . . .	Probably or partly true . . .	In doubt; divided; open question . . .	Probably or partly false . . .	Absolutely false . . .

a neutral position for two reasons. Without one, some people will leave the item blank or mark a mid-point anyway, and second, research has shown that the proportion of people responding to non-neutral positions when there is no neutral position is similar to the proportion so responding when there is a neutral point and the neutral responders are discarded. On certain items a category of 'not applicable' or 'don't know' category is sometimes added as an extra response option. It may be positioned to either the right or left of the other boxes.

Likert scales provide an excellent means of gathering opinions and attitudes and they can relate to terms other than agree or disagree. Other useful forms of Likert scales are presented in Exhibit 17.6.

Likert scales provide a great deal of information in a short period of time and they lend themselves to simple and effective analysis. Additionally the data can provide descriptive information, or it may be manipulated in more complex way. For example, one may list the findings or use a factor analysis to manipulate the data to look for underlying patterns of responses.

When using a Likert scale, you must include instructions that describe how to complete the scale. Typical instructions are included with the sample questionnaire in Appendix 17.3. In earlier times, much more extensive instructions were given, but today most respondents are familiar with Likert scales and how to complete them.

Exhibit 17.7: Sample rank item

Rank in order of importance the following five weaknesses of the training program. That is, place a 1 beside the weakness you consider most important, a 2 beside the next most important weakness and so forth, until you have ranked all five weaknesses.

<u>Rank</u>

The training program was too short.   _____

The content did not suit my needs.   _____

The content was too theoretical.   _____

The training group was too large.   _____

The training methods were poor.   _____

Rank

In this type of question the respondent is given a list of items and asked to rank them in order of importance (see Exhibit 17.7). A variation on the rank question asks the respondent to check all fitting answers. However, the true rank-order item is more powerful than asking the respondent to check all answers that apply because the act of ranking forces some difficult decisions. It is better to know that most people considered a certain problem the most serious with the training program rather than just one of 10 problems. When using rank questions one should not normally present more than 10 or 12 items since people can become confused. If more items are needed, try modifying the question by asking people to rank the five most important from the whole list and ignore the remainder. Be cautioned however that this may present difficulties. One difficulty with ranked items is the analysis since different respondents will rank more items than will others. Thus, one person's second choice may mean something quite different from another's.

When considering the visual presentation of the rank order question, it is imperative that all response items are listed on one page. Do not split the list between pages or you will get many response errors.

Step 3: Sequence the Items

Good questionnaires, unless they are very short, generally contain subsections. If questionnaire items have been developed within a research framework, then the major questions and subquestions will already be grouped to some degree. If not, you should attempt to refine the groupings into areas with common dimensions. The process is not unlike writing a report with subheadings and corresponding sections. Such sections give structure to the questionnaire and communicate a sense of purpose and order to the respondent. Within each section you will have to sequence the questions to accommodate two different principles. The first principle, related to a common debate about questionnaire writing, is whether or not to group questions on the same topic one after the other, or disperse them throughout the questionnaire. My experience indicates that questions on the same topic should be grouped together and questions of similar form should also be grouped. The second principle is particularly relevant for Likert scale items since one does not want to repeat the instructions too often. Since these two principles are not always compatible, you may have to rewrite some questions or perhaps change the sectioning of the questionnaire so that question types are not constantly shifting back and forth.

Sometimes it is necessary to use *filter questions*. Filter questions funnel out responses with common characteristics and guide the respondent to different branches. For example, participants who attended a particular management training course will be asked to answer questions about it; those who did not take the course will skip those questions and move to another section of the questionnaire. It is necessary when designing branches to make a flow chart from the filter questions. Extensive page flipping should be avoided and respondents should not become confused as they move forward through the questionnaire.

Another sequencing consideration concerns the overall organization of the questionnaire. It should begin with easy, non-threatening questions (see Sudman & Bradburn, 1982). Questions about age, gender, annual income can be threatening and are generally best asked at the end rather than the beginning. The various sections should be organized in logical fashion generally progressing from descriptive type information to more involved attitudes and opinions. Never start a questionnaire with an open question that requires much writing, as this will discourage people and lower the response rate.

Proper sequencing will involve question editing and will aid the overall construction of the questionnaire by identifying redundant or unnecessary questions that can be removed. The questionnaire should be as short as possible to achieve its purpose. Remember, lengthy questionnaires require lengthy analyzes. The permissible length is related to the respondents and their vested interest in the questionnaire. Typically, questionnaires should be limited to two to four pages unless the respondents are highly motivated, in which case up to 16 pages are possible. What motivates a respondent? Certainly, if a respondent believes that the results will affect them or something they believe in, they will be inclined to give it their full attention. Alternately, some respondents are motivated by the promise of a reward for returning the questionnaire.

Step 4: Design the Questionnaire

The format of a questionnaire is extremely important because it is a major factor in determining whether the questionnaire will be completed. An attractive, well laid-out and easy-to-use questionnaire is taken more seriously than one which is thrown together with a minimum of thought. There are two important aspects to design: individual questions and the whole questionnaire. For individual questions, certain types of questionnaire layouts can reduce confusion and contribute to valid responses. As noted earlier, response options for multiple choice, rank or list formats should be in a single column following the question stem. Fill-in-the-blanks or response boxes should follow the question rather than precede it. Likert scale responses can follow the sentence being rated or appear at the right of it.

The second consideration concerns the overall questionnaire format. Years of experience have proven that a booklet format is best. This format is efficient for several reasons. First, questionnaires printed on both sides will appear more slender and less onerous to complete than those which are printed on one side and stapled in the corner. Second, a booklet is simple to use and easy to produce. Third, booklets decrease the paper requirement and, if administered through the mail, they also diminish the postage costs; and finally, it can be produced in a range of sizes, depending on its purpose, but will need to be 4, 8, 12 or 16 pages. If there are more than four pages, it should be stapled in two places along the fold in the manner of a magazine. Because it has to be in four page multiples, the page size needs to be chosen so that the information will fit into a four page combination. Some tolerance regarding this restriction is afforded by the back cover, front cover and even the back and front inside cover pages.

Unless the questionnaire is short (four pages or less), it is advisable to use the first page as a cover. Whether or not a cover is used, the questionnaire should have a suitable title, and there should be an introductory paragraph. The paragraph not only introduces the purpose of the questionnaire, but it should mention whether the responses are confidential, indicate that all questions are to be completed and, in the case of mailed questionnaires, identify where to return the completed questionnaire.

The various sections and questions should be organized to make efficient use of the available space. Where possible, sections should be self-contained and begin at the top of a page. Care must be taken to ensure that individual questions are not split but are intact on a single page. As with any layout, there should be a visually pleasing amount of white space. Questions must not appear crowded. Open-ended comment questions can serve to open spaces and number of response lines can be expanded to fill the page. Generally, questions are numbered sequentially throughout the questionnaire.

In some situations, a questionnaire may need to be sent in two languages. For example, in Canada, French and English are often required. In such cases one questionnaire should be in two languages, one on the flip side of the other and both working into the centre. Some people may be inclined to send one copy of each unilingual questionnaire, however some respondents find this offensive and this can bias the results. Respondents, regardless of linguistic preference, should be treated identically and should be able to respond in their language of choice.

Occasionally, questionnaires are precoded. That is, they include numbers in small print adjacent to each possible answer to aid the data entry operator (Appendix 17.2). Personally, I try and avoid the use of precoding as it depersonalizes an instrument which is already somewhat cold. The procedure is not all that necessary when there are only 100 or 200 questionnaires. Once numbers get into the 1000's however, precoding is probably necessary. Exhibit 17.8 summarizes the fundamental steps in questionnaire design.

Exhibit 17.8: Six rules to aid questionnaire design

---

1 Lay out items to avoid confusion
- use the formats shown in the examples;
- do not change pages in the middle of a question;
- give instructions on what you want the respondent to do for each type of question;
- number the questions consecutively.

2 Use a booklet
- to make it professional;
- to facilitate flip side French/English versions.

3 Include a title and introductory explanation
- to let your clients know what you are doing;
- to help them fill it out properly.

4 Organize into sections, each with a title
- to help structure thinking;
- to facilitate analysis.

5 Group similar types of items together
- especially rating scales;
- fill-in-the-blank and multiple choice can be mixed.

6 Use all available space
- try to limit it to 4 pages;
- use space for comments to fill in pages;
- ensure it is visually appealing to the eye.

Step 5: Pilot-test the Questionnaire

It is always difficult to criticize your own written work and in developing questionnaires it is essential to obtain comments from at least a small group of the intended respondents. Pilot-testing will identify ambiguities in the instructions; it will help clarify the wording of questions, and it may alert you to omissions or unanticipated answers in multiple choice or ranking questions. Normally, individual questions will be vetted before the draft questionnaire is assembled. The pilot-testing permits overall reactions including comments on the length of the questionnaire.

An effective way to pilot-test a questionnaire is to assemble a group of 6 to 12 volunteers and have them complete the questionnaire individually. Encourage them to write marginal comments on the actual questionnaire, then follow-up with a group discussion. After the pilot-test, review the verbal and written comments, the questionnaire responses and evaluate its effectiveness. Then if required, revise the instrument. If major changes are necessary a second pilot test is advisable.

Step 6: Develop a Strategy for Data Collection and Analysis

Now you have a questionnaire ready to go! You will need to work out a strategy for how and where to send it. The first part of your strategy is to select a representative sample that represents all the subjects you want to reach. Then prepare a list. The second part of your strategy is to decide on the technology you will use to send out your questionnaire. There are three basic options:

1 *Standard*
   Questionnaires can be printed, in your office or by a printer, and mailed to respondents. Respondents fill them out and mail them back. Alternatively, sometimes it is possible to administer them in a group meeting with the targeted respondents. Results are manually entered into a database or statistical program for analysis.

2 *Optical Scanning*
   It is possible to print questionnaires so that they can be read by an optical scanner that picks up the responses automatically. This approach is only beneficial when you have hundreds of questionnaires. Smaller samples probably do not justify the printing and set-up costs.

3 *Electronic Questionnaires*
   The advent of electronic communication has created yet another way to administer a questionnaire. Sending questionnaires via electronic mail (e-mail) is growing in popularity for professionals, organizations and individuals networked through the Internet. This form of questionnaire is designed on a computer and sent as a computer file to the subject via e-mail. The respondent receives the file, completes the questionnaire on his or her computer, and e-mails the file back to you. This is most useful for in-house surveys, such as within a school system.

Develop Cover Letter and Send Questionnaire

Every successful questionnaire comes with a cover letter (Appendix 17.1). The letter should contain six pieces of information:

- the purpose of the questionnaire;
- who is sending it;
- why the respondent was selected;
- where, how and when to return it;
- whom to contact if there are further questions; and
- whether and how the results will be shared.

When contacting respondents ensure each subject receives a cover letter, a professionally developed questionnaire and a self-addressed return envelope, unless you are transmitting electronically.

Monitor Returns and Follow-up Distribution Strategies

You should count on four to six weeks to receive responses to your questionnaires. If your returns are slow, consider one or more follow-up strategies. First start by tracking the number of questionnaires returned daily (e-mail lets you know who has not yet replied). Then send a reminder two weeks after the first mailing. If this reminder does not stimulate an adequate return, consider an alternate distribution system such as developing a *pyramid network*. Pyramid networks use key people to pass out and collect questionnaires on your behalf. Generally, personal networks are the best way to get a high level of returns.

Data Entry

As soon as the first questionnaires are received you can begin entering the data into a data base. It is useful to number each questionnaire with a code number that can be used for such purposes as labeling qualitative comments or to verify a response if required. Precoded questionnaires can be entered directly. Questionnaires that have not been precoded should first be coded. To code a questionnaire, you simply write code numbers that correspond with the data entry template or code-book on each questionnaire. Code numbers can be used for quantitative or qualitative data.

A vital part of the data entry process is to check the validity of data entry. Many professionals enter the data twice and compare the two entries for accuracy. If you do not do this, it is essential to employ an expert to enter the data. My preference is to use an expert then a series of statistical analyzes which check for outliers (scores that fall beyond the normal expected range).

Data Analysis

There are many approaches to questionnaire data analysis. When using quantitative data, start your analysis when responses dry up. I like to begin with computing the basic statistics for all items on the questionnaire: frequency distributions, means, standard deviations and measures of skewness. This permits me to see that each item has variance (spread in responses) and that the patterns are reasonable. For example, if everyone checked the same answer category, there may be a coding error or the item may have been misunderstood. Sometimes respondents write comments on their questionnaire (e.g. 'I don't understand this question!') that help you figure out what is going on. This phases identifies the background characteristics of the respondents so that they can be compared to the target population. If there is a good match (assuming you know something about the target population), then you have some assurance that your sampling strategy worked.

The next phase probes the data in more statistically dynamic ways. My strategy is to begin by comparing groups (e.g. males vs. females) using cross-tabulations or graphs. I also examine interrelationships among variables using correlations and related statistics. This phase of analysis is the most interesting and soon highlights what is going on. Generally, you can tell pretty quickly whether you have findings that support your research agenda or not.

Qualitative data are generally scanned as they come in and reviewed immediately to get a feeling for the range of responses and to determine the context(s) from which people are responding. Once all the questionnaires have been processed, they are sorted into files for analysis. Sometimes, a predetermined group is prescribed, such as when you want to see how people in one region respond. In other cases, the sorts are derived from the quantitative analysis. Qualitative data often supplement quantitative findings by exposing information that might otherwise remain a mystery.

Conclusion

Well constructed questionnaires permit researchers to gather reasonably valid quantitative and qualitative data in a simple, timely and cost efficient manner. This chapter has presented how to develop and implement a questionnaire in six steps. These steps and their major components are summarized in Appendix 17.2. By following these six steps you should be able to produce an effective questionnaire for your research project. Because questionnaires are so important in educational research, I have included a complete sample questionnaire (Appendix 17.3) and the cover letter for a study that evaluated training taken by supervisors in industry (Appendix 17.1).

Developing a questionnaire requires thought, care and time, but the end product can be satisfying. Questionnaires lend themselves to logical and organized data entry and analysis for both quantitative and qualitative findings.

For Further Study

Sudan, S., & Bradburn, N.M. (1982). *Asking questions*. San Francisco: Jossey-Bass Publishers.

Chapter 18

Inquiry Protocols

Interviewing for research purposes must follow a plan related to the objectives one wants to achieve in the data collection. It is not sufficient merely to meet with people and conduct an informal chat. One should plan the interview in great detail and write down the questions in modified questionnaire form. This type of data collection tool is called an interview protocol or schedule. For some purposes I also use an interview guide that is merely a list of five or six topics. The subject of this chapter is protocols and schedules which are more elaborate forms of instrument. The purpose of this chapter is to provide guidance on how to develop an effective interview protocol.

Effective protocols vary greatly in detail and in the amount of research and development they require. An elite interview with a head of state may have relatively few planned and written questions, but these will be supported by weeks or months of careful research and planning on the part of the interviewer who is also the person intimately involved with preparation of the protocol. On the other extreme, a relatively routine protocol for a normative interview might require considerable planning and detailed instructions, including standardized replies for the interviewer and coding sheets to record the responses. Such interviews are frequently undertaken by a team of interviewers, so there needs to be standardization as well as a natural but explicit flow that suits all types of interviewers.

Unlike a questionnaire, the interview protocol must address process issues as well as content. The way that you plan to proceed with an interview is not typically shared with the respondent (though sometimes a summary of headings or list of issues is exchanged), so the respondent does not know what questions are coming later. One advantage for the interviewer is the ability to gain the respondent's confidence before asking what might otherwise be threatening questions. A disadvantage is the tendency of many respondents to get ahead of the interviewer and take the lead, destroying the sequence which has been prepared, resulting in a disjointed interview in which the interviewer may leave without critical information. You will have to judge the amount of detail your protocol requires, but these seven steps should help guide you through the process of organizing and creating an effective interview protocol.

Step 1: Determine your General and Specific Research Questions

As with all types of structured data collection one must have a clear idea of the objectives for the interview and the data needs of the researcher. Similar to constructing a questionnaire, your information needs can be determined effectively with a research framework that includes your questions and subquestions. If you have not done so, review steps 1 and 2 in Chapter 17 on questionnaire construction.

The interview is generally a one-time event, so if you miss essential data the first time you may not have a chance to get it later. Every part of the interview has a purpose and you should think about the reason for asking every question before you include it. At this stage you are focusing on the content concerns of the interview only. Process concerns will be addressed later.

Step 2: Draft the Interview Questions

Using a process similar to that involved in questionnaire construction, you can begin drafting the interview questions, however the form of questions may differ. As with questionnaires, all questions must be carefully drafted and worded to minimize ambiguity. It is useful when drafting questions for an interview to distinguish between open questions and closed questions.

Open questions ask for broad or general information. They put few restrictions on how the interviewee might answer. For example, 'How do you feel about the merger of the two schools?' Such open questions have a great value in many circumstances. They help discover the respondent's priorities and frame of reference. They give recognition to the respondent and satisfy a communication need by letting the individual talk through his or her ideas while you listen. They tend to be easy to answer and pose little threat since there are no right or wrong answers. They also reveal the depth of a person's knowledge and might enable you to evaluate the degree of emphasis to put on their response. These open questions are the major type used in key informant interviews. Open questions also have distinct limitations. They consume a lot of time and energy. They make it difficult to control the interview, placing more stress on the interviewer's skill; recording and tabulating answers is more difficult.

Closed questions, on the other hand, are specific and frequently restrict the options available to the respondent. There are three types of such questions: The multiple-choice question provides for a list of answers. The bipolar question essentially gives a yes or no option. Third is a specific factual question to which the interviewer does not know the possible response. For example, 'Where did you complete your undergraduate degree?' The advantages of closed questions is that they save you time and energy, they enable you to classify and record easily. They also apply well when there are multiple interviewers dealing with a large sample. Of course, these closed questions are limited in that they do not let you know how much information the respondent really has about the question and in some cases the respondent may not like the available options and cannot easily respond. In general, open and closed questions are complementary and often work together to provide a balanced, smooth-flowing yet controlled interview.

In some cases it is helpful to present the respondent with a rating scale or other device. In the case of a face-to-face interview, one can use cards made up as visual aids to show the respondent the rating scale, or to enable the respondent to sort options into choice-categories or otherwise to convey in-depth information. Such techniques are useful only with normative interviews — interviews that collect data to be classified and statistically analyzed.

There are various possible problems in how the questions are phrased. Exhibit 18.1 provides examples of five of the most common problems in interview questions. Interviewers often get into trouble because they violate basic rules. The following problems should be avoided:

Exhibit 18.1: Tips on asking questions

Question Type	Example and Recommendation
Double-barreled	• Have you ever experienced burn-out and what do you do to prevent it? • Avoid double-barreled questions. Ask one question at a time. Do not combine questions and expect an answer.
Two-in-one	• What are the advantages and disadvantages of working in a private school? • Do not combine opposite positions in one question. Separate out the parts and things will be much clearer.
Restrictive	• Do you think that female school administrators are as good as male school administrators? • The phraseology of this question eliminates the possibility that females might be better. Avoid questions which inherently eliminate some options.
Leading	• Bill 101 which forces 'immigrant' children into French schools in Quebec has been challenged in the courts on the grounds that it violates the Canadian charter of Rights and Freedoms. What do you think of Bill 101? • Do not precede questions with a position statement. In this type of question, the interviewer states a view or summarizes the position of a current or recent event and then asks for a response. This tends to lead the respondent in a given direction.
Loaded	• Would you favour or oppose murder by agreeing with a woman's free choice concerning abortion? • Avoid questions which are emotionally charged and use loaded words.

Step 3: Sequence the Questions

A variety of questions is essential if an interview is to be interesting and natural. Generally, it is best to organize the questions into blocks on various themes. Just like a questionnaire or research paper, each section stands on its own with its own inherent structure and integrity. Within this section you may vary the question types, though, in some sections it will make more sense to keep them all closed. It is generally a good rule to mix closed questions with open-format questions. By organizing the questions into sections you will also be in a position to convey the major themes to the interviewee and will be able to judge your timing.

Sometimes special question sequencing techniques are used for a particular purpose. Many structured interviews use *funneling techniques*, moving from general questions to specific questions, or vice versa. A funnel sequence, moving from the general to the specific, will help develop a logical progression for responses, and it will help the respondent to communicate pieces of information in a loosely connected fashion. If an inverted funneling sequence is used, the interviewer will begin with specific questions and then move to general questions. This type of sequence is often used with respondents who exhibit shyness. By answering specific questions, the respondent may gain confidence which will enhance the possibility for greater expression later.

As with questionnaires, interviews also frequently incorporate branches. Various *filter questions* are used to direct the interview along different paths. For example, a person might be asked which university program he or she has completed. A graduate in engineering might then be asked different questions than a graduate in the arts. You will, of course, have to try various orders among and within the sections in order to provide a natural flow to the interview.

Step 4: Consider your Process Needs

The interviewer must manage the interview process, and the protocol may also reflect this concern. A question as simple as 'How are you?' is asked for a reason. If you forget the reason, you might spend the whole afternoon discussing the respondent's state of health!

Between each block of questions you will need a transition which moves from one theme to the next. Transitions are useful in giving both the interviewer and interviewee a constant reminder of where the interview is going. Abrupt transitions leave the interviewee questioning whether you might not have liked the responses. Essentially, transitions provide a summary of where you have been, where you are going and perhaps why.

At strategic locations throughout the protocol it is often helpful to place personal reminders to paraphrase or summarize. It is also sometimes useful to list standard probes or questions, to move along the process, clarify what is intended, and so forth.

Step 5: Prepare the Introduction and Closing

The protocol begins with an introduction. It states the purpose of the interview, who the interviewer is and why the interview is taking place. It clarifies any questions about the research and informs the respondent about confidentiality and the use of data. Permission to use recording devices and so forth is obtained at this stage. The introduction indicates how long the interview will be and sometimes provides an overview of the major topics to be discussed. The issue here is to provide relevant information quickly and efficiently without cutting off the respondent's questions. This is very important in setting the tone of the interview and in establishing a rapport with the respondent.

Finally, the interview contains a closing. All interviews should be brought to a definite close so that the interviewee does not wonder whether this is the end. A verbal statement can be used to signify the end and a nonverbal gesture such as rising, shaking hands or opening the door will surely convey the message. The closing should be reinforcing and leave both people with a sense of accomplishment. A final summary or reference to a particularly helpful contribution will do this. Finally, the interviewer should thank the respondent, confirm any arrangements for follow-up or sharing the research results and enable the researcher to exit easily.

Step 6: Prepare for Recording the Responses

A final consideration is what is to be done about a record of the interview. If the interview is with a key informant respondent whose every word has potential significance, it would be wise to tape record the interaction. If you do so, be sure to get permission, preferably in advance of the session and use an unobtrusive recording device. Such things are easily forgotten and ignored, whereas a microphone in the centre of a table can put some interviewees on edge and affect their responses. The major difficulty with tape recording is the inordinate amount of time required to listen to the tapes. My preference is to record responses during the interview on the interview protocol or in a stenographic notebook. The latter is easy to use on one's knee and the spiral binding reduces it to a single page in front of you at any time. For normative interviews, the interview protocol can be organized with check-off boxes and space for efficient data recording.

Remember too, that taking copious notes may slow down the interview considerably. It is probably best to take brief notes and to reconstruct the interview later. My preferred method is to take written notes and immediately following the interview, dictate a summary into a portable mini-cassette recorder. The facts and perspectives are then fresh and can be dictated and forgotten, keeping the mind unencumbered for the next interview. This approach was critical for one of my doctoral students doing research with senior citizens. These respondents did not want to be quoted and would not even consent to a notebook! If you wait until the end of the day and have done several interviews, the responses become blurred and impossible to separate. On a couple of recent occasions both in Asia and Southern Africa, I brought a portable laptop computer and typed in a summary immediately following each interview. Two interviewers are a great advantage for reconstructing and validating what the interviewee said and intended.

Step 7: Pilot-test the Interview Protocol

While it is important to test a questionnaire to ensure that the wording will be understood, it is doubly important to validate an interview protocol. Here, as well as the content, you also have to validate the flow, the physical utility of the form of the protocol and the arrangements you have made to record the responses.

If you are using interviewers other than yourself, you have the added problem of ensuring that they can deal with your protocol. Such interviewers will need to be trained to use your protocol and ideally, they should be monitored in its use over several interviews or simulations.

Conduct the Interviews

The protocol will enable you to collect the data following the suggestions of the subsequent chapter.

Analyze the Data

Data analysis depends on the type of interviews you conduct. For normative interviews, similar techniques to those used for questionnaire analysis are used. For key informant interviews you need to use more analytic creativity to process what you have found. Ask yourself to portray the key views of these respondents as a group. What did you learn that you expected? What did you learn that was new? Which views are shared? Which views differ? Is it possible to account for differing views based on characteristics of the respondent? You may want to use direct quotes to illustrate the findings. Often such quotes tell more about the situation in few words than you can in a whole paragraph. Be sure, however, to select a balanced representation of comments.

Conclusion

By following the steps in Exhibit 18.2, you should be able to develop an effective interview protocol. The protocol used for the supervisory development needs assessment described in previous chapters is presented in Appendix 18.1.

A good interview schedule won't eliminate all the problems in this form of data collection, but it helps. I recently returned from a field mission in the Caribbean where I conducted many interviews. I began the trip with my protocols carefully pasted into my field notebook. The first interview is always the hardest because you are not yet immersed into the subject and its jargon. I arrived for my first interview and discovered that I had left my notebook at the hotel! On that occasion I was saved by good planning: a second set of protocols in my briefcase.

Exhibit 18.2:   Developing an interview protocol

1 Determine your general and specific research questions
   - what do you intend to find out?
   - what information is essential from the interview?

2 Draft the interview questions
   - draft open questions;
   - draft closed questions.

3 Sequence the questions
   - group into topic sections;
   - vary question type;
   - arrange sections in sequence.

4 Consider your process needs
   - prepare suitable transitions;
   - prepare probes, process questions.

5 Prepare the introduction and closing
   - record verbal statements;
   - note non-verbal statements.

6 Prepare for recording the responses
   - decide on general method;
   - organize protocol for written responses.

7 Pilot test the interview protocol
   - pilot-test;
   - revise as necessary.

For Further Study

Frey, James, H. (1983). *Survey research by telephone*. Vol. 150, Sage Library of Social Research, Thousand Oaks CA: Sage.

Sudan, S., & Bradburn, N.M. (1982). *Asking questions*. San Francisco: Jossey-Bass.

Chapter 19

Successful Interviews

The interview is probably the most widely used method of data collection in educational research. Interviews can be conducted on all subjects by all types of interviewers and they can range from informal incidental sources of data to the primary source of information used in a research study. When used with care and skill, interviews are an incomparably rich source of data, but seldom are inexperienced researchers sufficiently familiar with the requirements for a good interview or sufficiently practiced in the requisite interviewing skills. Perhaps the commonness of the interview is its major downfall. We use interviews in all walks of life for a wide range of purposes and to use it for research purposes requires more care and skill than is commonly exercised. While everyone conducts interviews to some degree, few do it well. This chapter discusses various types of interviews, describes the planning requirements and how to structure an interview protocol.

An interview is defined as a specialized form of communication between people for a specific purpose associated with some agreed subject matter. Thus, the interview is a highly purposeful task which goes beyond mere conversation. There are many advantages to the interview as a method of data collection. People are more easily engaged in an interview than in completing a questionnaire. Thus, there are fewer problems with people failing to respond. Second, the interviewer can clarify questions and probe the answers of the respondent, providing more complete information than would be available in written form. It is this opportunity for in-depth probing that makes the interview so attractive when dealing with informed respondents. Third, interviewing enables the interviewer to pick up non-verbal cues, including facial expressions, tones of voice and, in the case of interviews conducted on the respondent's turf, cues from the surroundings and context.

There are also disadvantages. It is often difficult to record responses, particularly if the interviewer is also responsible for writing them down. Second, the quality of responses, that is their reliability and validity, is dependent on the interviewer. Different interviewers may obtain different answers, particularly if questions, procedures and techniques are not standardized. Third, the context, which has the advantage of providing useful non-verbal information, has the disadvantage of sometimes affecting responses due to interruptions and pressures of time.

Types of Interview

There are basically two types of interviews categorized according to purpose: *normative* and *key informant*. Normative interviews are used to collect data which is classified and analyzed statistically. Common examples of normative interviews are those used in mass surveys by pollsters and researchers intent on finding the views of large numbers of people to fairly straightforward questions. In essence, these routine interviews are little more than a questionnaire but in oral form. Questions are always worked out carefully in advance and the interviewer codes the responses on a form.

The other type of interview is called a key informant interview and is for a different purpose. The researcher is not interested in statistical analysis of a large number of responses, but wants to probe the views of a small number of elite individuals. A key informant interview is one directed at a respondent who has particular experience or knowledge about the subject being discussed. The person might be a school principal who has in-depth knowledge of what goes on in the school or it could be a head of state or other significant person who is unique. In the latter case, there may be only one respondent in the sample and the key informant interview becomes of prime importance in collecting the necessary data. This is frequently used in historical research where someone involved with the history discusses it.

Normative interviews often include many interviewers all of whom are trained to ask questions in a similar way. Their own knowledge of the subject is of far less consequence than is their ability to interview for reliable and valid responses. On the contrary, with key informant interviews the interviewer should be expert in the subject under discussion. He or she must be in a position to grasp new information and use it to pursue new directions. The interviewer is interested in building understanding and in this sense the key informant interview is a teaching situation in which the respondent teaches the interviewer about events and personal perspectives. Unless the interviewee is unique, researchers generally combine approaches by collecting normative data on selected questions and continue the interview to obtain more elite type of information on questions requiring more personal and conceptual perspectives.

Interview Contexts

There can be many contexts for interviews which may encompass a variety of settings and from two to a large number of participants. The typical interview includes two people, and when face-to-face, most often takes place at the respondent's place of work, whether home, office or school. While I have interviewed busy people over lunch or on airplanes, it is preferable to conduct the interview in a setting where one's full attention can be devoted to the interview. My own research has included interviews in the Canadian bush, in mud huts in Africa and in the offices of prime ministers and many other highly placed government officials. All of these settings work, providing that the session is relatively uninterrupted and seating can be arranged to provide for the process needs of the interview as discussed later.

Interviewing by telephone is one of the most commonly used research techniques because it is quick and economical. No other data collection technique can provide such a fast return of data from geographically dispersed people. Sampling can be precisely targeted. One knows the refusal rate which is generally as low as 7 per cent in popular surveys and polls. People who are often difficult to reach in person can sometimes be reached by telephone, and the fact that one is not on view often facilitates people answering honestly. Of course, people require a telephone to be interviewed in this way. There are other disadvantages as well. The interview must be shorter for telephone use than for personal interviewing. Complicated explanations and visual aids such as response cards or diagrams cannot be used to aid the respondent nor can the interviewer depend on visual cues from respondents that might reveal a misunderstanding of the question or boredom with the interview. The effectiveness of research interviews by telephone can be greatly enhanced when there is precontact, either by letter or phone, arranging a precise time for the telephone interview to take place. In some cases, written information can be sent to the respondent in advance and it can be reviewed and considered prior to the phone call. With good planning and good techniques, there should not be a major difference between the validity of data obtained in telephone interviews and those obtained face-to-face. Telephone interviewing is greatly facilitated when one wears a telephone receptionist's headset as that frees up both hands for holding the protocol or writing. I have begun to conduct telephone interviews using a protocol on my computer screen and can type in the responses into appropriate spaces in the protocol. Once voice-activated word processing becomes commonplace, data recording should be a delight!

In some cases, there might be more than one interviewer and there can be more than one respondent. Key informant interviews are often highly effective when there are two interviewers who are experienced in working together and who can bounce the questioning back and forth so that one can pick up things that the other would have missed. When there is more than one respondent, one has the advantage of synergy within the group. The responses of one person trigger responses of another and one can get more complete data than if each individual were interviewed alone. Of course, in this case the responses within the group also bias what other people might have said and one must be careful to ensure that the overall group response is valid. One of the major difficulties when there are several respondents is the problem of recording responses. Often the responses come fast and furious and it is difficult for one person to record them, particularly when the interviewer is also responsible for pursuing points of interest and generally guiding the process.

Focus groups occur when a group of people focus on a particular topic and discuss it fully with the leader. I have sometimes used the technique following a 15-minute pre-session in which each participant completes a short written questionnaire. For example, in conducting a follow-up study on the effectiveness of a job-related training course, I was able to use such a procedure to obtain both normative and focus group data. On that occasion, I observed that the normative data in the written questionnaire disagreed with the central thrust elicited by the group, presumably because of the group sanction of critical and negative feedback.

One of the most challenging settings is in developing countries where government officials are being interviewed with respect to development assistance programs. There are generally several problems to overcome. In these cases, the interview may be highly formal, sometimes including a whole delegation of officials from the Canadian embassy and an equal number from the host government. The challenge for the team leader in such settings is to control the questioning and not let unbriefed members of the Canadian team interrupt the flow by asking questions which do not relate to the purpose of the visit. Of course, there is an added difficulty in that the respondents have a stake in the result and will try to portray things in a way that furthers their interests. The process itself is also a concern as it often follows official protocols and may not allow for a free and relaxed dynamic. Generally, the most senior person does most of the talking and one must direct questions to technical and support people through the senior official. Thus, the responses tend to be guarded rather than candid. At the extreme, such interviews are conducted in two languages and the exchange is filtered through a translator. Also, these are cross-cultural interviews in which for both linguistic and cultural reasons people may not easily understand one another's perspectives. Finally, there can be technical difficulties. I have found in Africa and the Caribbean that the low bass voice of many respondents, coupled with the din of an air conditioner makes it difficult to hear what the respondent says. Numbers are particularly problematic with 15 and 50 sounding identical. I recently interviewed a Ukrainian respondent who pronounced 'Italian' so it sounded like 'Thailand'. The only defense is to sit close, but even that is subject to social custom. On several occasions I have saved the day by inviting people to lunch where the central air conditioning, being less noisy, allowed for interpretable conversation.

Planning for a Successful Interview

The next chapter discusses the important step of developing an interview protocol. After the protocol has been developed and tested, several factors need to be considered in order to carry out an actual interview. One needs to arrange the appointment giving some idea of the interview's purpose and how long it is expected to take. On the question of length, most interviews should not exceed 40 minutes. Elite interviews, however, can last hours and may even be phased over several sessions. However, for normative interviews if you can not cut through to the substance in that length of time then there is probably a problem with planning or interviewing technique.

The location is important. If the interview is to be conducted in a busy office where there are many interruptions, the interview process could be affected profoundly. It is best then to find a quiet, uninterrupted place and time for the interview, or failing that, ask the respondent to hold phone calls and other interruptions. I once conducted an interview in Swaziland which was interrupted by five entrances of other people and seven phone calls! Needless to say, the process was more than a little discontinuous.

A second consideration is the physical arrangement of furnishings and seating. My experience includes an interview with a senior Permanent Secretary in Asia where we were seated at opposite ends of a small couch while photographers shot flash pictures throughout the interview. On many other occasions large desks or tables found themselves between me and the interviewee. In such instances protocol dictates that the senior official determine where people sit, so there is not much that can be done to control it. If one meets on neutral territory or the situation otherwise allows it, it is best to sit facing the interviewee.

Effective communication requires a degree of trust between interviewer and interviewee. It helps in establishing this trust to be like the person being interviewed. A common background of age, education, social class, employment status and manner of speech is helpful. It is very difficult for a 20-year-old researcher to interview a senior manager in his sixties. Be sure to dress the part. Few Canadian school principals would welcome being interviewed by someone wearing jeans and a T-shirt. School children might relate better if you were not wearing a tie. As a general rule, wear something similar to what you presume your interviewee will wear.

Conducting Effective Interviews

Effective interviewing relies on sound planning, skills which can be developed by practice, a cooperative interviewee and sometimes considerable good luck. For effective interviewing the interviewer needs to control both the content and the process of the interview. The content is controlled largely by the protocol and the nature of the questions. If the objectives are clear and one uses appropriate techniques there should be few occasions when you leave without the content you need. To help ensure validity and to accomplish the task pleasurably and efficiently, good process skills are required. The basic structure of the interview lies in the messages sent and the responses obtained about a particular subject and as such the two major roles are those of the interviewer and the interviewee or respondent. The interviewer and the respondent enter into a kind of interactive relationship in which communication becomes a two-way street. The interviewer sends a message which the respondent receives. The respondent processes the message and sends a response. The response is received and processed by the interviewer and so on. Both interviewer and respondent act as senders and receivers. It is this passing of messages from one party to the other which offers the greatest challenge for reliability and validity. As we all know, much distortion can occur when messages are communicated verbally. Sometimes the cause is in the way the message was sent and sometimes it is in the manner in which it is received. The researcher must be particularly sensitive to this source of error and must take steps to ensure valid responses.

Initial attitudes may influence the rapport between the interviewer and respondent. If a respondent dislikes an interviewer or has any negative feelings towards the interviewer, it is unlikely that the respondent will be open to the questions being posed. It is also important for the interviewer to know that he or she may reflect a particular attitude simply because of the tone that is used in phrasing a question. If as an interviewer, you are self-assured or lack confidence, these dispositions may also send certain messages to your respondent. The interviewer must be aware of the many ways that attitudes can shape an interview.

Cross-cultural interviews can be among the most challenging, and in this there is no substitute for adequate cross-cultural knowledge. For example, traditional Chinese respondents want to receive the questions days in advance, presumably so that they can ponder their response and not be put in an awkward position regarding 'face'. Unfortunately, in western culture, we rely on spontaneity to uncover underlying views; in China that does not work. In Thailand, you must not cross your legs so that the sole of your foot faces the person you are with. It is hard to conduct an interview if you transgress such a rule before you begin. Another difficulty can be the pattern of language used in different cultures. In India, and some other parts of Asia, people ask a question by giving a lengthy and unimportant introduction followed by the important aspect at the end of the paragraph. In our culture, we do just the reverse. Unless you understand and compensate for this difference, this results in a total mismatch in communication: the Indian expects the important aspect to be in our conclusion, whereas we present it up front, leaving the conclusion for redundant repetition. Even more difficult is to conduct interviews in cultures such as that of the Cree of northern Canada who have a culture that is not verbal. The Cree understand by careful observation and non-verbal interaction. In such a context, should one use the interview as the primary data collection tool? If you are involved in cross-cultural interviewing, be sure to learn about the culture and adjust your data collection approach before you begin.

Effective communication is also affected by expertise. Perhaps the greatest hallmark of effective communication is one's facility to use language. All of us have experienced a situation where we could not quite get someone to see a situation as we saw it. We were not able to make the description of a situation as vivid to our audience as it was to us. This was probably due to the fact that we could not find the proper words to serve us adequately. In the interview process, it is extremely important that questions are understood. Checks for clarity must be made to ensure the respondent's interpretation is correct. In the same way, the interviewer must also check whether he or she has understood the message that has been sent.

Basic Interviewing Skills

Active Listening

It is important to attend or listen actively to the respondent. Good attending behaviour demonstrates respect and that you are interested in what the respondent has to say. By utilizing attending behavior to enhance the individual's self-respect and to establish a secure atmosphere, the interviewer facilitates free expression thereby enhancing validity.

In order to attend to the interviewee, the interviewer should be physically relaxed and seated with natural posture. A comfortable interviewer is better able to listen to the person being interviewed. Also, if the interviewer is relaxed physically, his or her posture and movements will be natural, thus enhancing a sense of well-being. This sense of being comfortable better enables the interviewer to attend to and to communicate with the interviewee. Relax physically; feel the presence of the chair as you are sitting on it. Let your posture be comfortable and your movements natural; for example, if you usually move and gesture a good deal, feel free to do so at this time. Do not be overly relaxed however. By leaning forward occasionally you signify your attention.

The interviewer should initiate and maintain eye contact with the person. However, eye contact can be overdone. A varied use of eye contact is most effective, as staring fixedly or with undue intensity usually makes the respondent uneasy, and can be inappropriate in some cultures. This notwithstanding, if you are going to listen to someone, look at them.

The final characteristic of good attending behavior is the interviewer's use of comments which follow directly from what the person is saying. Follow what the other person is saying by taking your cues from what is said. Do not jump from subject to subject or interrupt. If you cannot think of anything to say, go back to something the person said earlier in the conversation and ask a question about that. There is no need to talk about yourself or your opinions when you are interviewing. By directing one's comments and questions to the topics provided by the individual, one not only helps develop an area of discussion, but reinforces the person's free expression, resulting in more spontaneity and animation.

In summary, the interviewer's goal is to listen actively and to communicate this attentiveness through a relaxed posture, use of varied eye contact, and verbal responses which indicate to the person that the interviewer is attempting to understand what is being communicated.

Openness and Empathy

Your purpose in an interview is to allow the interviewee to share his or her information with you. You should be open in posture and expression, willingly accepting the information offered. You should empathize, but in a non-leading way. Avoid value judgments and agreeing or disagreeing with the respondent. Accept what is said, but do not lead the person being interviewed further than he or she wants to go voluntarily. If you do not understand, get the message clarified, but resist taking sides. For example:

Respondent: The principal is a bastard.
Interviewer: Why do you say that?
Respondent: Because he says one thing to your face and another behind your back.
Interviewer: He's pretty inconsistent, then?

Being open should not mean that you are not assertive. You must control the interview while not condoning the opinions expressed. Be firm and direct while at the same time open.

Paraphrasing

Paraphrasing takes what the interviewee has just said and repeats it back in different words. It acknowledges your attention and it increases validity by checking whether what you heard the interviewee say was the intended message. Paraphrasing crystallizes comments by repeating them in a more concise manner. When your paraphrase differs from the interviewee's intent, he or she will clarify the statement and you will not have obtained an invalid response.

Summarizing Content

Summarization attempts to recapitulate, condense and crystallize the essence of what the interviewee has said. While a summary thus resembles a paraphrase, it differs in one fundamental respect — the period covered by a summary is substantially longer than that of a paraphrase. The latter deals with the individual's last few sentences or a short paragraph. A summary puts together a number of his paragraphs or an entire section of an interview. It may cover even an entire interview.

A summary serves at least these three major functions: it may crystallize in a more coherent and integrated manner what the interviewee has been talking about; it may help the respondent put facts together; it may serve as a stimulus for further exploration of a particular topic or area. Because it pulls together materials discussed over a substantial period of time, it frequently serves as a necessary perception check for the interviewer.

Summarizations are frequently used when the interviewer wishes to structure the beginning of a conversation by recalling the high points of a previous interview; when the interviewee's presentation of a topic has been either very confusing or just plain lengthy and rambling; when an interviewee has seemingly expressed everything of importance on a particular topic; when at the end of an interview, the interviewer wishes to emphasize what has been learned within it.

Controlling the Process

In my view, the interviewer must know how to control the interview, its process and its pace. By controlling, the interviewer need not always take the lead. Indeed, many key informant interviews are successful because the person being interviewed is so skilled at communicating and knows exactly what to say. You merely give a lead and the interviewee picks it up and carries on, often answering many of your other questions on the way. It can be many minutes before you probe or nudge the process in a new direction. However, you must be able to regain the lead at any time or the interview will no longer be yours and it may no longer suit your purpose.

In order to assume and maintain leadership in the interview it is important to set the stage right up front. Your introduction will do much to establish where you will be in the process. If you are insecure and unsure of where you are going you may easily get sidetracked into a friendly conversation or discussion which does not do much to produce the data you need. I find it helpful to outline an agenda for the interview which states the three or four major themes or sections and provides a lasting frame of reference to which you can refer later. This helps prevent the respondent from moving ahead of you as he or she knows that there will be a time later to make some point on that topic. The agenda also helps you speed up the interview when required using the interjection, 'that is very interesting, but as you know, we have three more topics to cover, so perhaps we should move on.'

A problem I recently experienced interviewing people in Russia and Eastern Europe was a tendency for some of them to rush forward. In fact, since they knew the general purpose of my visit, they often rushed to the punch line before I could even get a description of who they were. I discovered it to be futile to redirect them, but rather learned to let them shoot their bolt and then try to go back methodically and reconstruct the pieces. It was not easy, however, to then go back to their critical views in more depth as they felt that they had covered them already.

Once the interview begins, you should shape the behavior you expect by cutting off a response which gets too long. Once you establish how much you want on each question most interviewees learn to go to that level of detail and no more. At first this can seem awkward, but with practice, you should be able to do it authoritatively while not throwing cold water on the process. My advice is to study skilled TV interviewers and learn how they do it.

The opposite problem also presents itself. Sometimes the respondent does not respond, at least not easily or fully. In these cases you must invite a response. Learning to live with silence is fundamental. Many interviewers from the Canadian culture find this difficult, so end up doing all the talking themselves. Ask the question and wait patiently. If the respondent does not understand, he or she will eventually ask for clarification. Sometimes you should talk in an attempt to engage the respondent in conversation. This is all right, but it should not persist. Do it a little and then go back to silent waiting.

Humour is one of the most effective process tools if you know how to use it. I often get people laughing and then find that their natural resistance disappears. It can build trust and disarm the respondent. I use it frequently in cross-cultural settings and consider it an indispensable tool.

Conclusion

A data collection interview is a marvelous challenge and is always a test. No two interviews are ever alike and every interview teaches new lessons. I find that unless I am up for an interview, well briefed on what I need to know and conscious of the need to work at the process, I lose a unique opportunity for data collection. Plan each interview as carefully as possible, practice your interviewing skills and analyze each experience once it is over.

For Further Study

Downs, C.W., Smeyak, G.P., & Martin, E. (1980). *Professional interviewing*. New York: Harper & Row Publishers.

McCracken, G. (1988). *The long interview*. Qualitative Research Methods, Volume 13, Thousands Oaks, CA: Sage Publications.

Chapter 20

Focus Groups

As early as the 1930s, social scientists expressed concern about the interview as a data collection technique. Interviews were judged to be overly dominated by the questioner, and criticized as not leading to the true feelings of the respondents. Various approaches were attempted in response to this criticism, leading to such innovations as Carl Rogers' non-directive therapy, and later, invention of the T-group. Another approach that built on participant's feelings became known as the Focus Group. Since the 1960s, the technique has been adopted by market researchers who use it to determine what consumers think of products, or potential products. In the last two decades, social scientists, evaluators, planners and educators have also discovered the technique and are now using focus groups to collect data on a wide variety of issues and topics.

Description

A focus group is a carefully planned and moderated informal discussion where one person's ideas bounce off another's creating a chain reaction of informative dialogue. Its purpose is to address a specific topic, in depth, in a comfortable environment to illicit a wide range of opinions, attitudes, feelings or perceptions from a group of individuals who share some common experience relative to the dimension under study. The product of a focus group is a unique form of qualitative information which brings understanding about how people react to an experience or product.

The focus group has several distinct advantages over other data collection techniques such as the questionnaire or the interview. Questionnaires only allow input from the individual respondent. There is no opportunity for the respondent to clarify questions or expand his or her own perceptions by sharing and comparing them to those of others. Interviews allow some opportunity for clarification and additional input, for the interviewer might probe and suggest ideas which give rise to views and opinions which the respondent may not have shared in a written questionnaire. The focus group goes yet another step further. It not only discloses what is important to individual respondents, but the group setting attempts to create a synergistic environment resulting in a deeper, more insightful, discussion. Thus, the focus group elicits a unique type of in-depth qualitative data which could not be obtained as efficiently any other way. In this sense, focus groups have something in common with brainstorming techniques.

Focus groups have many uses. Depending on their *raison d'être*, focus groups can be used to gather insight, bridge communication, prepare for a larger study, obtain market research data, understand consumers and uncover complex motivations or behaviors. In education, focus groups can be useful to collect information on participant needs when planning, improving or evaluating programs. For example, focus groups are held to test reactions to possible program offerings or to examine the factors that help make people decide to enrol in programs before new social or educational programs are introduced. They are also used in the development of research procedures to test reactions to possible evaluation questions and procedures to be used later using quantitative methods. They are particularly useful in helping develop specific research questions and issues for further exploration. Focus groups are sometimes used during an on-going program in order to provide formative evaluation. They are increasingly being used after programs are conducted in order to provide a basis for evaluation and analysis. They provide a useful complement to other methods of summative program evaluation, permitting a judgement about the value and continued utility of a program.

Why do focus groups work? Focus groups work because they provide a natural, relaxed and secure setting where individuals are encouraged to share both positive and negative comments. Participant selection is based on commonality, and several people are engaged in the process at the same time. The group setting also allows questions to be clarified and modified, which in turn enhances the group discussion and assists the chain reaction of participant dialogue. In the end, the views on a particular topic or issue are exhausted, and the data collected have a high face value for they are supported by participants in *their* language. From a practical standpoint, focus groups are inexpensive, versatile and provide a way for organizations to stay in touch with their clients. The turn around time from conception to results can be quick; however, as with all forms of qualitative research, analyzing focus group data is a challenge.

While focus groups can be an extremely effective way to collect data in certain situations, there are times when they should not be used. Focus groups can be problematic when language poses a barrier or when the group forum for discussion is viewed as socially or politically inappropriate. Thus, for example, they have no place in formal, face-saving cultures such as those in some Asian countries. Also, focus groups are not recommended for situations where the sample population is emotionally charged, for the focus group may intensify the conflict. Finally, focus groups are inappropriate if quantitative data are required for statistical projections, when sensitive information must be preserved and remain confidential, or when other means of collecting data can produce similar results more economically.

Planning the Focus Group

As with all types of research and data collection, one must have a clear idea of the purpose of the exercise. In planning to use focus groups, you need a clear idea of what specific information is needed, who will use the information, and you should also have some notion of why the information is important.

It is vital to select an appropriate category of individuals to be included in the focus groups. It would be fallacious for the market researcher to involve people who do not use the product being researched. Similarly, in focus groups used for your research, you must decide who is in the best position to provide the information you require. Sometimes one single category of people can give you what you need, but be sure not to restrict your focus groups to only one target population when several may relate to the problem. In examining a training program, for example, you might like to involve program participants, possibly non-participants, instructors or program coordinators.

Participants are typically pre-screened, via telephone or letter of invitation, to ensure that they have the required characteristics. You do not invite people to attend a 'focus group', but merely to join a group discussion on the topic of interest. As with any method, you must make clear the arrangements concerning the time of the group, its purpose and how long it will last. It is best to meet in some neutral but convenient place where the intended participants can be expected to feel comfortable.

You will need more than one focus group. In practice, researchers typically collect data until they stop getting appreciable new information. In most situations, the first two groups give considerable new information. Thereafter, the new insights rapidly diminish. In my experience, by the third or fourth session, the topic has generally been exhausted unless, of course, the groups have some inherent difference. For example, in examining national training programs, I have conducted focus groups on the training program itself, but have also been interested in regional differences. In such cases, groups in various settings across the country permit insights into regional variations.

Developing the Focus Group Guide

One of the most difficult tasks with focus groups is constructing the questions. The quality of the responses are directly related to the quality of the questions; good answers dictate the need for good questions that have both a content and a process function. When you finish, the questions are deceptively simple, but in practice, they take considerable energy to develop. With respect to content, many focus groups include only five or six questions, but because of the group process, a great deal of discussion and elaboration can take place — much more than would be possible through interviewing individual participants. Focus group questions are always open-ended. For example, in an evaluation activity you might ask such questions as: 'What did you think of the program?' 'What did you like best about your training?' 'How have you been able to use your training back on the job?' Be sure to keep your questions of a qualitative nature, and avoid quantifiers such as 'how much?' These qualifiers tend to restrict answers, rather than allow for a full range of responses. Also, avoid questions that have a possible 'yes' or 'no' answer. Ironically, while the main purpose of focus groups is to discover why people hold certain views, the 'why' question is rarely asked in the focus group session. You are not interested in a rational answer to the question 'why'. Instead, you discover 'why' from a less direct approach based on questions about how people feel about the topic, product, service or program that is being discussed. It is often useful as part of your planning to brainstorm a large list of questions and systematically reduce and refine them, until you have the core. The questions must then be sequenced, and the sequence must ensure a natural flow and transition from one to the other. Participants should not feel that they have finished one question and are then being asked another. Instead, they should feel that the session is an overall discussion, exploring a variety of related issues and leading logically through the various topics. A sample focus group guide is included in Appendix 20.1 for a supervisory development evaluation that involved nine focus groups.

Group Composition

Group composition is fundamental to good focus group technique. First, the participants must have some common characteristic related to what is being focused upon. For example, participants in a training program have that as a common characteristic, regardless of gender, background, education or experience. This becomes the glue that bonds the group together, and it is advisable not to confuse this by having too many other common characteristics. People can be prescreened to ensure they fit the selection criteria. It is a mistake, generally speaking, to pick participants from memory or use intact groups — people who know one another outside the group context. Such people will not benefit as much from the ideas of colleagues as they would from those of complete strangers. In some types of evaluation, however, this is hard to avoid since those who participated in a program have generally come to know one another. There is particular danger dealing with intact groups who already have a life and personality of their own; this is rarely conducive to the focus group purpose. Wherever possible, one should involve a mix of relative strangers who will feel comfortable sharing their views without having to wonder what their friends and colleagues might think about their responses.

Focus groups generally range from 6–12 participants. You need enough people to achieve synergy and facilitate group dynamics, but not so many as to prevent everyone from having a full say. In practice, it is difficult to control groups greater than 12, which tend to break apart into various factions. Groups smaller than six generally do not have enough to provide the synergy required. The exception is where the topic needs to be explored in great depth, and where people have had lengthy experiences related to it. In those cases, mini-focus groups (3 to 5 people) are often best.

Conducting the Focus Group

To be effective, the focus group procedure requires a moderator, skilled at leading groups. Such a moderator should have sufficient group dynamics skills and techniques

Exhibit 20.1:   Tips for the focus group moderator

The Moderator must:

- Be comfortable with group processes
- Encourage discussion, balance the contributions
- Listen actively, paraphrase and summarize
- Be innocent, empathetic and sensitive
- Functions as a facilitator, not performer

- Be aware of past, present, future perspectives during the session
- Keep the discussion moving, focused and know when to wrap up
- Effectively use silence, pauses and probes
- Exert mild control, but avoid leading participants
- Remain flexible and adaptive

- Stay in the background — it is the opinions of the participants that are wanted
- Suspend his or her personal biases
- Acknowledge individual contributions
- Control dominant individuals

- Remain conscious of time
- Respect the participants and believe their contributions are important regardless of their background, experience or education
- Have adequate background knowledge on the topic
- Have effective communication skills
- Understand how to use humour and naïve questions

---

to be able to exercise control over the group, yet do so unobtrusively (see Exhibit 20.1). The skilled moderator will be able to draw out silent individuals and control those who dominate the conversation. Such a moderator will be skilled at asking the questions and keeping the flow directional, animated and relevant. The moderator has to be a good listener and know how to empathize. In my experience, it is most effective to have an assistant as well. The assistant frees up the moderator to focus entirely on the process, while the assistant is instrumental in overcoming logistical difficulties and is occupied with taking notes and sharing in the analysis phase. Remember, however, when selecting a moderator factors such as sex, age, gender, race, technical knowledge, socio-economic characteristics or a perceived power differential, between the moderator and participants may inhibit communication.

It is advisable to begin the session with some transitional period. For example, one can provide coffee and refreshments for those who arrive early, and the moderator and assistant can engage in appropriate small-talk. You will want to use this to put the participants at ease, but avoid talking about the issues until the group formally begins. This also provides an excellent context to assess who is in the group, and the skilled group leader will identify the dominant individuals who, whenever possible, should be seated at the moderator's side. Once the expected number of participants have arrived, it is best to seat them so that all members of the group have eye contact. Be sure to avoid the 'head table' approach as the moderator should always be seen as part of the group. As a moderator, you will want to control the seating and furniture arrangements to maximize and set the environment.

Begin the group by thanking the participants for coming, briefly state the purpose of the discussion and you might also inform people why they were selected. Be sure to emphasize the rules of confidentiality, and provide an opportunity for people to ask questions about why they are there. Tell the participants how the information will be recorded and reported. Participants generally ask whether or not they will receive the results, so you can anticipate this question. The first question should be an ice-breaker, designed to engage people in the process. As the process develops, the moderator will introduce relevant questions, provide probes, pauses, involve people in discussion, always without expressing any value on the answers received. Avoid closing a response with agreement or head-nodding. Even comments as innocuous as 'yes' imply a value to the response received.

The purpose of the focus group is not to achieve consensus but to exhaust an exploration of the various perspectives held. For this reason, I conclude by thanking the participants, rather than providing a summary. It is important to ask whether you have missed anything to give everyone the feeling that all their contributions have been heard. You might, of course, give some sort of comment on the great value of the contributions, then thank the participants and dismiss them. In my experience, most focus groups can be conducted in an hour and a half to two hours. A good rule of thumb is to allow about a half hour per question and slightly more for groups of more than eight.

Exhibit 20.2 summarizes what the moderator needs to animate the process successfully, move along the dialogue and trouble shoot problem situations which may arise.

Recording the Responses

Because of their intensity, focus groups lend themselves to recording. If you use a tape recorder, or video recorder (not as common), be sure to inform the participants and obtain their permission. The advantage of tape recording is that it gives you a full record of what has been shared, a potentially rich source of data. Its disadvantage is that it is time-consuming to listen to the tape. As with all such techniques, it is preferable to use an unobtrusive recording device. Use tapes of sufficient length so you do not have to make a change midway through the session, as this may destroy the group atmosphere. Whether or not you tape-record, detailed notes are indispensable, if only to assist in providing the location of information on the tape. The assistant moderator should take copious notes of the discussion and document any relevant observations which may enhance or contribute to the analysis. While writing, the recorder must avoid giving cues to participants about the value of their contributions by noting only the 'best' ones. In general, the recorder should be writing things at all times, or at least appear to be doing so. In recording the notes, it is useful to jot time references or tape recorder revolutions in the margin so that specific points can be located easily on the tape. It is also useful to underline or highlight particular reference points which seem, at the time, to be significant

Exhibit 20.2:   More tips for the focus group moderator

Techniques to Move Along the Dialogue

- **Direct phrases** to specific individuals:
  John, what do you think about what Sarah said?
  Why do you feel that way, Lisa?

- **Draw-out** participants by asking broad questions, for opinions and perspectives
  What did you think of . . . ?
  There are a couple of people we haven't heard from yet. Jack, do you have an opinion?
  Sandra, do you have a perspective on this?

- **Verify** what you are hearing by restating or paraphrasing:
  So what I hear you saying is . . .

- **Use silence** — ask a question then take time to wait and look around the group for a response. Be patient, 10 seconds is okay, but may seem a lifetime.

- Seek various **perspectives:**
  Think back to the time when . . . What did you think of that activity?
  Are there any other views?

- **Use probes** to expand on the question and stimulate discussion

Trouble Shooting

- Beware of the **loudmouth**, **joker** or **wisecracker** who interrupts with 'humorous' comments. You can either choose to ignore them, or incorporate their energy and humor in the discussion.

- The **storyteller** or **braggart** can be curtailed by avoiding eye contact and using your body language to signal an interruption. You may also speak directly to something that is said, 'Hold that idea, we'll return to that later. Now I'd like to move on to . . .'

- The **shy individual** who is reluctant to speak out can be encouraged by using positive body language that encourages and shows interest. Never force them to speak by putting them on the spot; they do have a right not to speak, but credit their contributions.

- Intervene and regain control if **everyone is talking** at one time; reestablish the ground rules, and recommend that people write down their ideas.

- The **manipulator** who sneers at others or tries to impose their views:
  - avoid getting frustrated
  - often the group will find methods to silence this person

- Establish a 'respect' rule at the onset to discourage those who may **belittle others**. Remind the group that all opinions are valid and may only make sense in the greater analysis of data with other focus groups.

- Recognize the expertise of a **genuine expert** who knows a lot about the subject but may intimidate others into silence. Emphasize the importance of all perspectives to greater understanding. As for the **pseudo experts**, those who *act* as if they know the topic well, redirect their conversation for they often annoy others.

contributions. In some instances you can pre-define categories and organize a page of your notebook to accommodate comments in the anticipated categories. Some people use shorthand or codes in order to prevent the participants from peeking at what was recorded.

Data Analysis

In doing the analysis you must constantly keep in mind the purpose of the focus group. Preliminary data analysis should take place as soon as possible after the group session concludes. The moderator and other researchers present should be involved in the analysis to systematically go through your data record, verify the audio recording, review the handwritten notes, collect and label auxiliary resources (i.e. flip chart notes), and record the big ideas and concepts that were heard. This list of ideas will be a valuable resource in later stages of the analysis.

Post session analysis refers to the merging, consolidating, organizing and ultimate interpretation of data from the multiple focus group discussions. During this phase the themes identified in the preliminary analysis become a starting point for organizing the multiple data sources into categories and subcategories. During this phase it is important to consider the words used, the context which gave rise to those words, whether people changed their views, or held them constantly throughout the session, and you need to assess the intensity of the responses; that is, the enthusiasm a participant holds for a given idea. As you explore the data, the categories initially identified will help you create a framework for understanding and working with your information. Into this framework you will refine your findings, select and edit quotations to support your discoveries, look for negative cases (themes or comments which go against the grain of your findings), draw your conclusions (see Exhibit 20.3).

Exhibit 20.3: Focus group data analysis tips

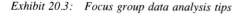

Data Analysis Tips

- Type up significant commentary from rough notes, record speaker's name if possible, and note the seating arrangement of participants.

- Content analysis: cut and past comments into themes.

- Order the comments within the themes into subthemes then arrange in order of importance. Look for negative cases.

- Edit the themes to eliminate redundancy, ensure comments are not one person's perspective only and to create a balanced, accurate reflection of what was actually said in the group.

- Write a summary statement for each theme.

- Select and edit actual quotations to illustrate each theme. Avoid extreme views, select statements that are typical, correct grammar and language usage where required and ensure that participant's identities are concealed.

Reporting on Focus Group Findings

Some focus groups have little or no written report. In marketing research, the client is sometimes invited to observe participants behind a one-way mirror or view video highlights of the session. This method is particularly powerful when assessing consumer reaction to a product. For other purposes a briefing and oral report is prepared.

For most research purposes, however, a written analysis is required. In general, there are two extremes to written forms of reporting focus group data. One is to conduct the analysis and report summaries of the major ideas and themes. The other is to use the participant's words verbatim. Which route you choose will depend on your purpose and the intended reader. Personally, I like to combine narrative summaries with actual quotes that illustrate views in the participant's own words. Unless your goal is to illuminate or advance a specific point, avoid using extreme quotations and attempt to include more general, representative statements. It is all right to edit individual quotes, laundering the swear words and correcting the grammar if you wish, as long as the intent is clear. Remember your purpose is to gain insight about the theme under investigation and understand why people hold the views they hold. Albeit a challenge, it is possible to distill a mountain of qualitative data into a concise form, notwithstanding the great depth of data collection and the analysis that precedes it.

Conclusion

Like all data collection techniques, focus groups are an indispensable tool for gathering information and insight on certain issues and questions. Focus groups are intended strictly for qualitative data and to help you understand why people hold the views they hold. For their purpose they are a good tool, and in the hands of trained researchers provide valid and reliable data. Focus groups can be an efficient data collection technique and with relatively little investment can often help us avoid asking the wrong questions, or embarking on things which are guaranteed to fail. Focus groups also provide a timely response and can suggest the futility of more elaborate forms of research. They may also help you sharpen your questions for complementary forms of data collection and analysis. Remember, however, that quality data requires trained and experienced researchers. Focus groups may have inherent appeal because they are in vogue, but are effective only if used properly.

For Further Study

Krueger, R.A. (1994). *Focus groups: A practical guide for applied research.* (2nd ed.) Thousand Oaks, CA: Sage.

Patton, M.Q. (1990). *Qualitative evaluation and research methods.* (2nd ed.) Thousand Oaks, CA: Sage.

Stewart, D.W., & Shamdasani, P.N. (1990). *Focus groups: Theory and practice.* Applied social Research Methods Series, Vol. 20. Thousand Oaks, CA: Sage.

Vaughn, S., Shay Schumm, J., & Sinagub, J. (1996). *Focus group interviews in education and psychology.* Thousand Oaks, CA: Sage.

Part IV

Appendixes

Choosing Your Advisor

Selecting a professor to supervise your graduate research is an extremely important decision. It is also a difficult activity that makes many students feel awkward and uncomfortable. To diminish your personal discomfort, turn the activity into a learning experience, and maximize the time you spend with each professor by preparing for every meeting. Your time, and the professors' time, is valuable and should not be wasted. Below is a list of activities that will help prepare you for this activity.

1   Investigate the professor's research background. Many university depart-
    ments have a list of their faculty that identifies the current research interests
    and activities of their professors. Ask the department secretary for informa-
    tion, ask the professor directly and ask your course instructors who they
    would recommend given your area of interest.
2   Familiarize yourself with the written work of the professor(s) you would
    like to interview.
    *   locate recent journal articles they have published;
    *   find out if they have written any books you can examine;
    *   ask to borrow a copy of a recent research report they have produced.
3   Examine a few theses or dissertations that the professor has supervised to
    get an idea of the range of their research interests, the scope of graduate
    studies they have supervised, and the type of written presentation they
    encourage or will accept. For example, some professors demand complete
    written prose, others encourage a more business style of writing.
4   Talk to other students:
    *   find out from students working with a specific professor what they
        like and dislike about working with this individual;
    *   find out from other students who are 'shopping' for a professor,
        why they have decided not to study with certain individuals.
5   Take a course from the professor to learn about their personality, the way
    he or she deals with students, communicates ideas, and provides feedback.
6   Enter each interview prepared to discuss your personal situation:
    *   the research topics that interest you (try and have a list of ques-
        tions prepared);
    *   your personal work habits, how you learn best;
    *   your career aspirations and how this ties in with your research
        interests;

- the time frame you have set to complete your research project;
- the frequencies of meetings and who initiates these sessions;
- any personal information that will impact on your research (i.e. currently working full-time, inability to work over the summer, moving out of town in 8 months, etc.).

7   Don't be shy to ask the professor personal questions as well:
- how often does he or she like to meet with students?
- does he or she like to see multiple draft copies of your work in progress?
- does his or her professional commitments require out-of-town trips, if so how do you work around this?
- is he or she planning a sabbatical leave? early retirement?
- does he or she have a full student load?
- what does he or she expect from their graduate students?

Working with a research advisor is a two-way street. Taking the time to shop around for a suitable professor who meets your learning needs is worth the time invested. Remember, graduate study is not merely taking additional courses and completing a study. It is an experience that offers a variety of opportunities for personal growth and development, many of which cannot be found in a textbook. Finding a research advisor is part of the graduate student experience and supervising students is part of a professor's job. Approach the task with a positive attitude, learn from each interview, respect the professor's time, limitations and interests, look for a personality match, ask for referrals elsewhere and most importantly, remember that often it is the student's responsibility to find a supervisor! If you wait for a personal invitation for a professor to supervise your research, you may be in graduate school a very long time.

Indicative Planning Parameters for a One-Year Research Study

Task/Activity	Total Hours per Month												Total Hrs	Major Milestones
	1	2	3	4	5	6	7	8	9	10	11	12		
Administration														
Buy supplies	32		1		1			2	4			4	15	
Organize work	4	4	4	4	4	4	4	4	4	4	4	4	48	
Develop systems to store and retrieve information		10		5		5			5				25	
Other														
Define the Problem														
General reading	20	10	10	10	10	10	10	10	10	10	10	10	130	Month 1: General problem decided
Discussions with colleagues	8	8	8	8	8	8	8	8	8	8	8	8	96	
Prepare statement (draft 1)	12												12	Month 2: Draft problem statement
Feedback from colleagues on statements	4		4										8	
Revise statement (draft 2)			6										6	
Discussions with supervisor(s)		2	2	2									6	Month 4: Submit complete proposal
Initial consideration of methodology			12	20									32	
Revise ideas			5		5								10	
Other														

Task/Activity	Total Hours per Month												Total Hrs	Major Milestones
	1	2	3	4	5	6	7	8	9	10	11	12		
Review of research														
Time in library	20	20	20	10	10	10				10			100	
ERIC search	10	10	5										25	
Journal search	20	10	10								5		45	
Other sources (i.e. experts, personal)	5	5	10		5	5		5					35	
Read material	40	40	20	20	10	10		5					145	
Write paragraphs				40	30	50							120	
Develop outline	5	5	5										15	
Prepare tables		10		10									20	Month 4: Draft lit review
Draft review #1			20	20									40	
Feedback from colleagues on #1 review				5									5	
Write revision, draft #2					20								20	
Feedback from supervisor				2									2	Month 8: Penultimate lit review
Write revision, draft #3								10					10	
Revision of problem statement, draft #3						5							5	
Other														
Methodology														
Define data sources		5	5										10	
Search for published instruments		10	5										15	Month 4: Select/develop instruments
Develop instruments			10										10	
Pilot-test instruments			10										10	
Revise instruments				10									10	
Layout and design instruments				10									10	
Prepare for printers				5									5	
Define sample			5										5	Month 5: Decide methodology
Select sample				5									5	
Write methodology, draft #1					25								25	
Revise methodology #2						20							20	Month 6
Revise methodology # 3									5	10			15	Month 10: Revise methodology
Other														

| Task/Activity | \
Total Hours per Month												Total Hrs	Major Milestones
	1	2	3	4	5	6	7	8	9	10	11	12		
Conducting the Research														
Collect data						40	40	40					120	Month 6–8
Code/process data						40	40						80	
Analyze data							80	80	80				240	Complete month 9
Computer interface							40						40	
Prepare tables								40					40	
Prepare figures								40					40	
Write results #1									60				60	Month 10: Draft preliminary results
Revise results #2										40			40	Month 11: Final results section
Revise results #3												20	20	
Obtain feedback/criticism								5	5	10	10	10	40	
Prepare report														
Edit manuscript										10	20	40	70	
Arrange typing							5		5	5	5	5	25	
Proofreading							5		5	5	5	5	25	
Format/layout										5	5	5	15	Month 12: Submit Dissertation
References						10		10		10		5	35	
Abstract											20		20	
Translate abstract												5	5	
Preliminaries (title pages, abstract, etc.)												5	5	
Appendixes											20	10	30	
Administration			5				5			5	5	5	25	
Totals:	151	189	217	191	68	177	212	209	211	147	147	161	2090	

Significant Educational Research Journals

Journals	Comment
Administrative Sciences Quarterly	The major theoretical journal about organizations. Includes some research on educational organizations.
Adult Education Quarterly	A referred journal that publishes research and theory in adult and continuing education.
Alberta Journal of Educational Research	One of the few good quality Canadian journals dealing with research. Mix of methodologies and topics related to all aspects of education.
American Educational Research Journal	One of the most rigorous journals devoted exclusively to research articles in all areas of education. Many articles esoteric, empirical and multi-variate statistics are generally used. This journal is now divided into two sections: 1) Social and Institutional Analysis and 2) Teaching, Learning, and Human Development.
American Journal of Education	Pursues themes and general issues emphasizing theory and research.
Australian Journal of Education	Contains largely research articles related to a wide range of topics related to Australia and education in general.
British Journal of Education Psychology	A high quality British journal containing largely empirical research on a wide range of topics in educational psychology.
British Journal of Educational Studies	Contains largely theoretical and axiological articles on contemporary issues related to Britain and the Commonwealth.
Canadian and International Education	Contains high quality articles, reviews, reports with some research on development.
Canadian Journal of Education	A major national refereed journal for professors and researchers in education. Published mixture of general articles and research of interest to Canadians.
Comparative Education	Provides information for general readers on significant trends throughout the world.

Journals	Comment
Comparative Education Review	The major research journal in comparative education.
Curriculum Inquiry	Publishes studies of curriculum research, development, education and theory.
Educational Administration Quarterly	Elementary and secondary schooling focus with mixture of conceptual studies and those with a traditional research focus.
Education Evaluation and Policy Analysis	Mixture of theoretical, analytic and research articles related to policy and evaluation.
Educational Gerontology	An international journal reflecting changes and new ideas in the study and practice of educational gerontology and related disciplines.
Elementary School Journal	Publishes original studies, reviews of research and conceptual analyzes for researchers and practitioners interested in elementary schooling.
Evaluation Research in Education	Aimed at making evaluation research methods available to educational administrators.
Harvard Educational Review	One of the most influential journals containing occasional research studies which tend to be milestones. Published by students.
History of Education Quarterly	A leading American journal on history of education.
Journal of Applied Behavioral Science	Emphasis on soft research such as case study, conceptual and opinion articles and action research.
Journal of Educational Psychology	One of the many psychology journals of interest to educators. Contains research studies, mostly empirical and many experimental.
Journal of Education Research	Emphasizes research with practical application to elementary and secondary schools.
Journal of Reading	A forum for current theory, research and practice in reading.
Review of Educational Research	Most significant quarterly devoted to reviews of research in all areas of education. Excellent conceptual and meta-analysis.
Journal of Research on Science Teaching	A leading journal devoted to research on science teaching.
New Zealand Journal of Educational Studies	Publishes essays, research studies and critical comment in all areas of education.
Research in the Teaching of English	Publishes research and discussion related to the teaching of English and the language arts.

Note: This summary is not intended to be definitive but rather is indicative of the range of journals of interest to researchers.

220

Some On-line Databases of Interest to Social Science Researchers

Data Base	Description
Bilingual Education Bibliographic Abstracts	Covers various aspects of bilingual education in the USA with some international coverage. The scope includes such topics as classroom instruction, teacher education, ethnic and minorities, linguistics, second language instruction and culture.
British Education Index	This file indexes the literature of education, covering not only traditional facets of primary, secondary, tertiary and further education but also adult and continuing education, student counseling, special and vocational education, and women's studies.
CINAHL	Indexes over 650 English journals related to nursing and the allied health disciplines.
Current Contents	It is one of the world's most timely current awareness services produced by the Institute for Scientific Information (ISI). This data base provides access to the tables of contents of more than 3800 international journals including: agriculture, biology and environmental sciences, arts and humanities, clinical medicine, engineering, technology, applied science, life science, physical/chemical/earth science, and social and behavioral sciences.
Educational Index (EDI)	EDI indexes 350 of the key English language periodicals in all areas of education.
Educational Resources Information Center (ERIC)	This major education data base consists of two files, *Current Index to Journals in Education* (CIJE) covering over 700 education and education-related journals, and *Resources in Education* (RIE) covering 16,000 non-journal materials including research reports, surveys, program descriptions and evaluations, curriculum and teaching guides, and instructional and resource materials.
Educational Sciences	Provides coverage of the history and philosophy of education, educational policy, teaching organization, educational research, teaching methods, teachers, orientation and goals and the sociology and psychology of education.

Data Base	Description
Exceptional Child Education Resources (ECER)	Provides coverage on exceptional child education.
General Science Index (GSI)	This index of 140 resources covers the fields of astronomy, botany, chemistry, earth science, environment, food science, genetics, mathematics, medicine and health, microbiology, oceanography, physics, physiology and zoology.
Humanities Index (HUM)	Covers the fields of archaeology, classical studies, art and photography, folklore, general scholarship, history, journalism and communications, language and literature, literature and political criticism, music, performing arts, philosophy, religion and theology.
International Development Research Centre (IDRC)	This file is a merge of several data bases related to international development. Among these data bases are the USAID data base and the UNESCO data base. The USAID data base contains technical research and development material produced by aid programs. Among the subject fields covered are education and human resources. The UNESCO data base includes worldwide coverage of literature written by or for UNESCO. It deals with a broad range of educational, scientific and cultural programs with an increasing emphasis on development issues.
Legal Periodicals Index (LPI)	Cites core legal periodicals from more than 645 journals. Topics include law reviews, bar association journals, university publications, yearbooks, institutes and government publications in Canada, Great Britain, the USA, Puerto Rico, Australia and New Zealand.
Medline	An international data base with literature on bio-medicine including the allied health fields, humanities, science information as it relates to medicine and health care, and the biological and physical sciences. References approximately 3600 journals.
PsycINFO	Is a major on-line data base for the field of psychology and related fields such as education, business, law, medicine and applied health disciplines. PsycINFO is a division of the American Psychological Association. It is the major resource for information on behavior sciences and related fields. The publications on record here include research proposals, technical reports, translations, annual publications, chapter/books, conference papers, surveys, literature reviews, case studies and bibliographies.

Data Base	Description
PsycFILE	This file is a portion of the PsycINFO data base. PsycFILE contains citations and summaries on such topics as personnel management, selection and training, managerial practices and characteristics, organizational behavior and changes, and occupational attitudes.
Social Sciences Index (SSI)	An index of 420 periodicals covering a wide range of interdisciplinary fields in the social sciences.
Social Sciences Citation Index (SSCI)	Contains references from more than 1500 of the most significant journals in the social sciences in the fields of education, psychology and sociology, as well as the other social science disciplines. SSCI also contains relevant source items from approximately 3000 additional journals in the biomedical, natural and physical sciences.

Note: This summary is not intended to be definitive but rather is indicative of the range of data bases available at the time of print. On-line data bases are a growth industry and therefore it is important to check your local library for current listings of the most useful data bases available when you are ready to begin a research project.

Appendix 8.1

Sample of a Tabular Literature Review

Summary of the Literature Reviewed

Contribution	Descriptive Summary	Author, Date
I. The Social Context		
	Definitions and boundaries in adult education, the Canadian movement in context	Selman & Dampier, 1991: pp. 1–69.
	The context and environment of adult learning	Merriam & Caffarella, 1991: pp. 1–56.
	Growth of a learning society	Cross, 1992: pp. 1–31.
II. Conceptual Framework		
Hierarchy	Hierarchy of needs	Maslow, 1954
	Bloom's taxonomy	Bloom, 1956
Continuum	Expressive-Instrumental Continuum (EIC)	Havighurst, 1969, 1976
	Revising the EIC with older adults	Wirtz & Charner, 1989
Typology	3-way typology of the adult learner	Houle, 1961
	Typologies as a consumer classification scheme	Holt, 1995
Classification	Educational Participation Scale	Boshier, 1971
	Understanding the decision to participate	Henry & Basile, 1994
III. The Quantitative Research Tradition		
Questionnaire	Analyze participation patterns of older adults	Heisel, Darkenwald & Anderson, 1981
Data bank analysis	Houle's typology after 22 years	Boshier & Collins, 1985
Educational participation scale (EPS)	Reasons for participation in adult education courses	Morstain & Smart, 1974
IV. The Qualitative Research Tradition		
Life-stories	Motivation and expectations of older adults	Wolf, 1990
Case Studies	An Elderhostel case study	Murk, 1992
In-depth interview	Learning as a strategy to negotiate retirement	Adiar & Mowsesian, 1993

Sample Ways to Table Your Literature While Collecting and Developing Literature to Review

Quantitative Studies

Type	Size per cent	Age	Analysis	Description	Author, Date
Educational participation scale (EPS)	611	college	multi-variate analysis	Reasons for participation in adult education courses	Morstain & Smart, 1974
Mail questionnaire	479 69.8%	$\bar{x}=34$	factor analysis	Identifying deterrents	Scanlan & Darkenwald, 1984
Questionnaire	458 89.2%	7%<60 93% between 61–89	descriptive stats, f-test, t-test, chi square	Motivation to participate in Atlantic Canada	Rice, 1986
Questionnaire	560	60+	multiple regression analysis	Predictive relationship between participation and learning outcomes	Brady & Fowler, 1988
EPS data bank	13442	—	cluster analysis	Houle's typology after 22 years	Boshier & Collins, 1985

Qualitative Studies

Research Design	Collection	Orientation Claim	Description	Author, Date
Life stories	40 In-depth Interviews	Psychological and gerontological framework	Motivation and expectations of older adults	Wolf, 1990
Case study	1 Program	—	An Elderhostel case study	Murk, 1992
Case study	7 In-depth Interviews	Phenomenology and Grounded Theory	Learning as a strategy to negotiate retirement	Adair & Mowsesian, 1993

(Arsenault, 1996)

227

Statistical Indicators for 50 Countries with the Highest Under-5 Mortality

Country	1987 Under-5 mortality rate	1985 Number of radio sets per 1000 population	1980–86 Per cent of grade 1 enrollment completing primary school	1985 Male adult literacy rate
Afghanistan	304	91	54	39
Mali	296	16	25	23
Mozambique	295	32	26	55
Angola	288	26	24	49
Sierra Leone	270	222	48	38
Malawi	267	245	28	52
Ethiopia	261	284	41	—
Guinea	252	30	37	40
Burkina Faso	237	21	75	21
Niger	232	49	67	19
Chad	227	219	29	40
Guinea-Bissau	227	34	18	46
Central African Republic	226	58	53	53
Somalia	225	43	33	18
Mauritania	223	132	80	—
Senegal	220	109	86	37
Rwanda	209	58	47	61
Kampuchea	208	110	50	85
Yemen Dem.	202	70	40	59
Bhutan	200	14	25	—
Nepal	200	30	27	39
Yemen	195	22	15	27
Burundi	192	53	—	43
Bangladesh	191	40	20	43
Benin	188	74	15	37
Madagascar	187	—	30	74

Country	1987 Under-5 mortality rate	1985 Number of radio sets per 1000 population	1980–86 Per cent of grade 1 enrollment completing primary school	1985 Male adult literacy rate
Sudan	184	251	61	33
Tanzania	179	89	76	93
Nigeria	177	85	31	54
Bolivia	176	581	32	84
Haiti	174	21	45	40
Gabon	172	96	59	70
Uganda	172	22	58	70
Pakistan	169	90	34	40
Zaire	164	100	65	79
Lao People's Dem. Rep.	163	104	14	92
Togo	156	206	43	53
Cameroon	156	95	70	68
India	152	66	38	57
Liberia	150	228	—	47
Ghana	149	184	75	64
Oman	—	644	60	47
Côte d'Ivoire	145	133	89	53
Lesotho	139	28	27	62
Zambia	130	30	85	84
Egypt	129	256	64	59
Peru	126	203	51	91
Libyan Arab Jamahirya	123	222	82	81
Morocco	123	175	70	45
Indonesia	120	117	80	83
Number of Cases	49	49	48	47
Mean	194.9	122.6	47.9	54.2
Standard deviation	49.5	126.4	22.1	20.3

Evaluation Matrix for the East/West Enterprise Exchange

Major evaluation issues/questions	Major subquestions	Evaluation indicators	Methods of data collection and analysis
Program Effectiveness 1 Has the E/WEE met the objectives of the university, the program sponsors and other stakeholders?	1 To what extent has the project contributed to transferring management skills, intellectual expertise and technical know-how? 2 Has the program led to sustainable business partnerships? 3 Has the program built and maintained networks? 4 To what extent has gender equity been satisfactorily addressed in the program?	• number of returned business delegates who have used the information they learned about Canadian business context and management practices • number of Canadian corporate hosts who obtained valuable knowledge about doing business with Central and Eastern Europeans • number and type of networks created and maintained • gender statistics; presence of gender equity in programming	• Descriptive analysis from data in reports, interviews, previous studies
Program Efficiency 1 How do program costs compare to those in other programs? 2 To what extent has the overall program been efficiently managed? 3 To what extent has the program met the needs of the participants? 4 To what extent has the E/WEE met the needs of participating Canadian companies?	1 What is the overall financial performance of the program? 2 To what extent has the program followed standard management practices [planning, implementation, monitoring]? 3 How effective have the financial and narrative reports been in responding to the funder's needs?	• average cost per delegate • average cost per business relationship established • comparison to other similar programmes (where they exist) • ratio of management costs to program costs • level of satisfaction of delegates, participating companies • ratio of applicants to participants • number of repeat participating Canadian businesses	• Comparative analysis and standard practice analysis

Major evaluation issues/questions	Major subquestions	Evaluation indicators	Methods of data collection and analysis
Program effects and impact 1 What did participants do as a result of the project?	1 To what extent has the project contributed to strengthening new business linkages between Canadian organizations and their overseas business partners? 2 What is the return on investment for the program? 3 What effects and impacts did the project have on its stakeholders?	• number and types of new business linkages developed (e.g. joint ventures, technology/ expertise transfers, trade, etc. with dollar value whenever possible) • return on investment • identified effects and impacts on European participants, Canadian businesses, the university	• Return on investment calculations • Case studies of four partnerships • Interview analyzes of effects and impact
Rationale for continued government funding	1 What is the rationale for funding continuation in light of contextual changes in Eastern Europe? 2 What is EWEE's distinctive niche? 3 Which programs are EWEE's major competitors? 4 How does the program mesh with other Canadian government activities in the region?	• estimated political, economic, social benefits relative to stakeholder needs • number and quality of aspects of comparative advantage of program • extent of compatibility, overlap, duplication with other Canadian programs	• Descriptive and comparative analyzes

Sample Letter to Accompany a Questionnaire

October 15, 1996

Dear _____:

ABC Inc. has completed the first phase of its supervisor training program and would like your assistance in evaluating the experience. The Human Resources Department has contracted Universalia, a well-known management consulting firm to conduct this independent evaluation. Universalia has worked with us to develop the enclosed questionnaire which we ask you to complete and return within two weeks.

You were selected to receive this questionnaire because you were on the first cohort of supervisors involved. We have carefully selected a sample of 20 supervisors to represent each department of the company, so it is important for us to have as complete a response as possible. Please assist our efforts to continue to make our company a leader in its field.

If you have any specific questions about the survey, please contact me or Gary Anderson, President of Universalia at 514–485–3565.

Once we have the questionnaires back, Universalia will analyze them and share their findings with the senior management team. We will be publishing the results in the company newsletter in January with an advance summary available on the e-mail network.

Thanks for your cooperation in this project.

Hugh Mann Resources
Vice President

A Six-Step Summary for Developing and Administering an Effective Questionnaire

1 Determine your research questions:
    - what do you intend to find out?
    - how will the information be helpful?
    - which issues will relate to the questionnaire?
    - specify your subquestions by listing all the things you want to find out
    - identify the subquestions to be included in the questionnaire
    - refine your list

2 Draft the items:
    - translate questions into items
    - formulate fill-in-the-blanks, multiple choice, comment-on, list, Likert scale, and rank questions

3 Sequence the items:
    - group into topic sections
    - group by question type
    - rewrite questions as necessary and eliminate any redundancies

4 Design the questionnaire:
    - lay out items
    - use a booklet and all available space
    - decide on the need for pre-coding
    - include a title and introductory explanation
    - organize into titled sections
    - group similar types of items together

5 Pilot-test the questionnaire:
    - test the questionnaire with a small representative group of the population
    - have respondents complete the question then discuss the draft questions, clarify wording, and identify ambiguity
    - revise and retest if necessary.

6 Develop a strategy for data collection and analysis:
    - select a sample
    - determine how you will send the questionnaire

- develop cover letter
- prepare distribution package and send
- monitor returns and follow-up as required
- enter data
- analyze data

A Sample Questionnaire

Evaluation of ABC Supervisor's Training

Questionnaire for New First Line Supervisors

ABC is interested in evaluating the Supervisory Development Training that has been introduced over the past year. Please help us by completing and returning this questionnaire. Be open and honest — we want to hear what you think, not what you think we want to hear. Do *not* sign your name. The results of the questionnaire will be grouped and individual questionnaires will be kept confidential.

BACKGROUND

1 Did you complete the Getting Results training for First Line supervisors (two 5-day sessions)?

☐ No ⇒ return the questionnaire unanswered. 4
☐ Yes ⇓ 5

2 On what region do you work?

☐ National Headquarters 6
☐ Eastern 7
☐ Central 8
☐ Mid-West 9
☐ Western 10
☐ Northern 11

3 How much of your work takes place:

In an office ___% 12
On the shop floor ___% 13
In the field ___% 14

4 How many employees do you supervise? ____ 15

237

5 In what ABC Department do you work?

☐ Strategic Operations	16	☐ Human Resources	17
☐ Sales & Marketing	18	☐ Information Systems & Accounting	19
☐ Engineering	20	☐ Purchases and Materials	21
☐ Equipment	22	☐ Other, specify _____	23

GETTING RESULTS TRAINING

6 Please rate each of the following aspects of the training. Circle the number that indicates how much you agree with each statement.

> 1 = *Not at all*　2 = *Minimally*
> 3 = *Somewhat*　4 = *Extensively*

⇒ My superior discussed the training with me in advance of the training session.

| 1 | 2 | 3 | 4 | 24 |

⇒ The program duplicated a lot of training I already had.

| 1 | 2 | 3 | 4 | 25 |

⇒ I learned new skills.

| 1 | 2 | 3 | 4 | 26 |

⇒ I have consulted my participant manual since the training.

| 1 | 2 | 3 | 4 | 27 |

⇒ The job aids were useful to me.

| 1 | 2 | 3 | 4 | 28 |

7 I discussed my personal development plan with my superior following the training session.

☐ No ⇒ go to question 8　　29
☐ Yes ⇓　　30

　　☐ I initiated this discussion.　　31
　　☐ My superior initiated this discussion.　　32

APPLICATION OF TRAINING ON THE JOB

Please complete the following questions about the various training modules.

8 Module: ABC's Mission, Vision and Values

After completing this module, did you act on what you learned?

☐ No ⇒ go to question 9　　33
☐ Yes ⇓　　34

Did you take steps to improve the performance of your unit?

    ☐ No   35
    ☐ Yes   36

Did you solicit ideas for improvement from your employees?

    ☐ No   37
    ☐ Yes   38

Did you use your implementation plan?

    ☐ No   39
    ☐ Yes   40

What has been the overall effect of your work on mission, vision and values on your employees' job performance?

    ☐ Mostly positive   41
    ☐ No observable change   42
    ☐ Mostly negative   43

9   Module: Managing a Diverse Workforce

Are you or any individuals in your work unit members of a target group (visible minority, aboriginal, religious group, disabled or female)?

☐ No ⇒ go to question 10   44
☐ Yes ⇓   45

    Does the training help you to promote a working environment that is sensitive to all?

    ☐ Yes   46
    ☐ No   47

    Do you feel the training has equipped you to deal with situations involving possible discrimination?

    ☐ Yes   48
    ☐ No   49

If you answered No to *both* of these questions ⇒ go to question 10

If you answered Yes to *either* of these questions ⇓

What has been the effect on your employees' job performance?

    ☐ Mostly positive   50
    ☐ No observable change   51
    ☐ Mostly negative   52

Modules 10–17 follow a similar pattern but are not included here

18 Module: Delegating Tasks

Since your training, do you delegate differently?

☐ No ⟹ go to question 19   113
☐ Yes ⇓   114

What has been the effect on the performance of your work group?

☐ Mostly positive   115
☐ No observable change   116
☐ Mostly negative   117

TRAINING FOLLOW UP

19 Please rate the different types of training follow-up that are listed below. Circle the number that shows how important that type of follow-up is to your future efforts to apply your supervisory training.

| 1 = *Not at all* | 2 = *Minimally* |
| 3 = *Somewhat* | 4 = *Extensively* |

How important is:

⟹ Direct support from your superior	1 2 3 4	118
⟹ Authority to set group goals affecting work unit	1 2 3 4	119
⟹ Authority to implement improvements within jurisdiction of work unit	1 2 3 4	120
⟹ Authority to provide tangible recognition (gifts, cash, etc.) for good performance	1 2 3 4	121
⟹ Training for your superior	1 2 3 4	122
⟹ Training for employees	1 2 3 4	123
⟹ Team-building with superior and employees	1 2 3 4	124
⟹ Other: _____	1 2 3 4	125

20 I feel additional training would be useful.

☐ No ⟹ go to question 21   126
☐ Yes ⇓   127

Please list the areas in which you would like more training:

1. _____

2. _____

3. _____

OTHER COMMENTS

21 Please share any other comments or suggestions you have on the Getting Results training program.

_____

_____

_____

_____

_____

_____

_____

Thank you for your cooperation.
Please return your completed questionnaire to:

Universalia

°/o Training and Development — Human Resources
ABC Headquarters

A Sample of an Executive Interview Protocol

ABC Inc. Supervisory Development
Program Needs Assessment Executive Interviews

Introduction

As you may know, we have been asked by System Training to conduct a Training Needs Assessment for first-line supervisors.

The assessment will interview a number of senior executives, will conduct group interviews with key managers, and will involve supervisors themselves in focus groups and a national survey.

The purpose of this interview is to help us understand your department as it relates to first level supervisors and to explore your vision for the type of supervisors you will need in the future.

We would like to discuss the present and evolving context of supervisors in your department, training priorities and what you feel might be the best approach for training.

1.0 Department context

    1.1   What are the major types of supervisors within your unit?

    1.2   What are the major corporate issues that are affecting the work of first-line supervisors?
        (probe for effects of downsizing on span of control)

2.0 Supervisors' roles

    2.1   What qualities characterize the best supervisors in your department?
        (probe for different requirements for different types of supervisor)

    2.2   What do you consider to be the most prevalent weaknesses of first-line supervisors?
        (probe for technical, managerial, human relations skills)

2.3 If a training course could be introduced to make all your supervisors competent in one area, what would it be?

3.0 Supervisors' roles in future

3.1 What are the major changes affecting your department?
(probe for effects on supervisors)

3.2 What new skills and competencies must supervisors acquire to prepare for these changes?
(probe for generic types of skills)

4.0 Training

4.1 What support exists within your department for supervisors to learn new things?
(probe for informal support, individualized and group)

4.2 Does your department provide support for alternative and informal ways of training?
(probe for use of posters, circulating articles, giving individuals relevant material)

4.3 What has been the most effective training at ABC Inc. in the past?
(probe for Managing Our Business; Leadership Centre; other models)

5.0 Supervisory development program

5.1 What would you consider the most important content areas in a training development program for first-line supervisors?
e.g. a. finance   d. marketing
      b. personnel   e. planning
      c. supervision

5.2 What training model do you consider most appropriate?
e.g. a. centralized short-course
      b. departmental/functional course
      c. non-course models (internships, rotations, etc.)

5.3 How can such a training program best be managed in terms of:
      a. releasing people for training (one vs. many at a time)
      b. phasing (one-shot vs. periodic)

6.0 Conclusion

6.1 In conclusion, what have been the most important experiences in helping you to become effective in supervising people who work with you?
(probe for both formal and informal methods of learning)

A Sample Focus Group Leader Guide

ABC Inc. Supervisory Development Focus Groups Leader's Guide

Introduction

Good morning, and thank you for agreeing to meet with us and share your views on ABC's supervisor training. My name is Gary Anderson and I represent Universalia, an independent consulting firm. Assisting me is Louise Pesant, also from Universalia. We are attempting to find out about the training and its effectiveness, and have invited people from different areas in ABC Inc. who have completed the training program.

Before we begin, let me review the ground rules. We are recording your responses, but will keep all individual comments confidential. Keep in mind that we are just as interested in negative comments as in positive comments, and often the negative comments are the most helpful. We will adjourn sharply at 11:00. I know that people at ABC are always inclined to agree with one another, but a diversity of views will help us understand what you really think.

First, could you introduce yourselves, and tell me when you completed the supervisor training.

[Self-introductions one-by-one]

What is your functional area?

When did you complete the training program?

1 What did you think of the ABC Supervisor training?

Probes:

Structure	What did you think of the group size; duration; venue; cross-functional mix?
Quality	Was there anything in this training that was really outstanding? Was anything a major problem?
Relevance	In general, did the training meet your needs?
Modules	What were the most/least pertinent modules? [Keep this VERY short]
	Mission, Vision and Values
	Overview

Supporting Results
Managing a diversified workforce
Leadership
Communication
Assigning Tasks
Motivation
Organizing your time
On-the-job coaching
Managing poor performance and behaviour
Employee assistance program
Delegating tasks

2 **What results of your training were you able to use back on the job?**

Probes:

Behaviour   Examples of things you did differently after training

Attitudes   Which? In what ways? What differences did these make?

Knowledge about ABC in general? Cross-functional?

3 **Think back to when you returned to your job after training. What were the major factors that helped your efforts to apply what you learned?**

Probes:

Support   From boss in preparation for training; in follow-up?
From subordinates?

4 **What were the major factors that hindered your efforts to apply what you learned?**

Probes:

Lack of Support   From your boss?
From your subordinates?
Subordinates not yet trained?

5 **After your training, did you have different expectations of your subordinates? How about expectations for your boss?**

Probes:

Demands   Higher expectations?

Support   More help?

6   What follow-up to the training would you recommend?

Probes:

Additional training	For you; for others?
	What would it focus on?
Corporate changes	Policies; culture; work methods; attitudes

7   How could we demonstrate to senior management that you are a better employee as a result of training?

Probes:

Could you keep a diary of the new behaviours?

Would other people notice? Could we ask them?

Conclusion

Let me tell you what else we are planning in our evaluation of supervisory development.

(a)   We are developing a Questionnaire.

- Your contributions today will help define the questions.
- Some of you may be asked to comment on a draft. Is that OK?

(b)   We want to do an in-depth study of a few supervisors.

- Here too, your suggestions will be used.

Is there anything you would like to add? Thanks for your help.

Glossary

Term	Definition
Accessible population	The members of a population who can realistically be included in a research sample (e.g. a specific group of individuals, organizations, events, communities or schools).
Analysis of variance (ANOVA)	A statistical procedure for determining whether the differences among variable means among two or more groups is what would be expected by chance alone.
Audit trail	A record of the procedures selected, the decision path followed, and sources of evidence used in qualitative research. Also used with computer data searching to record the path traveled to reach your findings (e.g. http locator).
Baseline	Describes the condition prior to an intervention. Periodic comparisons to the baseline state can determine progress, or lack thereof.
Benchmarking	Compares that which is being measured to best practices in the field, including a professional or scientific standard.
Case	The phenomenon to be investigated in case study research. The term is also used for clinical cases such as the behavior pattern of an individual.
Case study research	An empirical investigation that is defined by interest in a specific phenomenon, within its real-life context. It is a qualitative form of inquiry that relies on multiple sources of information.
Chain of evidence	Similar to the audit trail. A qualitative research technique that enhances the validity of the study by recording all aspects of the research process as they unfold and demonstrating how the links and conclusions between the data and the analysis were derived.
Chi-square (X^2)	A statistical procedure used to compare distributions of data across nominal categories.

Term	Definition
Citation	A written statement used in a bibliography or reference list that accurately describes information that an individual needs to locate a document or source. It includes the author, data, title, publisher and in some cases includes page numbers and volumes.
Complete observer	A qualitative researcher who enters a setting and remains physically detached from the activities and social interactions.
Complete participant	A qualitative researcher who enters a setting and actively participates in all activities and social interactions. This may be done covertly or overtly, depending on the nature of the investigation.
Concurrent validity	A method used to determine the validity of an inquiry instrument. The instrument is administered simultaneously to different sample populations and if consistent results are obtained, one can declare concurrent validity of the instrument.
Construct	A word or set of words used to describe an idea or concept derived from commonalities found by examining or observing phenomena.
Content analysis	An analysis of communication (e.g. speech, written documents, film, open-ended responses on a questionnaire) to determine what is included and in what proportion.
Content validity	The extent to which an instrument has statistical properties that suggest it actually measures what it purports to measure.
Control group	The group, in experimental research, that does not receive any treatment or intervention.
Correlation coefficient (r)	A statistic that measures the direction and magnitude of the relationship between two variables.
Correlational research	A type of quantitative research that explores the strength of the relationship between variables.
Critical theory	Principles designed to clarify forms of oppression and power relationships within a society or culture and that serve to emancipate (free) people from the oppression. A theoretical base for cultural study research.
Deception	The deliberate act, on the part of a researcher, to create a false impression in the minds of the subjects participating in a research activity.

Term	*Definition*
Dependent variable	A variable that is 'thought' to be affected/influenced by a treatment or intervention.
Descriptive research	Any research approach that attempts to truthfully and accurately describe phenomena.
Descriptive statistics	A group of statistical procedures used to describe numeric data (e.g. means, standard deviations, normal distribution, correlations).
Dual publication	Publication of one research report in more than one place. This is generally considered unethical.
Effectiveness	The extent to which objectives or planned outputs have been achieved.
Efficiency	The extent to which resources have been optimally used to achieve a goal or objective.
Emergent design	Refers to the evolution of the research design, or the need to change the design as information becomes available and the research experience unfolds. Particularly relevant to qualitative, policy, organization and evaluation research.
Emic perspective	The view held by research participants about their understanding of their social reality.
Epistemology	A branch of philosophy that studies how knowledge is acquired and validated. Asks the question, 'What is the relationship between the inquirer and the known?'
Empowerment evaluation	Empowers those involved in an evaluation study by giving them new knowledge of their performance.
Etic perspective	The view held by the researcher about their conceptual and theoretical understanding of the research participant's social reality.
Ethnographic research	A form of qualitative research based on anthropological research techniques.
Experiment	A type of research that randomly assigns subjects/objects to a control group and an experimental group and compares outcomes.
Experimental group	The group of individuals or objects that are randomly assigned to a treatment group in an experiment.
External validity	Refers to the degree to which research findings can be generalized from the sample population to the larger population.

Term	Definition
Face validity	Refers to the extent to which an instrument appears to measure the concepts which it purports to measure.
Factor analysis	A statistical procedure that reduces a large number of variables into reduced sets of variables called 'factors'.
Field notes	The researcher's detailed and descriptive record of the research experience, including observations, a reconstruction of dialogue, personal reflections, a physical description of the setting, and decisions made that alter or direct the research process.
Filter questions	A questioning technique that funnels out responses with a common characteristic and guides the respondent to a different line or branch of questioning.
Focus group	A carefully planned and moderated informal discussion where one person's ideas bounce off another's creating a chain reaction of informative dialogue. Its purpose is to address a specific topic, in depth, in a comfortable environment to elicit a wide range of opinion, attitudes, feelings or perceptions from a group of individuals who share some common experience relative to the dimension under study.
Framework	A model that allows the researcher to explore the relationships among variables in a logical and prescribed fashion. It clarifies questions by relating questions and their constituent subquestions and it summarizes the overall concept being investigated.
Gatekeepers	Gatekeepers are people who do not hold formal authority to approve or deny your access to a research setting, rather they are people within the setting who have influence in the form of informal authority.
Hawthorne effect	An obvious and observable change in a respondent's behavior based on the fact that a researcher is present, or the individual is knowingly participating in a research activity.
Hermeneutics	A field of inquiry that seeks to understand how individuals interpret text.
Historical research	The study of the past, using both qualitative and quantitative data, for the purpose of gaining a better understanding of phenomena within their original context.

Term	*Definition*
Hypothesis	A prediction about the outcome of a research activity.
Independent variable	The variable which is believed to cause or influence a dependent variable.
Indicators	Explicit measures that are used to determine performance.
Informed consent	The written or verbal permission of subjects stating that they (or their dependent minor) agree to participate in a research activity.
Inquiry protocol	A written questionnaire, interview guide, or focus group guide used to gather data from respondents in a research setting.
Institutional capacity	A concept that indicates what an organization is capable of doing.
Interval scale	A measurement scale with defined intervals that determine the degree of precision of a measurement (e.g. 5–10; 10–15; etc.).
Interview protocol	The written list of questions and probes used by a researcher to guide the conversation and when interviewing research subjects.
Internal validity	Refers to the degree to which an experimental treatment is in fact responsible for the observed effect.
Key-informant interview	An interview directed at a respondent who has particular experience or knowledge about the subject under investigation.
Likert scale	A scale which asks respondents to indicate the extent to which they agree or disagree with a statement. Five and seven-point scales are the most common, three can be used for special situations and children.
Longitudinal research	A type of research that investigates changes in a sample population over a specified period of time.
Mean	A measure of central tendency. Derived by dividing the sum of a set of scores by the number of scores in the set.
Median	A measure of central tendency that represents the middle point in a spread of scores.
Meta analysis	A statistical procedure that identifies trends in statistical results from a set of studies concerning the same research problem.

Term	Definition
Missing data	Data that the researcher intended to collect but was unable to do so for a variety reasons (e.g. the inability to interview a key informant, limited access to a research setting, blank items on a questionnaire, data entry errors).
Mode	A measure of central tendency that corresponds to the number that occurs most frequently in a set of scores.
Nominal scale	A scale where the categories have no quantitative value or order (e.g. pizza, beer, pickles and popsicles).
Normal curve	A distribution of scores which form a symmetrical bell curve (also known as a probability curve).
Normative interviews	Used to collect data which is classified and statistically analyzed.
Objective reality	A view of the world that asserts that certain features of the external environment exist independent of the perceptions and beliefs of individuals. (e.g. A falling tree will make a sound when it hits the ground, even if there is no one to hear the sound).
Ontology	A branch of philosophy concerned with the nature of reality.
Ordinal scale	A rank order scale with unequal measures (e.g. What aspect of physical fitness is most important to you? __ Strength __ Endurance __ Flexibility __ Cardio-vascular).
Paradigm	A set of basic beliefs that guides human action.
Participant observation	Involves the researcher watching or joining the activities of the community under investigation for the purpose of gaining observational data.
Pilot study	A study that uses a small sample of the population to test an inquiry protocol prior to its general application.
Population	The entire group of people or set of objects, including those not in the study.
Population validity	The degree to which the findings of a particular study can be generalized to a specific population at large.
Positivism	A view of the world that believes that objective accounts of the world can exist or be developed.
Post-positivism	A view of the world that believes in a partially objective world because no flawless method of inquiry exists.

Term	*Definition*
Post-modernism	A post World War II view of the world that does not assert a single authority, research method or research paradigm.
Predictive validity	Refers to the extent to which the results of a test administered at a specific point in time can accurately forecast future test scores administered on another population at a later date.
Pretest	Application of an inquiry instrument to a subject group before any experimental intervention.
Primary data	Information obtained first hand by the researcher.
Program rationale	The fundamental reason(s) why a program exists together with its underlying assumptions.
Program relevance	Asks the question 'Does anyone care if the program exists?'
Proposal	A written plan that describes a research project that includes an introduction, purpose, review of the literature, statement of significance, research design, data collection methods and proposed form of data analysis. It may also include a budget.
Pyramid network	A technique that uses people, connected to the research environment, to identify data elements that should be included.
Qualitative research	A form of research that explores phenomena in its natural setting and uses multi-methods to interpret, understand, explain and bring meaning to that which is being investigated.
Quantitative research	A form of research that describes, explains and reports on phenomena by collecting and statistically analyzing numeric data.
Quasi-experimental research	A form of research that examines differences between groups based on some natural characteristic using treatments or interventions, but not randomization. Also known as ex-post facto or causal comparative research.
Questionnaire	A set of written questions used to collect data from respondents.
Random sample	A research sample that ensures all members of a defined population have an equal opportunity of being selected for inclusion in a study and that all combinations of the same sample size are possible.

Term	Definition
Range	The highest and lowest scores in a set of numbers (e.g. 7–19).
Reflective analysis	The intuitive part of the research process, particularly in qualitative research, where the researcher relies on intuition or personal judgments when making statements about the phenomena studied.
Regression analysis	A statistical procedure that uses multiple correlation to predict a value in a dependent variable based on the battery of scores on independent variables.
Reliability	In quantitative research reliability refers to the extent that an instrument will yield the same results each time it is administered. In qualitative research reliability refers to the extent that different researchers, given exposure to the same situation, would reach the same conclusions.
Research tradition	A line of research and theory based on common epistemological assumptions.
Sample	A subset of a population.
Secondary data source	A source of information written by someone other than the researcher (e.g. witness, census data).
Semiotics	The science of signs or sign systems.
Sociometry	Attempts to assess the social structure within a group of individuals by ascertaining the status of each individual in the group.
Stakeholder	A person or group of people with a vested interest in the phenomena under study.
Standard deviation	A measure of the extent to which scores deviate from the mean.
Statistic	A statistical measure such as a median or mean used as an indicator in quantitative research.
Statistical significance	A statistical term that describes a result which is unlikely to have occurred by chance alone.
Terms of reference (TORs)	The focus and boundaries of a contract research project including a statement about who the research is for, the research objective, major issues and questions, and sometimes the schedule and available resources.
Thick description	A term frequently used in qualitative research to describe data that offer a complete description of a phenomenon.

Term	*Definition*
Tracer studies	Studies using longitudinal methods that involve locating people who were previously part of an educational program.
Triangulation	A process of using multiple data sources, data collection methods, and/or theories to validate research findings, help eliminate bias and detect errors or anomalies in your discoveries.
Unit of analysis	The actual thing being investigated (e.g. a teacher, a classroom, an organization, a nation).
Variable	A characteristic that can assume any one of a range of values. Variables can be nominal, ordinal, interval, ratio.
Validity	Refers to the extent to which what we measure reflects what we expected to measure (e.g. IQ test is assumed to be a valid measure of intelligence). Two forms exist: internal and external.
Workplan	A document that details the methodology to be used in conducting research.

Index